Iris Brecke
Ovid's Terence

Trends in Classics – Supplementary Volumes

———

Edited by
Franco Montanari and Antonios Rengakos

Volume 156

Iris Brecke

Ovid's Terence

—

Tradition and Allusion in the Love Elegies and Beyond

DE GRUYTER

ISBN 978-3-11-221544-9
e-ISBN (PDF) 978-3-11-130803-6
e-ISBN (EPUB) 978-3-11-130854-8
ISSN 1868-4785

Library of Congress Control Number: 2023945328

Bibliographic information published by the Deutsche Nationalbibliothek
The Deutsche Nationalbibliothek lists this publication in the Deutsche Nationalbibliografie;
detailed bibliographic data are available on the Internet at http://dnb.dnb.de.

© 2025 Walter de Gruyter GmbH, Berlin/Boston
This volume is text- and page-identical with the hardback published in 2024.
Editorial Office: Alessia Ferreccio and Katerina Zianna
Logo: Christopher Schneider, Laufen
Printing and binding: CPI books GmbH, Leck

www.degruyter.com

Acknowledgements

This book is a revision of my doctoral thesis from the Department of Historical and Classical Studies, the Norwegian University of Science and Technology (NTNU). I wish to thank my thesis supervisors, Thea Selliaas Thorsen (Department of Historical and Classical Studies, NTNU), and Stephen Harrison (Corpus Christi College, University of Oxford). I am grateful to Thea for all the things she has done for me from the very early stages of my work, as director of the project The Heterosexual Tradition of Homoerotic Poetics, in which I took part in my time as a PhD student from 2016 to 2020, and as an invaluable mentor, support and friend. My work has benefitted extensively from her insights, kind guidance and encouragement. I am thankful to Stephen for all his feedback, kind advice and encouragement through the process, for sharing of his vast knowledge with me, and for making my research stays in Oxford into such productive and memorable experiences. I am also thankful to my thesis examiners, Alison Sharrock and Laurel Fulkerson, for their insights and for the fruitful discussions of my work during my public defence in October 2020. I am honoured to say that I was awarded the Trends in Classics Book Prize for this book in its manuscript state: I wish to express my sincere gratitude to De Gruyter and the awarding committee.

I am very fortunate to have received comments and advice from a number of excellent scholars in the years I have worked on this project. I am indebted to Sharon L. James, who kindly accepted to comment on my thesis in the very final stages of the work; her remarks and insights added to its quality. Roy Gibson and Stephen Heyworth provided feedback on the project and offered valuable comments on a version of Chapter One. Tristan Franklinos shared observations on my work during a workshop in Trondheim, and thus aided me in further strengthening my arguments. I am thankful to the late Peter Brown, who met with me and shared with me his knowledge of Terence's works and thereby provided valuable input regarding my own thinking. I am grateful to the participants and audience at the conference 'Greek and Roman literature: the erotic connection' (Oxford, June 2016) for their comments on my talk on some of the main findings in Chapter Two; to the Classical Ages Research Group at NTNU; and to the participants of the Classical Ages Seminar, where I had the opportunity to present my work and receive feedback. A warm thank also to Jennifer Ingleheart, who kindly helped me and answered my questions when I could not access her commentary on *Tristia* 2 during the COVID-19 crisis in the spring of 2020. A warm thank is also due to all my colleagues and friends in Classics at NTNU, for scholarly advice and discussion, and for all the good times that we have shared.

https://doi.org/10.1515/9783111308036-202

I also want to express my thanks to Morten Moi and the Norwegian publishing house Gyldendal for allowing me to publish verse translations of Terence's *Eunuchus* and *Hecyra* in Norwegian in the book series *Kanon*, with Thea Selliaas Thorsen as editor in chief. The work with these publications has deepened my understanding of Terence's oeuvre and has been key to some of my main findings. I am grateful to Morten and Thea for all their help and feedback throughout the process.

The staff at the university libraries at NTNU and the Bodleian Libraries (University of Oxford) are also among those who have assisted me; I am thankful for all their aid throughout the research that has led up to this book.

I also wish to thank Carlo Vessella and Anne Hiller at De Gruyter for their patience and guidance, and copyeditor Carson Bay for all aid. All remaining errors are of course my own.

Lastly, I would like to thank my parents, Terje Brecke and May-Brit Aasen Brecke, for always being there for me, and my partner Magnus Eriksson, for all his encouragement and for always standing by my side.

Contents

Introduction

The love poetry of Ovid displays a high level of intertextuality, and his elegiac poems are closely connected both internally, and to the earlier poetic tradition, through references and allusions. Ovid is generally seen as the last and foremost writer within the genre of Roman love elegy, a genre that current scholarship sees as closely connected to Greek and Roman new comedy on a generic level.[1] This, I believe, is due largely to the fact that both genres are strongly rooted in social practice, presenting interpersonal relationships — heterosexual erotic connections in particular — in a non-mythological everyday setting. On the other hand, systematic research that traces direct links between the works of the individual Latin love elegists and those of the comic playwrights is, with some exceptions,[2] scarce. This book sets out to conduct such a study: it aims to conduct a thorough and systematic analysis of the reception of the comic playwright Terence in the elegiac works of Ovid. As I aim to show in the present study, a number of traces of Terence can be identified in Ovid's elegiac works; these traces will in most cases be defined as allusions, which points to an appreciation for and a complex reception of Terence in Ovid. This relationship has been understudied and underappreciated in previous research.[3]

Ovid is known for challenging the bounds of his genre, and as Harrison states, his 'consistently inventive and radical expansion of a highly conventional poetic kind suggests that "supergenre" might be a better term than "genre" in discussing the extraordinary Ovidian use of the elegiac form, beginning with traditional erotic discourse but expanding and diversifying to include practically every poetic topic.'[4] For the purpose of my investigation, I count among Ovid's

---

1 Of the recent research on the relationship between new comedy and Roman love elegy, see e.g. Barsby 1996; James 1998a; 2006; 2012; Piazzi 2013, 236–237. On Terence and love poetry, see Sharrock 2013, 61–63. Sharrock 2021, interestingly, argues that the genres of Roman comedy and Latin love elegy are more different than is often thought.
2 See e.g. Yardley 1972 (on Plautus' *Asinaria* in Propertius); 1987; Barsby 1996; James 2016a. The commentary editions of the works within the two genres identify a number of similar passages. See e.g. McKeown 1989 *ad Am.* 1.7 and 1.8. Barsby's commentary edition of Terence's *Eunuchus* (Barsby 1999) identifies a number of traits that point forward to the elegiac genre. Hanses 2014 treats Plautus' *Amphitruo* and Ovid's *Metamorphoses*; Hanses 2020, Chapter Four, treats the reception of Terence's *Eunuchus* in Roman love poetry, including Virgil, Catullus, and Roman elegy (Propertius, Tibullus, and Ovid).
3 James 2016a, demonstrating a connection between Terence's *Eunuchus* and the first book of Ovid's *Ars amatoria*, is an exception to this.
4 Harrison 2002, 79.

https://doi.org/10.1515/9783111308036-204

love elegies the *Heroides* (single and double), the *Amores*, the *Ars amatoria*, and the *Remedia amoris,* in line with recent studies of Ovid's love poetry.[5] As Dalzell points out, Ovid himself always refers to his erotodidactic *Ars amatoria* as elegy.[6] Dalzell also notes that there is a large didactic element present in the treatment of love in both Greek and Roman authors, including the works of Ovid's immediate precursors within the elegiac genre.[7] The *Heroides*, though, on the surface very different from the love elegies of Ovid's predecessors, have been shown to be closely tied to the elegiac genre,[8] perhaps most famously through their connection to Propertius' elegiac letter 4.3, which has been considered a possible model.[9] In addition, I include *Tristia* 2 in my study, due to its close connection to Ovid's earlier poetry in general and the *Ars amatoria* in particular, through its defence of it. All of Terence's six comedies are treated in this book, though to various degrees according to their thematic and allusive links with the Ovidian corpus.[10]

The relatively small amount of research conducted on the relationship between specific authors within the genres might be at least partially explained by the long-lasting scholarly pursuit of the possible sources of Latin love elegy and scholars' intensive focus on the relationship between new comedy and Latin love elegy on a generic level. Because of this, the comic genre has emerged as an important explaining factor and background against which Latin love elegy should be read. This mode of explanation might be labelled the 'comedy model'. However, the link between the comic genre and Latin love elegy is not straightforward, as there are a number of factors that separate the two genres on a fundamental level.[11] Perhaps most notably, Greek and Roman new comedy, in spite of the many erotic escapades of its *adulescentes amatores*, often to the despair of their fathers, ultimately underpin traditional and conservative values through the conventional happy ending: plays within the genre consummate in the marriage between a young man and woman of citizen status and often the birth of a legitimate child. This stands in stark contrast to the anti-marital, ele-

---

5 See e.g. Thorsen 2013b. Sharrock 2002 includes the *Amores*, the *Ars amatoria* and *Remedia amoris* when treating Ovid's amatory works.

6 Dalzell 1996, 137.

7 Dalzell 1996, 136–137.

8 On the *Heroides* as love elegies, see e.g. Thorsen 2013b, 117–120. See also Dalzell 1996, 136.

9 However, there are some issues of dating. See Dalzell 1996, note 18, for discussion.

10 As is pointed out by Hanses, the *Eunuchus* stands out as 'a special case in the reception of Roman comedy in Latin literature', Hanses 2020, 277. The *Eunuchus* is also central in my investigation.

11 See also Sharrock 2021.

giac ideal of love for its own sake.[12] The latter becomes particularly evident in the face of the reinforcement of conservative traditional values, such as proper marriage between elite Romans, under Augustus. In addition, the elegiac artistic 'I' and the strong female voice and perspective, sometimes conspicuously present in Ovid,[13] are traits of the elegiac genre that cannot necessarily be explained as deriving from the comic genre.[14]

Whereas a link between the two genres is now generally accepted, the problematic aspects of such a link remain in large part unexplored and unexplained. This constitutes a need for further research. As I hope to show in my investigation, Ovid's allusions to Terence both demonstrate the influence of the Terentian comedies, known for their elegance and humanity, on Ovid's development of central elegiac *topoi* such as the images of *seruitium amoris* and *militia amoris*. These allusions also take the reader straight to the core of more problematic themes, such as the violent origin of heavily politicized issues at the time of Ovid: namely, the Roman marriage institution vis-à-vis the legendary rape of the Sabine women, and the crucial issue of a woman's social status. As I aim to demonstrate, Ovid finds Terence particularly apt as a source for allusions that can be used to create double meaning in his texts when treating such issues. This is largely due to the playwright's genre-breaking focus upon excessively violent rapes in two of his marriage plots. Thus, this book both confirms the influence of the comic genre on love elegy when it comes to certain themes by highlighting the connection between Terence and Ovid, and also highlights some major differences between the genres. This latter point, furthermore, prompts a search for explanatory factors other than those of the 'comedy model' for understanding the connection between Ovid and Terence.

What are the dynamics of the relationship between Ovid and Terence, and in what ways can Ovid be said to revive the comic writer? How is Ovid's reception of Terence affected by his own social and political context? How does Ovid incorporate the comedies of Terence, bound by convention to steer towards a

---

12 On the nature of elegiac love, see Thorsen 2013a, 2–4.

13 For example, the single *Heroides* are all written in a female voice, and the third book of the *Ars amatoria* is famously addressed to women.

14 However, a link has been drawn between the *adulescens amator* Phaedria in Terence's *Eunuchus* and the elegiac poet lover; see Konstan 1986. One might also say that the *meretrix*, one of the stock beloved objects of new comedy, has a prominent voice in a number of plays, Thais in the *Eunuchus* being a good example, but her counterpart, the *uirgo*, has almost no lines, in spite of being an important character, most conspicuously in the rape-marriage plots of the genre. Both of these characters are beloved objects of the *adulescens amator*. As I will argue in Chapter Two, Ovid's *puella* cannot be linked straightforwardly to the comic *meretrix*.

marriage between a young man and the object of his love, in his own, anti-marital love poetry? At what points do their works overlap, where do they differ, and at what points can direct influence by Terence be traced in Ovid? These are some of the central questions on which my investigation will shed light as it explores how Ovid incorporates the comic playwright into his elegies. This book offers a systematic analysis devoted to Ovid's reception of Terence and will be the first extensive work to conduct such an investigation. By analysing Terentian allusions in Ovid and how they affect the meaning of the text when they are revealed to the reader, I also aim to modify the prevailing model of explanation for the common traits shared by the elegiac and comic genres; hopefully this will contribute to a deeper understanding of both genres, as well as of the relationship between them.

Background: new comedy and Latin love elegy

The relationship between the genres of Latin love elegy and Roman comedy in general has received a vast amount of attention in research within Classics and has been an area of much scholarly debate since the late 19th century. In recent research, what might be termed 'the comedy model' has established itself as one of the main explanations for the rise of the Latin love elegy of the pre-Augustan and Augustan age. In the words of James, 'the first thing for students of elegy to read is new comedy'.[15] The origin of the still ongoing scholarly debate on the sources of Roman love elegy can be said to have emerged with the works of the classical philologists Leo and Jacoby in the late 19th century and the beginning of the 20th century. Scholarship was for a long time focused on the relationship between Greek New comedy and the later Roman elegiac genre, as the prevailing opinion for a long time was that the elegiac poets did not read Plautus and Terence. Briefly outlined, Leo, in his *Plautinische Forschungen Zur Kritik Und Geschichte Der Komödie*, found that the poetry of the Latin elegists showed clear thematic similarities with Roman comedy; however, in his view these similarities should be explained as a result of influence from a common source, rather than direct influence from the Roman comic writers Plautus and Terence. According to him, the love elegists simply would not have read Plautine comedy. The comic motifs in Roman elegy rather came from Greek new comedy. However, Leo did not necessarily regard this genre as the direct source of inspiration for the Roman love elegists; his main theory was that the similari-

---

15 James 2012, 266.

ties with the comic genre came via the influence of Alexandrian poets and especially elegists, writers of a now lost subjective Greek love elegy who had taken up in their poetry the motifs from Greek new comedy.[16] Leo's theory about a Greek subjective love elegy was soon challenged by Jacoby, but his notion that the Roman love elegists did not read Plautus and Terence had a major influence on future debate, even among those who held that new comedy was a direct source for the love poets of the Augustan age; similarities between the Roman love elegists and Roman comedy continued to be generally perceived as a natural consequence of their common knowledge of the Greek playwrights, seemingly without considering that Tibullus, Propertius and Ovid might have had their Roman counterparts in mind.[17]

A shift of focus to the possible Roman sources emerges in 1985, as Griffin attacks the emphasis on Greek sources and lack of serious thought of Roman pre-

---

16 For the full argument, see Leo 1895, 126–141.

17 Jacoby 1905 argues that a Greek love elegy similar to Roman love elegy probably never existed, and that the writers of Roman love elegy, rather than imitating Greek love elegy, expanded the Hellenistic love epigram, but also made direct use of Attic new comedy. See Jacoby 1905, 38–105. The scholarly debate in the wake of the work of Jacoby further weakened Leo's theory regarding the influence of an Alexandrian subjective elegy. Wheeler sums up the ongoing scholarly debate (Wheeler 1910, 440–450) and ascribes to the Roman elegy direct influence from new comedy with regard to erotic teaching. According to his view, there is no need for an intermediary Alexandrian elegy to explain the existence of the erotic teaching of new comedy in Roman elegy; in this way, he allows the genre a greater degree of originality than did Leo (Wheeler 1911, 56–77). Day, carrying on the discussion regarding the predecessors of the Augustan love elegists, states that 'the fragments of Greek erotic elegy which have survived the singularly indiscriminating ravages of the centuries are so meagre in extent, and so doubtful of context, that an estimate of their importance as a source of Latin Elegy is of necessity based more upon the generosity of the critic's imagination that upon any direct conclusive evidence.' Day 1938, 1. He generally argues for a certain degree of direct influence from primarily Greek new comedy; he notices an admiration for Menander's *Thais*, and the transference of themes, such as the well-known similarity between Terence's *Heautontimorumenos* lines 279–307 and Tibullus 1.3.83–92 (see also Leo 1895, 129), which, as he argues, suggests that Tibullus had 'intimate knowledge of the original scene of Menander'(Day 1938, 89). Strong similarities of expression are also found in Propertius 3.6.1–18, and Day sees it as likely that Propertius and Tibullus derive directly from the same Menandrian source. That Tibullus might have known the Terentian passage, seems not to have been considered. For full discussion; see Day 1938, 85–101. Luck 1959 sees no influence from comedy on Tibullus and Propertius, whereas he allows that Ovid might have made 'occasional experiments' (Luck 1959, 38) with themes from the comic genre, as 'he was the last in the line of elegiac poets and had to explore new subjects in order to maintain the public's interest in this kind of writing' (38). See Luck 1959, 35–38 for full discussion.

decessors for the Roman love elegists apart from Catullus.[18] He criticises McKeown's view that even though material from comedy is present in the poetry of the elegists, the connection is probably an indirect one, since the elegists do not acknowledge a debt to comedy;[19] the elegists, Griffin argues, would not necessarily record their obligation to their predecessors in the same way as modern scholars would, but statements about predecessors are rather claims about the poets themselves, as 'they declare that they are worthy disciples of the most fashionable and distinguished masters'.[20] The fact that the elegists do not mention the comic dramatists as their predecessors only confirms that they were not fashionable at the time, and not that they were not influenced by them. Griffin also argues that 'the quest for "the origin" of Latin love elegy has often been put in too narrow terms. Such a literary genre as the epigram or the narrative elegy could be "the" origin of the developed elegy of Propertius or Ovid only in a restricted sense, since their poems are so different from the epigrams (in length and complexity), and from what we actually know of Hellenistic elegy (in tone and purpose)'.[21] In his investigation of the influence of drama, he points to contributions made by Roman comedy, and Plautus in particular, though he also makes mention of examples from Terence.[22]

In the wake of the work of Griffin one can see a definite change of direction in research concerning the relationship between Roman elegy and new comedy; it becomes impossible *not* to take the Roman playwrights into consideration, as there is not really any reason to assume that Plautus and Terence would not have been read by the elegists.[23] In fact, contemporary sources as well as recent research seem to indicate the opposite.[24] It is important in this context to mention is the work of Fantham,[25] who, though without arguing for a direct dependence of the Roman love elegists on Roman comedy, points to affinities of language and imagery in Terence in particular and the later Roman love poets. She argues that Terence's 'range of erotic, or rather, sentimental vocabulary, more

---

18 For full discussion, see Griffin 1985, 198–210. For a recent study on Latin love elegy and its Latin precursors in general, see Bessone 2013.

19 For McKeown's view, see McKeown 1979, 78.

20 Griffin 1985, 199.

21 Griffin 1985, 203–204.

22 See Griffin 1985, 204–208 in particular.

23 Yardley 1987 responds to Griffin's request for a serious consideration of the Roman comic genre. See also Barsby 1996 (pages 135–138 in particular) for a discussion of the research tradition.

24 See below.

25 Fantham 1972.

restricted and urbane than that of Plautus, embodied a norm which survives as the basis of usage in the Elegists',[26] and goes on to explore love imagery and *sermo amatorius* in Terence. It is left to the reader to estimate for themselves the degree of affinity between Terence and the love elegists, and whether their shared traits should be 'considered as the outcome of a continuing literary and spoken tradition, or of a direct debt, based on familiarity with Terentian comedy.'[27] Fantham points to a number of images used by Terence, such as the image of love as combat, war and peace in love, love as insanity, the lover as 'burning' with passion, love-sickness and its medicine, the lover's torture and self-torture, but also more positive love-images, such as the use of the words *ludus* and *ludere*. These are all images, it is argued, that are to be found in the language of the Terentian lovers, and which are developed by the later elegiac love poets.[28]

A central contribution to the scholarly debate and what has become today's prevailing view on the nature of the relationship between the comic and elegiac genres is the work of Konstan, who goes far in linking Roman love elegy directly to Roman comedy.[29] Furthermore, he places the focus upon Terence and the *Eunuchus* in particular, in which he identifies a structure of feeling that he is inclined to believe is more Roman than Greek.[30] He argues that 'an anticipation of elegiac subjectivity' might be found here,[31] as he proposes 'to locate in the tradition of the *Eunuch* the complex of themes that constitutes Roman elegy: the ambiguous status of the mistress, who remains aloof from marriage; the problem of greed and gifts; the necessary role of the rival; and the emphasis on sincerity and inner feeling, for which the Roman elegists have been honoured as the inventors of subjective love lyric.'[32] The work of Konstan remains vital for the present-day debate on the thematic relationship between Roman love elegy and new comedy. Within this debate, it is James who perhaps goes furthest in

---

26 Fantham 1972, 82. Fantham recognises that scholars since Leo have agreed that the affinities of subject matter and treatment between the Roman elegists and Plautus and Terence derive from Greek sources (such as Greek new comedy, Hellenistic epic, epigram and bucolic, if not from the Greek subjective love elegy proposed by Leo and rejected by Jacoby), but states that 'independence of treatment and subject matter does not preclude affinities of language'. Fantham 1972, 82.

27 Fantham 1972, 82–83.

28 For full discussion, see Fantham 1972, 82–91.

29 Konstan 1986, 369–393.

30 Konstan 1986, 390.

31 Konstan 1986, 391.

32 Konstan 1986, 391.

suggesting a constitutional connection between the two genres,[33] presenting her work on the interrelationship between Terence's *Eunuchus* and the first book of Ovid's *Ars amatoria* as a case study illustrating a comprehensive thematic relationship between Roman love elegy to new comedy in general.[34]

Konstan's work is, however, also a significant forerunner for later research that investigates the type of love that is presented in the Terentian comedies in particular, as something different from the representation of love found in Menander and Plautus; important here is the work of Barsby, who identifies Terence, especially his *Eunuchus*, as a forerunner of Catullus and the Roman elegists when it comes to his development of the imagery of love.[35] It is against this backdrop that my analysis is conducted, and it is my opinion that Konstan and Barsby are right in pointing out the *Eunuchus* as a particularly rich source for later writers in general when it comes to the Roman development of a type of subjective love, and as the comic play that perhaps most prominently points forward to the elegiac genre (especially the play's famous opening scene, which will be thoroughly discussed in my study). As will become evident, the *Eunuchus* is a central work in Ovid's reception of Terence, and its Ovidian reception will be a common thread throughout my study. I believe that the strong reception of Terence in Ovid is a sign of the special position of Terence — famous for his elegance, humanity and unique character portrayals, but also for offering shocking and explicit descriptions of rape, focusing on the devastating effect on the victim — in a larger context of texts and genres that lead forward to the elegiac genre in general, peaking with Ovid. On this note, it is interesting to notice the Terentian connection with Sappho suggested by Sharrock: Sappho's poem 31 acts as an early expression of love drawn on by Terence as he develops a 'new way of talking about emotions.'[36] The connection highlights Terence's role in a larger network of texts about love, and it works to highlight Terence's position in conveying the notion of subjective 'romantic' love to the Romans.[37] By this I

---

33 E.g. James 1998a; 2006; 2012; 2016a, note 2.
34 James 2016a, n. 2.
35 See Barsby 1999b, 5–29.
36 Sharrock 2009, 226–228.
37 As Sharrock states, 'two lines of arguments contribute to an intertextual relationship between Terence and Sappho, one going forwards from the Hellenistic reception of Sappho, and one backwards from Catullus and the later Roman elegiac lover'. Sharrock 2009, 226. As precursors to identifying the allusive presence of Sappho in Terence, Sharrock points to the already established role of the fictional Sappho in Greek comedy (see Most 1996), and Traill's argumentation for reading the braggart soldier of Plautus' *Miles gloriosus*, Pyrgopolynices, as a parody of Phaon and the *meretrix* Acroteleutium as taking on the role of Sappho (Traill 2005).

do not mean to deny the influence of Greek new comedy and Plautus on the Roman elegiac genre in general,[38] but rather to suggest that Terence stands in a special position, not only when it comes to expressions of love, but also when it comes to conveying more problematic aspects of sexual relationships, such as violence and rape. Furthermore, as will be argued throughout this book, there is a particularly rich reception of him in Ovid, who in addition to the specific Terentian expression of love deploys a number of Terentian motifs in his elegies, especially the problematic aspects that are famously highlighted in Terence.

Terence in the early principate

Research has already well established that the Romans continued to read and appreciate the works of Terence well after the 160s BCE. [39] After his death in 159 BCE, he seems immediately to have become an exemplar for other comic playwrights, and his plays continued to be read, imitated and praised in later times.[40] Cicero is known for citing Terence repeatedly in his works,[41] and Horace famously adapts the opening scene of the *Eunuchus* in his *Sat.* 2.3 (Hor. *Sat.* 2.3.258–271). Terence's father characters seems also to have functioned as models for the role and function of Horace's father in the *Sat.* (Hor. *Sat.* 1.4),[42] and Horace states how Terence is known for his *ars* at *Epist.* 2.1.59, followed up by the claim that the Romans still in his day and age both learn by heart and go to

---

Sharrock 2009, 227. For a recent study on the reception of Sappho in Roman literature (including chapters on the reception of Sappho in Catullus and the elegists), see Thorsen and Harrison 2019.

38 See Introduction, note 2, for examples of research treating Plautus and Latin love elegy.

39 On Terence in Latin literature in the period from the second century BCE to the second century CE, see e.g. Müller 2013. On Terence in late antiquity, see Cain 2013. On Terence in late antiquity onward, see Hill and Turner 2015. For a recent study on the reception of Republican theatre in Antiquity, see Manuwald 2019. Beacham 1991 offers a study on the Roman theatre and its audience through antiquity. For Terentian *testimonia* in antiquity, see Marti, 1974. Hanses 2020 examines the reception of Roman comedy in Latin literature in the late republic and early Empire, and argues for the continued performance of Plautus and Terence during the late Roman Republic and into the Julio-Claudian and Flavian eras.

40 According to Suetonius' *Vita Terenti* (preserved by Donatus), togata writer Afranius, who lived shortly after Terence, claimed that no one was Terence's equal as he praised him in his *Compitalia*. See Müller 2013, 366. By the fourth century CE, Terence had become one of the four canonical school authors; the three others were Cicero, Vergil and Sallust: see Cain 2013, 382.

41 Monda 2015, 115, states that Cicero quotes Terence 37 times in total.

42 Manuwald 2019, 268, cf. Leach 1971.

the theatre to enjoy the plays of the old authors (*hos ediscit et hos arto stipata teatro / spectat Roma potens*, Hor. *Epist.* 2.1.60–61, 'These authors mighty Rome learns by heart; these she views, when packed in her narrow theatre'), which indicates that the comic playwrights were a part of cultural education and points to the continued performance of Roman comedy in the time of Horace.

Friedländer sums up the evidence of the continued popularity and performance of new comedy under the Empire in the following manner:

> Of artistic dramas, however, the New Comedy of the Greeks (represented chiefly by Menander, and imitated by Plautus and Terence) retained the firmest hold on popular favour. In Rome, in Italy and the provinces, the stock figures travestied gods, doddering kindly fathers, mawkish sons, cunning slaves, braggarts, whores, etc. delighted audiences for centuries. To keep interest alive in these well-worn plays, known to most of the spectators, at least at Rome, good acting must have been essential.[43]

Similarly, Beacham sums up the status of Roman drama after the second century BCE in the following manner:

> Although there continue to be references to its performance, the composition of comedy seems virtually to have ceased after the end of the second century BCE and, like tragedy, it evidently lost its appeal as a subject for new writing for the stage. Although dramatic composition appears to have devolved to scholars and dilettantes, and away from professional playwrights, staged revivals of earlier works were abundant in the late Republic and well into the Empire. Cicero, for example, frequently records performances of tragedy, and refers to a production of Plautus' *Pseudolus* in the first quarter of the first century BCE. Later Horace indicates (in his epistle to Augustus written towards the end of the century) that the works of other Roman playwrights including Ennius, Naevius, Pacuvius, Accius, Plautus, Caecilius, and Terence continue to hold the stage.[44]

Ovid himself mentions Terence by name once, at *Tristia* 2.359, as part of his critique of Augustus' interpretation of the *Ars amatoria*.[45] However, in spite of the ancient indications of the popularity of restagings and Friedländer and Beacham's positive assessments of the continued popularity of Terence's genre, at least on stage, it remains impossible to determine whether Ovid actually saw a restaging of a Terentian play, even though it seems likely, in light of the evidence for Terence's continued performance. That he would have known them

---

43 Friedländer 1908–1913, 2.96. As proof for the continued performance of new comedy in the first period of the principate (down to the second century CE), Friedländer refers to Quintilian and Juvenal; Friedländer 1908–1913, 4.255.

44 Beacham 1991, 127. See Hor. *Epist.* 2.1.50–61 for the quote.

45 Ovid's mention of Terence in *Tristia* 2 will be treated thoroughly in Chapter One.

and had access to them in written form can, on the other hand, hardy be doubt-
ed, given the evidence for the continued appreciation of the playwright and the
acknowledgement of him as standard reading matter by Horace and others. It is
safe to say that Terence remained an integral part of the Latin literary tradition
in the increasingly urbane Rome, well into Ovid's day and beyond.

Allusive Ovid: approaches

Ovid is known as a writer of intricate poetry, with multiple layers of meaning
created through intratextuality,[46] general intertextuality and allusions to the
preceding poetic tradition. Much research has been conducted on Ovid and his
relationship to his models and predecessors, and several studies on Ovid's intertextual connection to previous authors both within his own genre and in others
has been published over the last decades.[47] Through such studies, a complex
intertextual relationship with both the Greek and the Roman literary traditions
has been revealed through the whole of the poet's extensive output, from the
earliest poems to his exilic works. This relationship has given rise to a deeper
understanding of and a new appreciation for Ovid's works; with the present
study, I aim to contribute further to this line of research and to the understanding of Ovid's multi-layered poetry. The purpose of such studies, the present one
included, is not merely to list the many allusions Ovid makes to previous literary works. Rather, these are studies of reception and intertextuality that aim to
explain a new and deeper understanding of the text in light of its connection to
its literary tradition. Simultaneously, the preceding text, or 'source', is also
inevitably reconsidered in the process, and a more profound understanding of
its meaning, influence, and literary position results. Over the last decades, the
works of scholars such as Conte, Hinds and Martindale have set the agenda in
delivering a new theory on how to approach these very matters,[48] and studies

---

46 On intratextuality in Ovid, see Hinds 1987; Sharrock 1994; and Thorsen 2014; 2018b. On
intratextuality in Latin literature in general, see Sharrock and Morales 2000; Harrison, Frangoulidis and Papanghelis, 2018.
47 Some important studies are e.g. Tarrant 2002 (on Ovid and the ancient literary history);
Harrison 2002 (on Ovid and his relationship to his genre); Hardie 1988; 1995; 2007 (on Ovid and
Lucretius); Thorsen 2014 and 2019a (on Ovid and Sappho); Ziogas 2013 (on Ovid and Hesiod);
and Boyd 2017 (on Ovid and Homer).
48 See e.g. Conte 1986; 1994; Martindale 1993; and Hinds 1998.

concerning intertextuality and reception within Classics, including my own, benefit greatly from this research.[49]

An important and more recent contribution to the field is Harrison's work on what is labelled 'generic enrichment', defined as 'the way in which generically identifiable texts gain literary depth and texture from detailed confrontation with, and consequent inclusion of elements from, texts which appear to belong to other literary genres', or 'the creative confrontation of different literary genres'.[50] Harrison's study investigates the effect of the concept as a characteristic and key feature of the poetry of Vergil and Horace in particular. But, as Harrison also states, the argument could be applied to the Augustan period in general, and to Tibullus, Propertius and Ovid in particular.[51] I find it useful to think of Ovid's incorporation of certain *topoi* and situations from the comedies of Terence into his elegies as 'generic enrichment', comedy being the 'guest' genre and elegy the 'host'.[52]

The allusions to Terence in Ovid involve similarities in wording as well as in literary settings and situations; they are not necessarily verbatim correspondences, and might be revealed by small similarities in wording that, due to the poetic context, can be linked to a particular scene in the Terentian corpus. This might partly be an effect of metre, and the difference between Ovid's elegiac meter and the freer comic meter may hinder more extensive verbatim allusion, even though, as I will argue, such allusions also do occur. An example of what I argue is that a small Terentian allusion, consisting only of two words, but with

---

49 The term intertextuality generally indicates reader-generated connections, whereas allusion suggest a connection that is author-generated; see e.g. Conte 1986; 1994, Hinds 1998, Harrison 2007b. Harrison 2007b, 8–19 sums up Conte's methodological approach and its evolution over time, which he describes as having gone from 'a pronounced structuralist/formalist flavour in his early work to a position which allows more to the intentions of the author as well as to the interpretative role of the reader.' Harrison 2007b, 8. I use both 'intertext/intertextuality' and 'allusion' in my book, though I am aware of this difference in use. I take an agnostic position, as I acknowledge that all connections are generated by me, but still assume that their meaning can be intended by the author. One can of course never reach a full understanding of Ovid's intentions and what he 'really meant', and neither is that the aim. The aim of my study is rather to provide evidence to substantiate the connection between Ovid and Terence, and thus shed light on how this connection affects the intended *and* received meanings of the texts.
50 Harrison 2007a, 1. See pages 1–33 for his general introduction.
51 Harrison 2007a, 1.
52 An example would be what I argue is an incorporation of the comic rape-marriage plot in the first book of the *Ars amatoria* in Chapter Two.

an important meaning, can be found in *Tristia* 2, which is treated in Chapter One. Such small allusions might also be termed 'micro allusions.'[53]

Outline of chapters

Chapter One investigates an intricate allusive play in the central exilic poem, *Tristia* 2, addressed to Augustus, and how Ovid invokes Terence, and the *Eunuchus* in particular, in a way that adds to the double meaning beneath the surface of the poem and Ovid's apparent *apologia*. I will argue that the only explicit mention of Terence in the works of Ovid, which occurs at *Tr.* 2.359, alludes to Horace's epistle 2.1, also addressed to Augustus, and the mentioning of the same playwright there. The allusion simultaneously invokes Horace's defence of contemporary art and artists in his epistle 2.1, and the unique Terentian prologue, adding to Ovid's own defence for the poet in *Tristia* 2.[54] However, it also hints at the emperor's double standards when he, according to Ovid himself, exiled him in part for prompting imitation of immoral behaviour through his *Ars amatoria*. Furthermore, I will argue for a striking allusion in the opening of *Tristia* 2 to Terence's most unconventional and shocking rape scene, i.e. the young man Chaerea's violent rape of the girl Pamphila, inspired by a painting of Jupiter and his rape of Danae in the *Eunuchus*. The allusion adds to the double meaning of the poem, as Ovid plays on the image of Augustus following the *mores* of Jupiter and what it really means to act like the king of the gods, as ruler on the one hand and rapist in disguise on the other. By extension, this implies what kind of example Augustus himself sets for the people when they follow his *mores*. This is perfectly in line with what seems to be the main message of *Tristia* 2: if art in fact can prompt imitation, this would be true for all art, and singling out the *Ars amatoria* would be a case of double standards. Furthermore, the emperor would himself be equally guilty, if not more so, for conveying to the people far more 'immoral' artistic representations, such as e.g. mime performances.

Chapter Two explores the crucial issues of marriage, rape, and status in the comedies of Terence and the first book of Ovid's *Ars amatoria*, with related ex-

---

53 I am grateful to Roy Gibson for making me aware of this useful term, referring me to Christopher Whitton, who kindly clarified to me his thoughts on this phenomenon in private correspondence. See also Whitton 2018; 2019. A recent study on the use of micro allusions as such is Hanaghan 2017.

54 An interesting study of the Terentian prologue and its position in the Roman literary tradition is Goldberg 1983.

amples from the *Heroides* and the *Amores*. As I will argue, Ovid exploits the rape scene in the *Eunuchus* and includes elements from the stock comic rape-marriage plot in his version of the Rape of the Sabine Women, the legendary origin of the Roman marriage institution, in the first book of the *Ars amatoria*. This works to highlight problematic aspects such as the fear and terror experienced by rape victims, a prominent feature in Terence's *Hecyra* and the *Eunuchus* in particular, and the forced nature of much Roman marriage, far from the ideal of elegiac love. This is closely linked to the issue of female status in Ovid, where the blurred status of the elegiac *puella* stands in contrast to the strict social categories of Roman society, especially in light of the newly-instated Augustan laws on adultery and marriage, aimed at regulating sexual activity and promoting marriage and childbirth among Roman citizens. This is reflected in the new comedy universe, where the same strict social categories are present; the young rape victims of the genre almost always turn out to be of citizen status and thus eligible for marriage, and are subsequently married off to their rapist.

Chapter Three latches onto the findings in Chapter One and Chapter Two and identifies several allusions to Terence in the *Remedia amoris*. These allusions connect the poem to Ovid's previous works, but also foreshadow the allusive play with Terence in *Tristia* 2. In the *Remedia amoris*, Ovid deploys Terence in a way that highlights current societal issues and the status of art and the artist. I addition, I argue that several notions of the image of love as a type of disease with a cure can be traced back to Terence, the *Andria* and the *Eunuchus* in particular, and that the Terentian slave, cast in a role similar to Ovid's *magister* or *praeceptor*, plays an important role also when it comes to aiding the young men in falling out of love. However, while there is a rich reception of Terentian language and concepts in the *Remedia amoris*, major differences between the genres are at the same time highlighted; the love cure, suggested by a *senex* in *Andria*, in the Terentian universe is marriage, which helps reinstate proper societal order. This cannot occur within the bounds of elegy; there is no real cure for love in Ovid.

Chapter Four investigates the elegiac image of *seruitium amoris* in Ovid and its link to Terence's slavelike lovers. One can find slavelike lovers in the *Heautontimorumenos* and *Phormio*, and, as I will argue, in the *Eunuchus*. Here one can discern clear notions of what become features of the elegiac *seruitium amoris*, such as a version of the *paraclausithyron*, with the young man Phaedria in the role of the *exclusus*, shut out due to a *diues amator*, and perhaps most importantly, a young man of citizen status who takes on the role of slave and performs slave duties to gain access to the girl of his dreams; this latter reference is to the other young man of the play, Chaerea. As I will show, this reading is supported by an allusion in Horace, and picked up by Ovid in the second book of the *Ars amatoria* as he advises young men to act the slave so as to come closer to their respective objects of desire. It is slaves, after all, who have the privilege of being in immediate proximity to the *puella*. This point is well demonstrated in the *Eunuchus*. Furthermore, I argue that Ovid makes a twist to this image, developing it from its conventional form and engaging Terence in doing so. This is also demonstrated in one of his most famous *seruitium*-passages in the Acontius-Cydippe letters (*Her.* 20/21), which occurs after Acontius has described himself in words associated with the stock comic *seruus callidus*, in a story that shares many features with the comic rape-marriage plot. Furthermore, I argue for a strong presence of the comic slave, Parmeno in the *Eunuchus* in particular, in Ovid's elegiac didactics.

Chapter Five explores how Terence stands in a special position in developing the image of *militia amoris*, which becomes a stock trait of Roman love elegy, in Ovid in particular. I will argue that there are direct links between Ovid's *militia*-poems *Amores* 1.9 and 3.8 and concepts found in Terence. Furthermore, I will show how both Ovid and Terence convey both male and female perspectives on the battle of the sexes; the female perspective is particularly clear in Ovid's *Heroides* and the third book of the *Ars amatoria*, and strong female voices are famously featured in Terence's *Eunuchus* and *Hecyra*, the battle of the sexes being programmatic for the latter comedy. There is a strong affinity between the *Hecyra* and Ovid's third book of the *Ars amatoria*, where in a similar manner love is described as a battle and in which the aim is to provide women with the proper weapons to secure a fair fight. The issue of perspective is further highlighted by a striking allusive play between particular passages. Furthermore, I will argue that Terence's *Adelphoe* plays a crucial role in an 'elegiac discussion' that takes place between Tibullus, Propertius and Ovid regarding amatory violence.

Chapter Six summarises my findings and shows how they affect our understanding of the two authors, their genres and the relationship between them.

Note on texts and editions

All the Latin texts cited are from the Oxford Classical Texts series (OCT) unless otherwise stated. When I dissent from the OCT-edition, this will be clarified in the footnotes. All translations are from the Loeb Classical Library, with some modifications, unless otherwise stated. Abbreviations follow the Oxford Classical Dictionary, 4th Edition — Abbreviations List.

1 Defending *artes*: Terentian allusions in *Tristia* 2

Introduction

Ovid mentions Terence by name only once in his *oeuvre*, and it occurs in the exile poetry, in the second book of *Tristia*: *Accius esset atrox, conuiua Terentius esset* (Ov. *Tr.* 2.359, 'else would Accius be cruel, Terence a reveller').[1] Therefore, this first chapter begins towards the end of the poet's career, and it begins with Ovid's retrospective view of his own literary production and his role as a poet in his contemporary society. *Tristia* 2 is both exceptional and central among the exilic works. One can assume that Ovid would choose his words with particular care in this poem, written at an early stage of his exile and addressing Augustus, the man responsible for his exile who still holds the poet's fate in his hands.[2] *Tristia* 2 takes the form of one long elegiac epistle, consisting of 578 lines, and is the only poem written in exile where the *princeps* is openly addressed. This makes it unique among Ovid's exilic works, which mainly consists of collections of shorter epistles to varying addressees. In the epistle, Ovid concerns himself with the role of poetry and the poet in society, in Augustan Rome in particular. *Tristia* 2 is ultimately a defence of the poet and poetry in general, and the *Ars amatoria* above all, as it was deemed to be immoral and at least partly the reason for the harsh punishment inflicted on the poet.[3] As a part

---

1 Even though this is the only explicit mention of Terence by name in Ovid (and in elegy in general), he might also be hinted at in the third book of the *Ars amatoria* behind the phrase *cuiue pater uafri luditur arte Getae* (Ov. *Ars am.* 3.332, 'or he whose sire is deceived by the crafty Geta's cunning'). Here, Ovid offers a list of poets with which the *puella* should be familiar, and even though Ovid appears to refer to Menander in this context (he has so far only mentioned Greek poets), the reference is not completely clear. The *fallax seruus* is most notable in the Roman comedies, and given that Ovid later in *Tristia* 2 links Terence with the *conuiua* character, even though this character is much more typical for Plautus' comedies (see e.g. Ingleheart 2010 and Owen 1924 *ad loc.*), Terence might be implied by Ovid also in *Ars amatoria* 3.332, on which see Gibson 2003 *ad loc.* I thank Roy Gibson for drawing my attention to this. Menander is linked with the *fallax seruus* at *Amores* 1.15.17–18: *dum fallax seruus, durus pater, improba lena / uiuent et meretrix blanda, Menandros erit* (Ov. *Am.* 1.15.17–18, 'as long as tricky slave, hard father, treacherous bawd, and wheedling harlot shall be found, Menander will endure'). However, the mention of Menander here seems to signal the genre in general; as long as the genre lives on, Menander lives on through it. See Fantham 1984, 302–303 and n. 14.
2 Claassen 2012 [2008] divides Ovid's exile poetry into five phases, of which *Tristia* 1 and 2 belong to the first. See pages 13–28 for an overview of the different phases.
3 Ovid was relegated to Tomis (modern Constanza in Romania) on the Black Sea by emperor Augustus in 8 or 9 CE due to *duo crimina, carmen et error* (Ov. *Tr.* 2.207, 'two crimes, a poem

https://doi.org/10.1515/9783111308036-001

of his justification for the *Ars amatoria*, Ovid compares his work and himself as a poet with a number of preceding poetic works and their authors throughout the poem. He places himself within a literary tradition as one of many producers of poems about love and erotic passion, and it is in this context that Terence becomes relevant.[4] Ovid's mentioning of Terence, or rather his comparing himself to the comic playwright, is neither accidental nor insignificant. As I will argue in this chapter, it is hardly a coincidence that Terence is Ovid's choice of representative for the Roman comic genre, and furthermore, as I aim to show, Ovid's mention invokes the mentioning of the same author in Horace's *Epist.* 2.1, also addressed to Augustus, but on the emperor's personal request (at least according to the biographical tradition).[5]

Moreover, I will argue for the presence of a striking Terentian allusion in the opening of the epistle, which has not been pointed out in previous scholarship. This allusion creates a link between the Ovidian image of Augustus as Jupiter, 'the angry god', the recurring image of Jupiter as serial adulterer or rapist and the infamous rape scene in Terence's *Eunuchus*. This is certainly the most shocking and unconventional rape scene in the corpus of Roman comedy, where a painting of Jupiter's rape of Danae inspires a young man to rape a young *uirgo* while she is asleep, and thus was presumably one that the Roman audience would easily recognise. In addition, as I will demonstrate in Chapter Two, Ovid engages in an allusion to the very same rape scene in the first book of the *Ars amatoria*.[6] Both the Terentian allusion in the opening of *Tristia* 2 and the

---

and a blunder'). In the opening of *Tristia* 2, it becomes evident that the poem is the *Ars amatoria*: *carmina fecerunt ut me moresque notaret / iam pridem demi iussa Caesar ab Arte meos* (Ov. *Tr.* 2.7–8 'verse caused Caesar to brand me and my ways by commanding that my "Art" be forthwith taken away'). Ovid was charged with being an *obsceni doctor adulterii* (Ov. *Tr.* 2.212, 'a teacher of obscene adultery'), which he himself denies: *at si, quod mallem, uacuum tibi forte fuisset, / nullum legisses crimen in Arte mea* (Ov. *Tr.* 2.240, 'Yet if, as I could wish, you had by chance had the leisure, you would have read no crimes in my "Art."'); *ecquid ab hac omnes rigide summouimus Arte, / quas stola contigi uittaque sumpta uetat?* (Ov. *Tr.* 2.251–252, 'Have I not strictly excluded from this "Art" all women whom the assumption of the robe and fillet of wedlock protect?'); and *et procul a scripta solis meretricibus Arte / summouet ingenuas pagina prima manus* (Ov. *Tr.* 2.303–304, 'Far from the "Art," written for courtesans alone, its first page warns the hands of upright women.').

4 *Tristia* 2 contains a catalogue of Greek and Latin poets within different genres who had also written about love and erotic passion but, unlike himself, without being punished for it (Ov. *Tr.* 2.361–470.)

5 See Suet. *Poet. Hor.*

6 This allusion is also discussed in James 2016a.

explicit mention of Terence later in the poem add to the double meaning of the poem. It is on the one hand an *apologia* for the *Ars amatoria* and the poet's claim of innocence from having prompted behaviour that conflicted with the *Lex Iulia de adulteriis coercendis*,[7] and it offers more than a hint at the emperor's double standards in singling out the *Ars amatoria* for inciting immoral behaviour.

Poet *versus* poetry: Ovid, Terence and Horace

An important argument in *Tristia* 2 is that literary works cannot serve as proof of the writer's mind and intentions, and subsequently, that Ovid as a private person cannot be likened to the *praeceptor amoris* of the *Ars*. What he writes in his playful poems, Ovid states, cannot be taken as his personal opinion or as reflecting his lifestyle, even if one were to interpret his teachings as immoral or even illegal. To highlight this point, he refers to Roman tragedy, represented by Accius, Roman comedy, represented by Terence, and writers within the epic genre, and the fact that these writers are not generally believed to have a personal character fitting the themes and values of their respective genres:

> crede mihi, distant mores a carmine nostro
>   (uita uerecunda est, Musa iocosa mea)
> magnaque pars mendax operum est et ficta meorum:
>   plus sibi permisit compositore suo.
> nec liber indicium est animi sed honesta uoluntas:
>   plurima mulcendis auribus apta feret.
> Accius esset atrox, conuiua Terentius esset,
>   essent pugnaces qui fera bella canunt.
>   Ov. *Tr.* 2.353–360

> I assure you, my character differs from my verse (my life is moral, my muse is playful), and most of my work, unreal and fictitious, has allowed itself more licence than its author has had. A book is not evidence of the writer's mind, but respectable entertainment; it will offer many things suited to charm the ear. Else would Accius be cruel, Terence a reveller, or those would be quarrelsome who sing of fierce war.

The apparent meaning of the Terentian reference in this context is that if one were to believe that Terence had behaved in the same manner as the characters of his comedies, he would be known for having frequented parties and everything

---

7 Passed shortly after the *Lex Iulia de maritandis ordinibus* of 18 BCE. On the *Lex Iulia*, see e.g. Csillag 1976 and Treggiari 1991, 88 and 277–298. On the sources on adultery at Rome, see e.g. Richlin 1981, 225–250.

that follows from that within his genre, i.e. excessive eating and drinking and the general behaviour associated with the typical comic dinner-guest. This is, according to Ovid, obviously not the case, and it is equally wrong to link the poet as a private person to the made-up character the *praeceptor* of the *Ars amatoria*.

In his commentary on the passage, Owen points to the fact that it has been supposed that *conuiua* in this context is equivalent to the comic stock character the *parasitus*. He also notes the allusion to the famous Terentian parasites Phormio, the *parasitus* in the comedy by the same name, and Gnatho from the *Eunuchus*. Owen, however, argues that the allusion should not necessarily be limited to these two characters, and that it is rather a reference to all 'gluttonies and carouses dear to the pleasure-loving characters in Terence's comedies', before he goes on to list multiple references to eating and drinking in Terence.[8] However, as Jennifer Ingleheart points out in her commentary on the same passage, when Owen argues for a more general connection between Ovid's reference to the *conuiua* and various Terentian characters, he points to many examples that prove the popularity of both *Phormio* and the *Eunuchus* and the famous parasites of these plays. This would, she states, tend to confirm that this allusion in fact is to these exact plays and characters.[9]

Either way, at first glance the choice of Terence in this particular context seems somewhat curious, as one might think that Ovid would have chosen Plautus to illustrate the point more effectively: he is famous for this type of character, far more prominent in his plays than in those of Terence. However, as Owen goes on to argue, Ovid names Terence here as the most refined and artistic of the Roman comic playwrights, as opposed to Plautus, whom he never mentions by name, and in the same way that Accius is mentioned because he is known as the greatest of the Roman tragedy writers.[10] If this is the case, it might indicate Ovid's preference for Terence over Plautus in general, but it also might signal a highly conscious choice, as a reference to the Plautine glutton would have been more compelling had he just wanted to make an easy point. Furthermore, this would in fact not be the first time Ovid made use of a reference to a Terentian dinner-party guest, as in the first book of the *Ars amatoria* he alludes to the character Chremes in the *Eunuchus* and uses him as an example for his readers. Lines 589–590 of the first book of the *Ars amatoria*, warning young men against drinking too much at parties, *certa tibi a nobis dabitur mensura bibendi: / officium praestent mensque pedesque suum* (Ov. Ars am. 1.589–590, 'I will give

---

8 Owen 1924, *ad loc.*
9 Ingleheart 2010, *ad loc.*
10 See full discussion in Owen 1924, *ad loc.*

you a sure measure of drinking: let mind and feet perform their duty.'), bear a striking resemblance to line 729 of the *Eunuchus*, and the character Chremes' description of negative physical reactions to drinking too much wine at a dinner party: *postquam surrexi neque pes neque mens sati' suom officium facit* (Ter. *Eun.* 729, 'Since I got up, neither foot nor mind has been functioning as it should.').[11] Chremes is, however, not a parasitic character, but a young Attic citizen of respectable family, who therefore might serve particularly well as an example for Ovid's readers, as he will be more relatable to them than the typical *parasitus* in this context.[12]

As Ingleheart also points out, Ovid's reference to Terence in *Tristia* 2 has the potential to have been written with a certain irony.[13] According to Suetonius, Terence, a freed slave, was famously accused of frequenting the circles of more powerful and wealthy men and benefitting greatly from these connections.[14] This would make the author into a figure not too far from the comic hanger-on/ flatterer character or a *conuiua*, who makes a living by flattering or performing other services for richer and more influential men in his real, everyday life. If this is the case, or rather if this was a common conception about Terence in Ovid's day, the reference does not work very well as the straightforward defence of the poet that it seems to be at first glance.[15] Furthermore, that there are certain parallels between the Ovidian elegiac lover and the comic dinner-guest (the *kolax*, or the related characters the *scurra* and the *parasitus*), as suggested by Labate,[16] adds to the irony, or double meaning, of the Terentian reference. How-

---

11 Hollis 2009 [1977] *ad loc.* also compares the passage to *Eunuchus* 729. As was pointed out to me by the examiners of my doctoral thesis, Plautus' *Pseudolus* should probably also be taken into the intertextual network here. I am grateful for this remark, and I am sure it is right. See e.g. Pseudolus' druken monody (lines 1246–1285 in the eponymous play). I still believe that the textual resemblance indicates an allusion to Terence, and perhaps also underscores a preference for him over Plautus, but both Ovid and Terence would surely have recognised Plautus' influence on the image, and probably also had his *Pseudolus* in mind.

12 In the *Eunuchus*, Chremes has attended a dinner-party at the soldier Thraso's house, where the parasite Gnatho and the *meretrix* Thais were among the guests. However, see Labate 1984, 175–226, who discusses the parallel between Ovid's lover and the *kolax* (or the related characters the *scurra* and the *parasitus*). The *parasitus* character might not be so far removed from the character of the young elegiac lover after all.

13 Ingleheart 2010, *ad loc.*

14 See Suet. *Poet. Ter.* 1.

15 As Ingleheart also points out, the reference to Accius might be read with the same type of irony, given the anecdotes about his aggressive behaviour. See Ingleheart 2010, *ad loc.*

16 See discussion in Labate 1984, 175–226. I am grateful to Roy Gibson for bringing this to my attention.

ever, as I will show in what follows, that 'nothing is as it first seems' can be said to be almost a stock trait of Ovidian texts, and the same goes for his defence of himself and his poetry in *Tristia* 2. The choice of Terence, somewhat curious at first glance, to illustrate the comic *conuiua* character in fact makes perfect sense if we pierce through the layers and double entendre of the text and its allusive network.

To shed further light on this passage and the choice of Terence as the foremost illustrator of the Roman comic genre (as Owen argues), it is useful to see it in the light of a similar mention of the playwright in what is generally accepted to be Ovid's main model for the second book of *Tristia*, Horace's *Epist.* 2.1.[17] The epistles share the same addressee (Augustus) and have a major theme in common, as both epistles ultimately constitute a defence of the poet, poetry, and its role in contemporary society. Moreover, Ovid effectively alludes to Horace's epistle throughout his *Tristia* 2. Of particular interest in the present context is that both works mention Terence by name and, what is more, both texts put the comic playwright in a special position, as the most illustrious representative of his genre.[18]

In epistle 2.1, Horace criticises the Roman people for exhibiting 'bad taste' when they still prefer old dramatic productions to more recently written poetry and for still learning by heart the works of Ennius, Naevius, Pacuvius, Afranius, Plautus, Caecilius and Terence, and for viewing their plays when they visit the theatre:

> *Naeuius in manibus non est et mentibus haeret*
> *paene recens? adeo sanctum est uetus omne poema.*
> *ambigitur quotiens, uter utro sit prior, aufert*
> *Pacuuius docti famam senis, Accius alti,*
> *dicitur Afrani toga conuenisse Menandro,*
> *Plautus ad exemplar Siculi properare Epicharmi,*
> *uincere Caecilius grauitate, Terentius arte.*
> *hos ediscit et hos arto stipata teatro*
> *spectat Roma potens; habet nos numeratque poetas*
> *ad nostrum tempus Liui scriptoris ab aeuo.*
>
> Hor. *Epist.* 2.1.53–62

---

17 On the connection between *Tristia* 2 and Horace's epistle 2.1., see e.g. Ingleheart 2010, 8–10; Barchiesi 2001 [1993], 79–104.

18 For a discussion of the positive position of Terence in Horace's epistle 2.1, see Müller 2013, 366–368. For the position of Terence (contra Plautus) in *Tristia* 2, see Owen 1924, commentary on line 359.

Is not Naevius in our hands, and clinging to our minds, almost as of yesterday? So holy a thing is every ancient poem. As often as the question is raised, which is the better of the two, Pacuvius gains fame as the learned old writer, Accius as the lofty one. The gown of Afranius, it is said, was of Menander's fit; Plautus hurries along like his model, Epicharmus of Sicily. Caecilius wins the prize for dignity, Terence for art. These authors mighty Rome learns by heart; these she views, when packed in her narrow theatre; these she counts as her muster-roll of poets from the days of Livius the writer to our own.

Müller investigates the information on Terence's language and style provided by Horace in his epistle to Augustus and explores what it actually means when Horace writes that Terence was known for his *ars*.[19] He points out that Terence is the one writer in Horace's list that stands out from Plautus and the other comedians in the catalogue for having a new distinctive style. What is more, Terence was misunderstood and underappreciated by his contemporary audience. This fact fits well with the point that Horace is making in the epistle, i.e. that it is wrong of his own contemporary audience to rank the poetry of the past over the works of modern poets. As famously stated in the prologues of his plays, Terence was criticised by e.g. a *poeta uetus* and those favouring the old ways of writing,[20] much as Horace complains concerning the poets of his day. Horace thus implicitly separates Terence from the ancient authors that he is criticizing, as he is highlighting his *ars,* which was underappreciated by his contemporaries. Müller here points to the fact that Horace, directly after the passage quoted above, states that the masses are wrong to prefer the old poets*: interdum uulgus rectum uidet, est ubi peccat. / si ueteres ita miratur laudatque poetas / ut nihil anteferat, nihil illis comparet, errat;* (Hor. *Epist.* 2.1.63–65, 'At times the public see straight; sometimes they make mistakes. If they admire the ancient poets and cry them up so as to put nothing above them, nothing on their level, they are wrong.'). Horace on the other hand, would have the masses be not so hostile to *nouitas* (Hor. *Epist.* 2.1.90).[21] I would here like to add to the argument that the

---

19 Müller 2013, 367–370.
20 E.g. *nam in prologis scribundis operam abutitur, / non qui argumentum narret sed qui male-uoli / ueteris poetae maledictis respondeat* (Ter. *An.* 5–7, 'He is wasting his time writing prologues, not to explain the plot but to respond to the slanders of a malicious old playwright.') and *tum quod maleuolu' uetu' poeta dictitat / repente ad studium hunc se adplicasse musicum, / amicum ingenio fretum, haud natura sua* (Ter. *Haut.* 22–24, 'The malicious old playwright further asserts that our author has taken up the dramatic art rather suddenly, relying on the talent of his friends and not on his natural ability'); cf. e.g. *si ueteres ita miratur laudatque poetas / ut nihil anteferat, nihil illis comparet, errat* (Hor. *Epist.* 2.1.64–65, 'If they admire the ancient poets and cry them up so as to put nothing above them, nothing on their level, they are wrong.').
21 See Müller 2013, 366–368 for his full argument.

distinction between the *ueteres ... poetas* and Horace's defence for the new poets of his own day (*nouitas*) might be a mirror of Terence's particularly marked distinction between the *poeta uetus* and himself as the *poeta nouus*, e.g. in the prologue to *Phormio*: *nunc siquis est qui hoc dicat aut sic cogitet: / 'uetu' si poeta non lacessisset prior, / nullum inuenire prologum po[tui]sset nouos / quem diceret, nisi haberet cui male diceret' / is sibi responsum hoc habeat, in medio omnibus / palmam esse positam qui Artem tractent musicam.* (Ter. *Phorm.* 13–17, 'Now if there is anyone who is saying or thinking that, if the old playwright had not provoked him first, the young one would not have had the material for a prologue, not having anyone to abuse, let him take this as an answer, that the prize is freely available to everybody who practises the dramatic art.').[22]

Later in the epistle, Horace goes on to claim that writing comedy is a more stylistically demanding task than writing tragedy, but that Plautus does not live up to this as he only cares about the money that comes his way. Shortly afterwards he gives the foremost example of popular bad taste by referring to the interruption of theatrical performances by people, *indocti stolidique* (Hor. *Epist.* 2.1.184, 'unlearned and stupid'), calling for other types of entertainment, namely *aut ursum aut pugilis; his nam plebecula gaudet* (Hor. *Epist.* 2.1.186, 'for a bear or for boxers: it is in such things the rabble delights.'). This passage, Müller claims, recalls the failures of Terence's *Hecyra*, famously featured in Terence's prologues, as the play was interrupted by the crowd the two first times it was put on stage, at the first performance because the crowd preferred a boxing match and a rope-dancer over the play:

> *quom primum eam agere coepi, pugilum gloria*
> *(funambuli eodem accessit expectatio),*
> *comitum conuentu', strepitu', clamor mulierum*
> *fecere ut ante tempus exirem foras.*
>
> Ter. Hec. 33–36

> The first time I tried to perform the play, I was forced off the stage early; there was talk of boxers — and added to that a promise of a tightrope walker — crowds of supporters, general uproar, and women screaming.

The allusion, Müller argues, further points to Terence as a victim of the bad taste of the uneducated masses, and suggests that he was underappreciated by his

---

22 The distinction between 'old' and 'new' is particularly emphasised in the text's structure, with *uetus* in the beginning of line 13, and *nouos* at the end of line 14. See Maltby 2012 *ad loc.*

contemporary audience, just like Horace and his contemporaries.[23] The 'un-learned and stupid' audience at Hor. *Epist.* 2.1.184 might also mirror the '*populu*' ... *stupidus*' or foolish audience at Ter. *Hec.* 4.[24] This would indicate that Horace saw in the works of Terence a certain modernity of style and maybe the foreshadow-ing of the poetics of his own day, and that he saw him as an example of 'good taste', as opposed to the 'bad taste' of the masses.

Being moulded on Horace's second epistle, it might also be natural for Ovid's poem to make mention of the same example as its model and choose Terence over Plautus as a suitable comparison for himself. This seems especially likely bearing Müller's point in mind, as Horace in a similar way singled out Terence as a fitting parallel to himself and his fellow poets and their situation in present-day Rome, as opposed to Plautus, who was favoured by critics that were more old-fashioned. In Horace, Terence is appreciated for his *ars* in Augustan Rome, but was underappreciated and misunderstood by his contemporary audience, a point highlighted by the allusion to the prologue of *Hecyra* and the interruption of the two first attempts to perform it. In an allusive play on Horace's epistle, which was written, at least according to the biographical tradition, at the re-quest of Augustus himself, Ovid now mentions the same author in an elegiac epistle defending his own *Ars*, addressed to the very same man. *Ars* might also be a more general feature of Ovid's verse,[25] one that he shares with Terence, who was also, like Ovid, the prime example of his own, fundamentally erotic genre, as opposed to the less sophisticated Plautus. I would like to argue, then, that the point of Ovid's reference to Terence is not only that he was not a *conuiua* in real life, just as he himself is not an immoral person, a point which in itself must be read with a certain irony given Terence's reputation of being a real-life *conui-ua* and the connection between the *praeceptor amoris* and the *kolax/parasitus*. Terence and *his ars* also fell victim to misunderstanding, which is exactly what Ovid accuses Augustus of doing now, i.e. misreading and misunderstanding his *Ars* when he deems it to be immoral. Furthermore, that the people who man-aged to remove Terence from the stage during the performance of *Hecyra* are labelled *indocti stolidique* in Horace's allusion adds to the fact that *Tristia* 2 is not as straightforward an appeal to the emperor as it seems on the surface. Thus

---

23 See Müller 2013, 367–368 for further discussion on Horace's allusion to the prologue of *Hecyra* in epistle 2.1. See also Rudd 1989, *ad loc.*

24 I am grateful to Sharon L. James for pointing me in direction of this connection.

25 One that he shares with e.g. Callimachus, cf. *quamuis ingenio non ualet, arte ualet* (Ov. *Am.* 1.15.14, 'though he sway not through genius, he sways through art.'), and in opposition to e.g. the cruder Ennius, cf. *Ennius ingenio maximus, arte rudis* (Ov. *Tr.* 2.424, 'Ennius mighty in genius, rude in art.').

Ovid's mention of Terence, seen in light of the Horatian passage, takes on several new levels of meaning.

Godlike *mores*: anger, pity and rape

As will be further argued in this section, an allusion to Terence also plays a key role in Ovid's address to Augustus in the opening of *Tristia* 2, in his comparing him to Jupiter. The Terentian allusion adds to the ironic and potentially dangerous aspects of *Tristia* 2 as it hints at Augustus' double standards in singling out the *Ars amatoria* as immoral and at the moral licence found in Rome's mythological past, in the emperor's divine lineage and in Augustan Rome.

Augustus is repeatedly associated with Jupiter in Ovid's exile poetry,[26] and the connection between them is made explicitly clear also in *Tristia* 2. Here, Ovid urges the emperor to follow the *mores* of the god that he shares a supreme role with when it comes to being lenient to the victims of his anger:

> *si, quotiens peccant homines, sua fulmina mittat*
>   *Iuppiter, exiguo tempore inermis erit;*
> *nunc ubi detonuit strepituque exterruit orbem,*
>   *purum discussis aera reddit aquis.*
> *iure igitur genitorque deum rectorque uocatur,*
>   *iure capax mundus nil Ioue maius habet.*
> *tu quoque, cum patriae rector dicare paterque,*
>   *utere more dei nomen habentis idem.*
> *idque facis, nec te quisquam moderatius umquam*
>   *imperii potuit frena tenere sui.*
>
>   Ov. *Tr.* 2.33–42

If at every human error Jupiter should hurl his thunderbolts, he would in a brief space be weaponless. But as it is, when the roll of his thunder has died away, affrighting the world with its roar, he scatters the rain-clouds and clears the air. Just it is, then, to call him the father and ruler of the gods, just it is that in the spacious universe there is no one mightier than Jove. Do you also, seeing that you are called ruler and father of our native land, follow the way of the god who has the same title. And that you do; no one has ever been able to hold the reins of his power with more restraint.

In her commentary on the passage, Ingleheart states that it is allegorical and that the parallels between Jupiter and Augustus suggest a metaphorical read-

---

26 Claassen 2012 [2008] treats Augustus as 'the angry god' Jupiter in Ovid's exilic works; see e.g. 29–33.

ing, the point being that Augustus has the right to be angry, but should not have taken further action against the poet.[27] She adds to this that asking the emperor to follow the *mores* of Jupiter can be read with a certain irony, in light of Ovid's previous representations of Jupiter and the picture of him as a 'serial adulterer' throughout his earlier poetic works.[28] This is also an aspect of the god of which the reader is reminded later in *Tristia* 2.

The quoted passage contains the only occurrence of the verb *detono* in Ovid, and is an allusion to *Iupiter Tonans*. This aspect of the god played an important part in justifying Augustan power, as it defined Augustus as the one chosen by Jupiter, miraculously spared from a lightning bolt that grazed him and struck a slave lighting the way in front of him during the campaign against the Cantabri in the 20s BCE. This was seen as a sign that he was the one chosen by the mighty god, and Augustus had immediately built a marble temple to *Iupiter Tonans* on the Capitol near the temple of *Iupiter Optimus Maximus*.[29] However, in the context of Ovid's exile poetry and especially *Tristia* 2, it is hard not to read the picture of the thundering Jupiter in light of the present tension between Augustus as Jupiter and Jupiter as 'serial adulterer' or rapist, known to take on different forms or disguises and rape mortal women. This aspect of the god was fully demonstrated in the *Metamorphoses*, e.g. in the catalogue of Jupiter's victims in *Met.* 6.103–128, as part of the poet's depiction of Arachne's metamorphic tapestry, presenting immoral actions conducted by the gods and their ill deeds towards mortals.[30]

The connection between these very two aspects of the god, the mighty thundering god and the rapist in disguise, had been made previously, in Terence's *Eunuchus*. Here Jupiter, through a painting of his rape of Danae in the form of golden rain on an internal wall in the house of the *meretrix* Thais, offers the *adulescens* Chaerea inspiration to rape the *uirgo* Pamphila in the same manner while she is asleep. He does so after having gained access to Thais' house and the inner rooms by disguising himself as a eunuch:

---

27 Ingleheart 2010, *ad loc.*

28 Ingleheart 2010, *ad loc.* Davis 1989, Chapter Three, discusses how Ovid in several poems throughout the *Amores* uses Jupiter as *exemplum*, and model for illicit sex.

29 See Zanker 2003 [1988], 108.

30 Ovid's and Arachne's situations are in fact very much alike; Harries argues that Arachne, whose '*ars* by which she wins her *nomen memorabile* becomes the cause of her own destruction', is 'a prototype of the exiled poet' and that they are both destroyed by their talent: *ingenio est poena reperta meo* (Ov. *Tr.* 2.12, 'a penalty has been found for my talent.'). See full discussion in Harries 1990, 64–82.

> ibi inerat pictura haec, Iouem
quo pacto Danaae misisse aiunt quondam in gremium imbrem aureum.
egomet quoque id spectare coepi, et quia consimilem luserat
iam olim ille ludum, impendio magis animu' gaudebat mihi,
deum sese in hominem conuortisse atque in alienas tegulas
uenisse clanculum per inpluuium fucum factum mulieri.
at quem deum ! 'qui templa caeli summa sonitu concutit.'
ego homuncio hoc non facerem? Ego **illuduero ita feci** – ac lubens.

Ter. Eun. 584–591

It depicted the story of how Jupiter sent a shower of gold into Danae's bosom. I began to look at it myself, and the fact that he had played a similar game long ago made me all the more excited: a god had turned himself into human shape, made his way by stealth on to another man's roof, and come through the skylight to play a trick on a woman. And what a god! The one who shakes the lofty vaults of heaven with his thunder! Was I, a mere mortal, not to do the same? I did just that — and gladly.

In the comic scene, Chaerea explains to a friend how he had been left alone with the girl, who was sitting on a bed after a bath and staring at the painting. He then started to stare at it himself, and was inspired to recreate the deed; he thus imitated Jupiter and raped the girl, who had now fallen asleep, in the same manner that he imagined the god to have raped Danae. When he describes to his friend how his plan was set in motion by divine inspiration, he brings forth the image of the thundering Jupiter, and he is positive that he acted in a godlike manner. The image of the thundering Jupiter here adds to the explanation and justification for what he has done; he, merely a little man, had imitated the most powerful god of them all when he, in disguise, raped a girl, and he had therefore done it happily.

Only differing in word choice, the invocation of *Iupiter Tonans* is effectively the same in Ovid's text and the comic passage. Furthermore, the allusion offers an explanation to the at first somewhat puzzling formulation in Ovid's line 40–41, *utere more dei nomen habentis idem. / idque facis* (Ov. *Tr.* 2.40–41). Gareth Williams argues that Ovid first praises Augustus for acting like the god, but that line 40 implies that in this one matter, i.e. in being lenient towards a victim of his anger, he is in fact *not* acting like Jupiter. He quickly removes this implication again by adding *idque facis*, but only after having made the implication in the first place.[31] Ingleheart adds to this that the passage can be read ironically in light of the extensive attention Ovid gives to Jupiter's many adulterous affairs in

---

31 Williams 1994, 171–172.

Tristia 2 and in his work in general.[32] It is to this ironical aspect of *Tristia* 2 that the Terentian allusion adds. The introduction of *Iupiter Tonans* and the reassurance that Augustus is in fact following Jupiter's *mores* with the phrase *idque facis* is effectively a repetition of the way Chaerea explains how he was inspired by Jupiter to imitate him and rape the girl Pamphila. It affirms that he in fact did it, with *illud ... feci* in line 591 in the *Eunuchus*, and Ovid's choice of words here conjure the earlier passage to mind. Just as Chaerea imagines thundering Jupiter — and this image adds to his motivation for imitating him and to the reason for why he in the end actually did it — Ovid states that Augustus should imitate *Iupiter Tonans*, and adds shortly after that he indeed does do so. As Augustus has not actually followed the *mores* of Jupiter in his actions towards the poet as victim of his anger, the phrase *idque facis* stands out as somewhat puzzling at first. However, the double meaning of the passage comes out when the allusion to the *Eunuchus* and Chaerea's Jovian rape becomes clear. It is also worth noting the assonance created by the repetition of the vowels *u* and *i* in the phrase *sonitu concutit* in line 590 of the Terentian text, and how a parallel effect is created in *detonuit, strepituque* and *discussis* in line 35–36 of the Ovidian passage.[33] Thus, Ovid's presentation of Augustus' imitation of Jupiter is made ambivalent through the intertextual recall of Chaerea's imitation of Jupiter in Terence: Jovian power can be wielded for purposes both good (ruling Rome) and bad (raping girls/committing adultery and exiling Ovid).

In this way, Ovid connects the recurring image of Augustus as Jupiter and Jupiter's sexual *mores* at yet another level in the text, in an allusive play on Terence. The irony gains yet another level when Ovid later in the poem states that Augustus wants the people to imitate him and his *mores*, e.g. in lines 233–234, *urbs quoque te et legum lassat tutela tuarum / et morum, similes quos cupis esse tuis* (Ov. *Tr.* 2.233–234, 'The city also wearies you, and the guardianship of your laws and of the morals which you desire to be like your own.'). If the people were to imitate Augustus' *mores*, in light of him imitating the *mores* of Jupiter, this could easily prompt actions in conflict with the Augustan law, which brings Augustus back to one of the reasons that allegedly made him introduce the laws in the first place — i.e. increasing sexual licence among elite Romans. Furthermore, prompting this kind of behaviour is exactly what he accuses Ovid of doing in his *Ars amatoria*. In essence, Ovid is accused for providing a poem — the *Ars amatoria* — that through its didactic explanations and multiple *exempla*

---

32 Ingleheart 2010, *ad loc.*
33 I am indebted to Tristan Franklinos for pointing this out to me.

prompts the reader to imitate the actions described — actions that break with the *Lex Iulia de adulteriis coercendis*.

The irony in the connection between Augustus as an imitator of Jupiter and the Terentian scene and the rape inspired by Jupiter's rape of Danae depends fully on the social standing of the victim of the rape. As the comedy convention dictates, the victims of comic rapes in the end turn out to be long lost respectable citizen daughters, a type of character denoted by the term *uirgo* throughout the plays, who contrasts with the comic *meretrix*.[34] The validity of the accusations made against Ovid is entirely dependent on the status of the women involved, as the law that he has allegedly broken concerns Roman matrons and marriageable women. Ovid also makes it explicit in *Tristia* 2 that Augustus must have misread (or maybe not read at all) his *Ars*, when he says that it teaches adultery and hence is criminal, as he there only addresses *meretrices*. He had in the opening of the book, he says, even made sure to state explicitly that it does not address Roman wives and marriageable women and that such women should stay away, and that no *crimen* can be found in his poem.[35] This is, however, exactly the type of woman that is involved in the comic rape scene and that is invoked in the allusion to Chaerea's rape, placing the emperor himself in the role of the Jovian imitator, and, given the status of the girl, the author of a *crimen*.

The Terentian image blends in with the message that follows when Ovid states that if he were to admit that the *Ars amatoria* could prompt imitation and promote illicit behaviour among elite women when they read it, this would also be true of many other things as well, such as public celebrations and certain locations at Rome. Through an allusive play with the first book of the *Ars amatoria*, he demonstrates over lines 279–300 that the *ludi* and the theatres, the Circus and porticos would have to be shut down, as these locations suggest many opportunities for improper behaviour.[36] The occasions and places mentioned play simultaneously with their suitability for flirting, as the poet demonstrated in the *Ars amatoria*, and Augustus' fondness for and boosting of public spectacles and his construction of porticos and temples. They also engage with the fact that if Ovid through his eroto-didactic poetry is guilty of promoting

---

34 For a discussion of the term *uirgo* in comedy, see Watson 1983, 120–123.

35 Quoted in Chapter One, note 3.

36 *Tristia* 2.279–300 points to the first book of the *Ars amatoria* and Ovid's listing of porticos, theatres, the Circus, gladiatorial shows and temples as suitable locations and occasions for young men to find suitable love-interests. Cf. also *Ars am.* 3.387–398.

illicit behaviour, Augustus is equally guilty for providing the occasions and locations where such behaviour could take place.[37]

Ovid's argument follows the same pattern in the lines to follow: When he states that it would be inadvisable to visit the temples, the reader is again reminded of the double meaning in Ovid's likening of Augustus to Jupiter in the opening of the letter. Standing in Jupiter's temple, any woman would quickly remember how many women this god had made mothers (*quam multas matres fecerit ille deus*, Ov. *Tr.* 2.290), and likewise in the temple of Juno, where one would be reminded of how the queen of the gods grieved over her husband's many adulterous affairs, i.e. many of the same *caelestia crimina* (heavenly crimes, Ov. *Met.* 6.131) already listed e.g. in Arachne's tapestry in the *Metamorphoses*:

> Maeonis elusam designat imagine tauri
> Europen; uerum taurum, freta uera putares;
> ipsa uidebatur terras spectare relictas   105
> et comites clamare suas tactumque uereri
> adsilientis aquae timidasque reducere plantas.
> fecit et Asterien aquila luctante teneri,
> fecit olorinis Ledam recubare sub alis;
> addidit ut satyri celatus imagine pulchram   110
> Iuppiter inplerit gemino Nycteida fetu,
> Amphitryon fuerit cum te, Tirynthia, cepit,
> aureus ut Danaen, Asopida luserit ignis,
> Mnemosynen pastor, uarius Deoida serpens.
>
>   Ov. *Met.* 6.103–114

Arachne pictures Europa cheated by the disguise of the bull: a real bull and real waves you would think them. The girl seems to be looking back upon the land she has left, calling on her companions, and, fearful of the touch of the leaping waves, to be drawing back her timid feet. She wrought Asterie, held by the struggling eagle; she wrought Leda, beneath the swan's wings. She added how, in a satyr's image hidden, Jove filled lovely Antiope with twin offspring; how he was Amphitryon when he cheated you, Alcmena; how in a golden shower he tricked Danae; Aegina, as a flame; Mnemosyne, as a shepherd; Deo's daughter, as a spotted snake.

Arachne — a character condemned due to her art and her depiction of the moral wrongdoings conducted by a more powerful party, i.e. the *crimina* of the gods and most prominently those of Jupiter — is regarded as closely associated with

---

37 See also discussion in Owen 1924 *ad loc.* and Ingleheart 2010, *ad loc.*

the poet Ovid in exile.[38] Given this association, the tapestry will be brought to mind through the many reminders of Jupiter's rapes in disguise throughout *Tristia* 2. The fact that the rape of Danae is featured in the tapestry also plays well with the Terentian allusion in the opening of the poem. It is worth noting the use of *luserit* (to play/trick, but also with sexual undertones, depending on context)[39] to describe Jupiter's action as shown in Arachne's tapestry in line 113, and how it recalls how the same verb is deployed in the *Eunuchus* to denote the exact same mythological story depicted in a painting in line 586–587: *et quia consimilem **luserat** / iam olim ille ludum* ('and, because he once had played the same game').[40] In Terence, Jupiter is described in line 585 as *imbrem aureum*, 'golden rain,' which can be compared to Jupiter's description as *aureus* in *Met*. 6.113.

The tapestry continues to be present when Ovid moves on and reminds the reader of the vices found in the stories of different gods, and he fittingly starts with Minerva: in his list of temples, he starts with hers, placed on the Aventine, then those of Mars Ultor and Venus, placed in the Forum Augustum and that of Isis in the Forum Iulium. The virgin goddess Minerva's temple recalls her attempted rape by Vulcan, the temples of Mars and Venus, the ancestors of the *gens Iulia*, recall their adulterous affair, and Isis/Io's temple brings Jupiter's love for her and Juno's rage to mind. Furthermore, the goddesses Venus, Diana and Ceres all had affairs with mortal men. This passage too hints at the *crimina* immanent in Rome's mythological founding and the divine lineage of the emperor. This is a recurrent theme throughout Ovid's poetry, also exemplified shortly before in the lines leading up to the passage. Here it is part of the argument that *all* poetry, including Roman poetry, has the power to corrupt the minds of readers, i.e., inspire illicit behaviour, when approached in the wrong way. In lines 259–260, Ovid reminded his addressee that if a married woman were to read Ennius' *Annales*, she would soon learn the way in which Ilia became the mother of Romulus, i.e. by being raped by Mars. If she were to read Lucretius' *De rerum natura*, she would be left wondering how Venus became the mother of Aeneas, the ancestor of the emperor himself. The reader is again explicitly reminded of this in lines 299–300, where Ovid lists famous relationships between goddesses and mortal men: *in Venerem Anchises, in Lunam Latmius heros, / in Cererem Iasion, qui referatur, erit* (Ov. *Tr*. 2.299–300, 'Anchises will remind her of Venus, the Latmian hero of Luna, Iasion of Ceres.'). It is worth

---

38 See e.g. Harries 1990; Johnson 2008, 118–119; and Thorsen 2018b, 265–268.
39 See Adams 1982, 162–163.
40 Cf. also the use of the same verb in *Amores* 1.3, of Jupiter's rape of Leda while he is disguised as a swan, see Davis 1989, 71.

noting that all three goddesses mentioned — Venus, Diana and Ceres — are closely tied to Augustus; Venus as the foremother of the *gens Iulia*, Diana as the twin sister of Apollo who, together with her twin brother, was invoked by Augustus as protector of the new Golden Age, and Ceres, as symbol of the fertility that flourished under the *Pax Augusta*.[41] Throughout this section, Ovid shows that the very behaviour that he is accused of prompting through the *Ars* can just as easily be promoted by the stories of the foundation of Rome, upon which the validation of Augustan rule rests, and by the mythology that surrounds it.

The reference to theatres in lines 279–280 works in a similar manner: *ut tamen hoc fatear, ludi quoque semina praebent / nequitiae: tolli tota theatra iube* (Ov. *Tr.* 2.279–280, 'Even should I admit this charge, the games also furnish the seeds of wrong doing; order the abolition of all the theatres!') clearly points to the theatrical performances provided at the *ludi*. But it also invokes the *Ars*, and the *praeceptor's* lecture on how the theatre is the perfect place to find a mistress: *sed tu praecipue curuis uenare theatris; / haec loca sunt uoto fertiliora tuo* (Ov. *Ars am.* 1.89–90, 'But specially do your hunting in the round theatres: more bountifully do these repay your vows.'). Here, having established that young men should hunt for a *puella* in the theatres, Ovid uses the odd *exemplum* of the rape of the Sabine women, the first Roman wives and the mythological foundation for the institution of Roman marriage, in this context presented as having taken place at the theatre and not at the *Consualia*. Within Ovid's anti-marital love elegy, this *exemplum* represents a clear paradox. The focus on the brutality of the actions and the fear of the women, referred to as *uirgines*, the type of women for whom Ovid both in the *Ars amatoria* and repeatedly in *Tristia* 2 argues the *Ars amatoria* is not intended, has little to do with the way of wooing the elegiac *puella*. However, as I will argue in Chapter Two, on marriage, this passage too alludes to Terence's *Eunuchus* and what to our knowledge arguably constitutes the most brutal rape scene of new comedy, and works to highlight the brutal origin of Roman marriage and the dangers of being a young mar-

---

41 The connection between the Augustan peace and Ceres is highlighted by Ovid, e.g. in the *Fasti*: *gratia dis domuique tuae, religata catenis / iam pridem uestro sub pede bella iacent. / sub iuga bos ueniat, sub terras semen aratas. / pax Cererem nutrit, pacis alumna Ceres* (Ov. *Fast.* 1.701–704, 'Thanks be to the gods and to your house! Under your foot long time War has been laid in chains. Yoke the ox, commit the seed to the ploughed earth. Peace is the nurse of Ceres, and Ceres is the foster-child of Peace.') and *pace Ceres laeta est, et uos orate, coloni, / perpetuam pacem pacificumque ducem!* (Ov. *Fast.* 4.407–408, 'Ceres delights in peace; and you, ye husbandmen, pray for perpetual peace and for a pacific prince.'). My text for the Fasti is Bömer 1957.

riageable woman in Rome.[42] Furthermore, in the mythological *exemplum* in the *Ars amatoria*, Romulus himself is given the role of *praeceptor amoris*, a fact that plays well with Ovid's tactics in this section of *Tristia* 2.

Mimicking *artes*

The idea that art can prompt imitation has been shown to be a widespread conception in the ancient Western world, and the theme is explored both in Ovid's *Tristia* 2 and Terence' *Eunuchus*. This idea is explained by Germany as 'mimetic contagion', defined as 'the viewer's tendency to imitate or absorb behaviours or ethical qualities from an artwork'.[43] This theory functions as an explanation of how life can imitate visual art, i.e. a reversal of the conventional pattern of *mimesis*, the creation of artwork in correspondence with life and the physical world. Germany provides a lengthy treatment of the concept in antiquity in general within e.g. cultic and erotic art and the philosophical tradition, and in Roman society. The starting point and key focus for this investigation is the unconventional rape scene in Terence's *Eunuchus*, particularly the implications of the fact that Chaerea imitates an erotic painting when he commits rape. Germany argues that it is the painting itself that suggests and facilitates the rape and, consequently, that the action was not planned prior to the young man's discovery of the painting. Germany posits that this sequence of events is in line with the ancient phenomenon described as 'mimetic contagion'. Whether or not the painting in the *Eunuchus* is the direct inspiration for the rape itself,[44] it offers

---

42 Chapter Two argues for a connection between the violent comic rape-marriage plots found in Terence and Ovid's portrayal of rape and marriage in his love elegies. The argument is largely based on allusions to Terence in the opening of the first book of *Ars amatoria*. Thorsen 2018a argues that one key message of the *Ars amatoria*, on a deeper level, is that marriage is ultimately dangerous for women. See Thorsen 2018a, 141–168.

43 Germany 2016, 81.

44 The leading view in the extensive research on the rape scene in the *Eunuchus* is that one of the most unconventional and shocking traits of this particular rape is that it is not a spur of the moment action, but rather planned out in advance by the rapist; see e.g. Rosivach 1998, 46 and Sharrock 2009, 222. James 2016a convincingly argues that Chaerea's plan is to 'get sex', i.e. commit rape, from the beginning. Germany's position seems to be backed up by Donatus's commentary on line 584 of the *Eunuchus*, where the painting is introduced in the play: *RESPECTENS TABVLAM QVANDAM PICTAM: bene accedit repente pictura ad hortamenta aggrediendae uirginis, ideo quia non ad hoc uenerat Chaerea, ut uitiaret puellam sed ut uideret, audiret essetque una, cum nihil amplius cogitare ausus fuerit, usque dum picturam cerneret.* (Donat. *Commentum Terenti ad loc.*, 'LOOKING AT A CERTAIN PICTURE: that the painting sudden-

divine inspiration for and justification of the manner in which the sexual en-
counter/rape is executed, and it holds a central position in the action of the play
and the unique rape scene in the middle of it.

Germany's definition of 'mimetic contagion', i.e. the ancient experience of
the fact that visual artistic representations can inspire imitation, might also be
said to be a theme throughout *Tristia* 2. In fact, the concept of life imitating art is
related to what Ovid's own *Ars amatoria* is being accused of, i.e. inspiring his
audience by teaching them how to to commit adultery. Ovid first insists that
claiming that the *Ars amatoria* has the power to prompt imitation in the reader
claims too much on behalf of his poetry (*'at quasdam uitio.' quicumque hoc con-
cipit, errat, / et nimium scriptis arrogat ille meis.* Ov. *Tr.* 2.277–278, 'Whoever
believes that this has resulted in depravity is mistaken and attributes too much
to my works.'). However, he goes on to say that if he *were* to admit that his poetry could prompt imitation, in this case illicit behaviour, this would obviously go
for all poetry and indeed the other art forms invoking love and erotic passion as
well.[45] This would include presentations of the gods and the mythology by
which the emperor justifies his own regime, as discussed above. In light of this,
the emperor's singling out of Ovid and his *Ars amatoria* as the only artist and
work of art that merit punishment for being immoral, or rather for inspiring
immoral behaviour, does not make much sense. This becomes clear in the
lengthy catalogue of Greek and Latin poets, who have all concerned themselves
with themes involving love and erotic passion, that appears in lines 363–470.
Ovid's claim is that he is merely following their example.

---

ly comes up to offer incitement to rape the virgin fits well, since Chaerea had not come to immediately rape the girl, but to "see her, hear her and be together with her", as he would have
dared to think of nothing more up until the moment he saw the painting.'). Germany adds that
several modern critics (e.g. Philippides 1995 and Barsby 1999) have quoted the passage from
Donatus 'with tentative approval' or have made a related point, i.e. that rape is not mentioned
in a clear way before this moment in the play, but without trying to answer the majority of the
critics who either ignore or try to refute Donatus' statement. See full discussion in Germany
2016, 28–48. Whether we see the rape as fully motivated by the painting or whether we see the
painting more as encouraging the consummation of an already planned or at least hoped for
opportunity to commit rape by offering inspiration to do it in the same way as Jupiter had once
done, the ancient's overall concern for art's impact on people, as demonstrated by Germany, is
relevant in the context of the present discussion. For the text of Donatus, see also Wessner
1902–1908.

45 Over lines 363–468 of *Tristia* 2, Ovid provides a lengthy, non-chronological catalogue of
Greek and Latin poets within different genres who in some way have written about love in ways
that could inspire the reader to commit allegedly immoral acts in the same manner as the *Ars
amatoria* is accused of doing.

The *Ars amatoria* is not a visual work of art. In this sense it does not fit directly in with the 'contagious' visual arts as defined by Germany. Ovid does, however, bring in the visual arts as a comparison in his defence of his eroto-didactic poem. Over lines 497–520 he discusses mime and insists that this art form, at least, must have a much greater potential for corruption than his *Ars amatoria*: It contains obscene jokes, and always includes *uetiti crimen amoris* (Ov. *Tr.* 2.498, 'the crime of forbidden love'), i.e. adultery. Still, Ovid claims, marriageable girls, married women, husbands, boys, and members of the senate are present at mime acts. At mime shows, he states, it is not only the ears that are violated by impure words (*nec satis incestis temerari uocibus aures*, Ov. *Tr.* 2.503, 'Nor is it enough that the ear is outraged with impure words'), but also the eyes become accustomed to shameful things (*adsuescunt oculi multa pudenda pati*, Ov. *Tr.* 2.504, 'the eyes grow accustomed to many shameful sights'). Thus, mime is not only morally damaging due to its obscene content, but also because it as a theatrical performance has a direct effect on its audience both aurally and visually.[46] What is more, Augustus himself pays for such performances. Is it the stage then, Ovid wonders, that makes this genre safe? In that case, his own poems have also often been performed, even before the eyes of Augustus himself: *et mea sunt populo saltata poemata saepe, / saepe oculos etiam detinuere tuos* (Ov. *Tr.* 2.519–520, 'My poems too have often been presented to the people with dancing, often they have even beguiled your own eyes.'). Thus, Ovid effectively makes it clear that he is not really arguing that art — his own in particular — has no effect on people, but rather that his art cannot possibly be held as worse than the visual artistic representations favoured by Augustus: What is more, he here for the first time unambiguously insinuates that the emperor, in insisting on Ovid's ability to write poetry that prompts imitation, is himself guilty of promoting adultery, by financing mime shows containing adulterous themes, forbidden by his own laws.[47]

It is worth noting that it has been claimed that Chaerea's account of his rape of Pamphila might be seen in connection with mime. One such argument is proposed by Germany, who argues that the rape scene in the *Eunuchus* evokes a scene from mime 'in order to comment on the generic boundary of Terence's art',[48] as the scene include features that are common to mime, but not to new comedy, such as 'violent physicality, extreme sexuality and female nudity'.[49]

---

46 See Germany 2016, 57.
47 He has also implied it earlier in the poem; see Ingleheart 2010, commentary to line 509–514.
48 Germany 2016, 121.
49 Germany 2016, 150.

For instance, according to Germany, Chaerea, dressed up as a eunuch, is given the task of fanning Pamphila, who has been placed on a bed after a bath, and thus it is natural to imagine that she must be naked at this point. If the audience were actually to view the rape scene, Pamphila could not have been played by a male actor, as she would in the comic play, but rather by a naked *mima*.[50] Even though the later description of the girl's torn clothes (*uestem ... discidit* at 646 and *conscissa ueste* at 820) might indicate that the girl had some clothes on immediately prior to the rape after all,[51] I would still suggest that the scene can be read in light of a stock scene from adultery mime, i.e. a scene in which a citizen man disguises himself as a slave to be able to enter his mistress' house, which is indicated by what I argue is an allusion to it in Horace's satire 2.7.[52]

After his over 20-line consideration of mime, Ovid moves on to another visual artform and considers the effect on the viewer of various sorts of paintings, among them didactic erotic paintings. Furthermore, he points out that such paintings can in fact be found in Augustus' own houses:[53]

> *scilicet in domibus uestris ut prisca uirorum*
> *artifici fulgent corpora picta manu,*
> *sic quae concubitus uarios Venerisque figuras*
> *exprimat, est aliquo parua tabella loco:*

---

50 In the comic play, everything of course happens backstage, and not onstage, as it would in a true mime, but still in what is described by Germany as not 'not some vague interior space, but in a room as discretely bounded as a stage'. Germany 2016, 149.

51 I am indebted to Sharon L. James for pointing this important detail out to me, and that there is some incoherence, as it seems to be suggested that the girl's clothes were torn after the rape (*postquam ludificatust uirginem*, Ter. *Eun.* 645, 'after he'd had his fun and games with the poor girl').

52 I treat this in full in Chapter Four.

53 The OCT-edition, which I elsewhere follow, prints *in domibus nostris* for *in domibus uestris* in line 521. I follow Ingleheart's text and the reading *in domibus uestris* here and interpret it to refer to the houses of Augustus, as I believe that this fits the overall context and the tone of the poem. See also Ingleheart 2010 *ad loc.* Owen, on the other hand, favours the reading *in domibus nostris*, 'in our houses', as 'in attempting to conciliate a sovereign offended by his indecency, Ovid would hardly have dared to inform him [i.e. Augustus] that, following the fashion, he himself possessed an indecent picture in his palace.' See Owen 1924 *ad loc.* The painting of Venus in lines 527–528 is probably a reference to Apelles' painting of Venus Anadyomene, put on display in the temple that Augustus built in honour of the Deified Julius Caesar in the Roman Forum (Plin. *NH* XXXV 91), which would count as one of his houses. I am indebted to Thea Selliaas Thorsen for pointing this out to me. Ingleheart also makes this link: see Ingleheart 2010, *ad loc.* On the painting of Venus Anadyomene, see also Thorsen 2016, 161–162. See Myerowitz 1992, 155–156 (note 2) for an overview over manuscripts containing the versions *nostris* and *uestris* and the choices of different editors.

> *utque sedet uultu fassus Telamonius iram,*
> *inque oculis facinus barbara mater habet,*
> *sic madidos siccat digitis Venus uda capillos,*
> *et modo maternis tecta uidetur aquis.*

Ov. Tr. 2.521–528

Surely in your houses, even as figures of old heroes shine, painted by an artist's hand, so in some place a small tablet depicts the varying unions and forms of love; there sits not only the Telamonian with features confessing wrath and the barbarian mother with crime in her eyes, but Venus as well, wringing her damp hair with her hands and seeming barely covered by her maternal waves.

What Ovid does through his treatment of the visual (and aural) arts is accuse Augustus of being corrupted himself, through mimetic contagion, by being the spectator of mime and performances of Ovid's own poetry. Accusing Augustus of owning suggestive paintings fits well in this context, especially in light of the allusion to the rape scene in the *Eunuchus* inspired by a painting of Jupiter's rape of Danae. This enhances the implications of what it means that Augustus should act like the god, in the opening of the poem.[54]

Conclusion

As I have argued in this chapter, Ovid invokes Terence, and his *Eunuchus* in particular, in an allusive play that adds to the double meaning of *Tristia* 2, addressed directly to Augustus. Ovid's only explicit mention of the comic playwright in his entire oeuvre occurs at line *Tr.* 2.359. This citation, as I argue, is strongly connected to Horace's *Epist.* 2.1, also addressed to Augustus, and his treatment of Terence there. This allusive play, simultaneously invoking Horace's defence for contemporary artists and Terence's carefully crafted prologues, constitutes a potent part of Ovid's own defence for his poetry and his role as a poet, but at the same time hints at the emperor's double standards in exiling the poet on the basis of the alleged immorality of his *Ars amatoria*. This aspect of the poem is strengthened by a striking allusion, in the poem's opening address to Augustus, to Terence's most shocking rape scene: the *adulescens*

---

54 The painting in the *Eunuchus* is not a part of a series of erotic illustrations of sexual positions, as the paintings hinted at in the Ovidian text are, but it is still, as Germany points out, 'a sex scene painted above a bed in a brothel. By its placement if not by its nature alone it is clearly intended to arouse, and once aroused, the bedmates in such a *cubiculum* may be presumed to enact their own love scene.' Germany 2016, 60.

Chaerea's rape of the *uirgo* Pamphila inspired by Jupiter's rape of Danae in the *Eunuchus*. This allusion plays on the image of Augustus as Jupiter and what it really means when Ovid urges the emperor to follow the *mores* of the king of the Roman gods, his many rapes of mortal women being a favourite Ovidian *topos*,[55] and the effect on the people who will ostensibly follow the *mores* of Augustus. The allusive nexus in the letter is perfectly aligned with the overall theme that rounds it out, that is the ancient notion that art could prompt imitation (as demonstrated in the *Eunuchus*), the emperor's role in conveying 'immoral' art to the people, and lastly, that Augustus also surrounds himself with sexually ex- plicit and 'contagious' art. As will become evident in Chapter Two, there is fit- tingly striking allusion to the very same Terentian rape scene in the first book of the *Ars amatoria*, which, as I will argue, hints at problematic aspects of tradi- tional Roman notions concerning marriage, status, and rape. At the same time, Ovid's overall defence of art in *Tristia* 2 plays a part in a larger intratextual net- work, as it latches onto and elaborates a similar defence proposed in the *Remedia amoris*, which will be further treated in Chapter Three.

---

55 E.g. *Am.* 1.3.21–24, 1.10.1–8, *Met.* 6.103–114, *Tr.* 2.289–292.

2 Marriage, rape and status: the Roman tradition

Introduction

As shown in the first chapter, the allusive play and mention of Terence in *Tristia* 2 represent a rich starting point for further exploration of Terentian intertexts in Ovid's treatment of central topics that go straight to the core of his authorship.[1] One of the most significant among such topics is marriage, which was in Ovid's day and age also a central political topic. Marriage is a prominent feature within both the New Comic genre and elegiac poetry, and a point of focus for both Terence and Ovid. Whereas the defence of *artes* works as a connection between Ovid and Terence, as demonstrated in Chapter One, marriage, on the other hand, seems on the surface to be a point of incompatibility between the two poets: it is the ultimate goal for young lovers within Terence's genre, yet something that should be avoided by the elegiac lover. However, as will be demonstrated in this chapter, the Terentian construction of marriage-plots fits perfectly well with Ovid's treatment of marriage as a Roman institution.

Marriage was a particularly crucial topic in Ovid's day and age, when Augustus, after a period of both political and social chaos and what was perceived as a moral decline, sought to strengthen the morality of the upper classes and bring Roman society back to its proper order.[2] Laws were passed to regulate sexuality and promote marriage and childbirth, manifesting that such issues now were very public matters.[3] In the present chapter, my aim is to demonstrate that a number of Terentian allusions occur in Ovid's treatment of marriage that affect the reading of his works when they are exposed, and that through these allusions, Ovid reveals important notions about Roman culture and tradition. By this I hope to show that there is present in Ovid a tension between the ideal of reciprocal elegiac love and traditional Roman values concerning sexual relationships, recently reinforced by Augustan law, which highlights and criticises the forced and violent nature of traditional Roman marriage as well as the strict

---

1 I presented some of the findings in Chapter Two at a talk at the conference 'Greek and Roman literature: The erotic connection' in Oxford, June 11, 2016. Some of the argument thus overlaps with Brecke 2021, which is based on the conference talk. James 2016a, which was not published at the time of the conference, also argues for a close intertextual relationship between the first book of the *Ars amatoria* and the *Eunuchus*, pointing to several allusions. I touch upon some of the same allusions as James.
2 See e.g. Eder 2005, 28.
3 An important study on Roman marriage is Treggiari 1991.

https://doi.org/10.1515/9783111308036-002

social categories that limit what kind of erotic relationship that women in particular may enter into without having to face the danger of punishment. The deployment of allusions to Terence's most shocking rape-marriage plot highlights this tension further.

To understand the relationship between Ovid and Terence, it is crucial to understand the role of marriage within their genres and writings. The treatment of and attitude towards marriage found in their respective genres is at first sight separating factor between the two authors. But at the same time, both authors devote much attention to the theme of marriage and the marriage institution itself. In Terence, as in comedy generally, marriage is the conventional solution to the plot revolving around an *adulescens amator*'s love affair with a young girl or a pseudo-*meretrix*. Marriage marks the young man's entry into adulthood and a traditional Roman lifestyle[4] and solves the conflict that emerges in many of the plays between him and his father, typically a *durus senex*, because of the *adulescens*' affair. On the other hand, the idea of married life itself is not generally portrayed in a positive or desirable manner, and is something that must be tolerated rather than something pleasant.[5] In this way, the comic genre can be said to reflect the traditional Roman view that marriage is a duty and the obvious and correct way of living, and that everyone should marry; thus, the young lover of comedy almost always marries his girl if he can, i.e. if she turns out to be of citizen status and thus eligible for marriage. This stands in stark contrast to Ovid's elegiac notion of love, which challenges these exact traditional values by treating marriage as something that should be avoided rather than sought after. This contrast is further underlined by the fact that Ovid writes in a time where these traditional values are very much in focus, with the Augustan reinforcement of them via new conservative moral legislation.

In the ancient Roman world, marriage and love did not necessarily go hand in hand, or have much to do with each other at all, even though a successful marriage was considered a happy marriage and it was commonly thought that love would facilitate this.[6] The goal of the Roman marriage institution was, from its aetiological origin, procreation, i.e. the production of legitimate Roman citizens. It was established as a way of securing a steady growth of the population

---

4 On the Roman notion of love in marriage, see Treggiari 1991, 229–261.

5 On love and marriage in Roman comedy, see e.g. Duckworth 1994 [1952], 279–285; Konstan 1983, 18; 24–25; 1986 (on Terence's *Eunuchus*); Anderson 1984; Rosivach 1998 (on sexual exploitation of women in new comedy); Brown 2001 (on love and marriage in Greek new comedy).

6 The relationship between love and marriage in ancient Rome is discussed in Treggiari 1991, 260. See also Grimal 1967 and Lyne 1980, 1–18.

from the very beginning of the Roman state, and was conventionally thought of as a way to ensure that children would be legitimate.[7] From a more pragmatic point of view, for individual families the main concern was to marry off children to spouses of the right birth and rank to secure the future of the family, rather than letting them marry out of love. Thus, for most young Roman men and women, marrying was a duty and something they owed to their family and to the state itself. One can easily see how love could act as a hindrance to a marriage wanted by the family, and marriage as a hindrance to what we might call 'true' love. These traditional ideas were further strengthened by legislation in Ovid's time, under Augustan rule, allegedly as a result of a rising concern for the reduced marriage and fertility rate among the elite classes, combined with what was perceived as increased sexual licence and a lack of respect for the Roman tradition. The *Lex Iulia de maritandis ordinibus* of 18 BCE and the *Lex Iulia de adulteriis coercendis* passed shortly after made it disadvantageous to stay unmarried and childless, both socially and economically, and adultery was established as a public crime and a crime against the state, and not just a private offence against one's spouse or family.[8] Ovid's elegiac poetry claims, on the other hand, to have everything to do with love and nothing to do with duty, procreation and the (re)building of the Roman society. Saying that a husband was too *rusticus* if he was offended by his wife's extramarital affairs (Ov. *Am.* 3.4.37) must surely have been seen as highly provocative in light of the new law, and even illegal, as a husband who failed to accuse his wife of adultery if he knew about it would break the law of *lenocinium*, and he would be defined as a *leno*, a pimp.[9] In the end, Ovid's poetry was regarded as a threat to the state, as undermining public morality and its newly revitalized values, and was at least partially the reason for his exile in 8 CE.[10]

Thus, the views on marriage promoted in Terence and Ovid, and in comedy and Roman love elegy in general, differ dramatically on the surface. However, as this chapter will argue, marriage also functions as a bond between Terence and Ovid. They both write within a tradition where there is a strong interrelationship between rape and marriage, and they both devote much attention to this connection. The strong interrelationship between rape and marriage is

---

7 On the origin and function of Roman *matrimonium*, see e.g Treggiari 1991, 3–80.

8 On the *Lex Iulia*, see e.g. Csillag 1976 and Treggiari 1991, 88 and 277–298. On the sources on adultery at Rome, see e.g. Richlin 1981, 225–250. On prostitution and Roman law, see also McGinn 1998.

9 On the law on *lenocinium*, see Csillag 1976, 182, McGinn 1998, 171–193.

10 See e.g. White 2002, 16–17.

immanent in the Roman marriage institution in itself, whose foundation is inextricably tied to rape. At the same time, marriage plays a crucial part in the founding history of Rome and how the city evolved from just a small group of men surrounding the founding father Romulus to become the leading city of an empire. According to Rome's aetiological history, marriage did not exist among the earliest inhabitants of the newly founded city. According to Livy,[11] there was a shortage of women, and the Romans were rejected everywhere when they asked for alliances and *conubium* rights with neighbouring peoples. Thus, to be able to escape a crisis of population shortage and secure the growth of the city through the birth of new citizens, Romulus arranged for the Romans to kidnap suitable women for this purpose. Romulus invited people living nearby in the Sabine country to a festival, and under the supervision of their founding father, the Romans grabbed and carried off Sabine virgins. To reassure the women of their safety in the Roman city, Romulus pointed to the wrong done by their fathers when they denied the Romans the right to intermarriage and promised them honourable *matrimonium* and children. Thus, even though the rape of the Sabine women was illicit *raptus*, it was also crucial to the founding of the Roman Empire and very much considered at Rome as a fortunate event, for the women as well as for the Romans.[12]

In this specifically Roman context, then, rape is marriage and marriage is rape. This is mirrored in elements of the Roman marriage ceremony, where marriage can be seen as a symbolic re-enactment of rape, with the bride's notional hesitation or unwillingness to leave her parents, possibly a mock abduction of the bride, the wedding cry *Talassio* and the carrying of the bride over the threshold.[13] In his epithalamia, Catullus describes symbolic abductions of brides at weddings, e.g. in poem 61, where Hymenaeus snatches the crying virgin bride Junia and hands her over to her husband (*qui rapis teneram ad uirum / uirginem,* Catull. 61.3–4, 'you who carry off the tender virgin to her bridegroom')[14] and in poem 62 Hesperus tears the bride from the arms of her mother (*qui natam possis complexu auellere matris, / complexu matris retinentem auellere natam, / et iuueni*

---

11 Liv. 1.9. Ovid mentions the rape and the events that followed at *Fast.* 3.195–234. A fuller account of the rape is featured in Dion. Hal. *Ant. Rom.* 2.30–31.

12 On the Sabine rape and Roman *matrimonium*, see Treggiari 1991, 3–4.

13 It is hard to know exactly how an actual Roman wedding ceremony was performed, but there are various descriptions within the different genres (e.g. law, history, comedy, tragedy, epithalamia, and elegy). Hersch 2010 treats Roman wedding customs, see e.g. 61–65, 140–150. See also Hersch 2014. Legally though, women's consent was necessary, see Treggiari 1991, 147 and 170–180.

14 My text for Catullus is Mynors 1958.

ardenti castam donare puellam, Catull. 62.21–23, 'for you can endure to tear the daughter from her mother's embrace, from her mother's embrace to tear the close-clinging daughter, and give the chaste girl to the burning youth.'). Later Festus, in his epitome of Verrius Flaccus' treatise *De uerborum significatu,* describes a simulated bride kidnap performed at a wedding, where the bride is snatched from her mother's lap and handed over to her husband. The scene is performed as a mime in honour of Romulus, as he had done the very same thing with a happy outcome: *Rapi simulatur uirgo ex gremio matris, aut, si ea non est, ex proxima necessitudine, cum ad uirum traditur, quod uidelicet ea res feliciter Romulo cessit* (Fest. 364–365, 'it is pretended that a virgin is snatched from her mother's lap, or if she is not available, from the closest female relative, when handed over to the husband, because this thing evidently turned out happily for Romulus.').[15] In fact, many ancient authors concluded that several of the events conducted at a Roman wedding originated in the abduction of the Sabine women, and as Hersch states, 'historically, marriage by capture may be an exceedingly rare occurrence, but the story of the captive Sabine women was probably the one tale about Roman marriage that every Roman knew by heart (...)'.[16]

This connection between marriage and rape is reflected in the works of both Terence and Ovid, which is only natural since they are both writing within what are arguably two of the Roman literary genres most rooted in social practice and they treat themes such as interpersonal relationships in a real-life, everyday setting. Ovid, however, distinguishes between forced sex with a husband and that which is given freely, e.g. in *Amores* 1.4, *oscula iam sumet, iam non tantum oscula sumet: / quod mihi das furtim, iure coacta dabis* (Ov. Am. 1.4.63–64, 'Then he will take kisses from you, yes, then he will take not only kisses; what you give me in secret, you will give him as a right, because you must.').[17] Ovid also uses an *exemplum* involving a rape leading to a fortunate marriage union to illustrate his teachings, where the forced nature of the latter act creates a tension. The same can be said about the crucial issue of status, as Ovid seemingly claims only to address women not eligible for marriage. This becomes most apparent in his treatment of the rape of the Sabine women, the first Roman wives, used as an *exemplum* for his pupils on how to hunt for women in the first

---

15 My text for Festus is Lindsay 1913.

16 Hersch 2010, 148. Hersch also states that the quote from Festus is the only instance where a real or simulated seizing of the bride from her mother at a wedding is tied directly with the Sabine rape, though many events and items in the Roman wedding ceremony were said to have their origin in this story. See also Hersch 2010, 143 and 145.

17 McKeown argues that the *uir* in the poem might also be the patron of a freedwoman. See McKeown 1989, commentary to Ov. Am. 1.4, introduction.

book of *Ars amatoria*. This tension is highlighted by the manner in which he lets his treatment of the legendary abduction/marriage of the *uirgines*, as will be argued, be reflected in Terence and the rape of a young *uirgo* in his popular *Eunuchus*. On the other hand, it has been argued that Terence presents rape in the worst possible light,[18] especially in the *Eunuchus*, a play that contains a rape scene in many ways unique within the new comedy genre as it is known to us.

The Terentian rape-marriage plot

Rape leading to marriage is considered a general feature, or in the words of Leisner-Jensen, a 'convenient convention',[19] of the Roman comedy genre, and the rape of a citizen girl always, on every occasion, promotes the marriage between the girl and the rapist or, alternatively, a rape in the parental generation leads to a marriage in the next generation. Hence, rape in the comedy genre in one way or another facilitates marriage. Rape of citizen *uirgines* was considered a general trait of new comedy ever since Hellenistic times,[20] and it is generally not problematized as a wrongdoing or crime in the genre, as the outcome of the action is always considered fortunate for all parties. The marriage between rapist and victim eliminates the problematic aspect of the assault on what in almost all cases turns out to be the body of a citizen girl,[21] or a rape in the parental generation provides the female child born as a consequence of the rape with citizen status, thus giving her the opportunity to marry into a citizen family (as in e.g. Terence's *Phormio*). In several cases, the rape also gives the victim the opportunity to 'marry up' into a well-off family, as in e.g. Terence's *Adelphoe*.[22] The conventional comic rape is committed prior to the action of the play, by a drunk young man during a nocturnal religious festival. In accordance with the comedy convention, the rape is never acted out on stage, but rather narrated by one of

---

18 See James 1998.
19 Leisner-Jensen 2002, 173.
20 Leisner-Jensen 2002, 191.
21 In Terence's *Adelphoe*, the family of the raped girl do actually threaten to take the offender to court, but only insofar as they at this point believe that he will abandon his promise to marry the girl.
22 As Rosivach points out, the comic rapist never comes from a poor family, even though there are many poor families in the plays. See Rosivach 1998, 13–14.

the characters or outlined in the prologue, and in this way forms a part of the backdrop of the plot of the play.[23]

Even though the rape-marriage plot was considered a stock theme of the comic genre, it does not occur in more than nine of the 26 known comedies of Plautus and Terence, and it is demonstrably more common in the comedies of Terence than in Plautus. Whereas eleven of the total 20 known plays by Plautus at some point during the action address the issue of marriage or marriageability, all of Terence's six comedies involves at least one marriage or intended marriage in the plot. What is more, four of the Terentian marriage plots (*Andria, Hecyra, Eunuchus, Adelphoe*) involve the rape of a citizen girl, and one play involves a rape in the parental generation that facilitates the marriage between the victim's daughter and a young citizen man (*Phormio*). To compare, rape is not nearly as common in Plautus, and only four of the twenty known Plautine plays involve rape as part of the plot.[24]

Another factor that functions to highlight the rape aspect of the Terentian marriage plots is the unconventional way in which he represents some of the rapes that take place, most notably the brutal and explicitly described rapes of Philumena in the *Hecyra* and Pamphila in the *Eunuchus*.[25] The rape in *Hecyra* does contain many of the conventional traits of comic rapes; it was committed prior to the action of the play, after dark, by the drunk *adulescens* Pamphilus. The rape was not planned, but rather a spur of the moment attack on a young girl, whom he met on his way over to the house of the *meretrix* Bacchis, his long-term mistress. However, as the rape is narrated by Bacchis, the focus in her account is the shocking amount of violence used in the attack and the fact that there was a fight between attacker and victim, in which the perpetrator ripped a ring from the victim's finger, which he later gave to Bacchis herself as a gift. The focus on the violence and the detailed description is unconventional for the genre. Furthermore, instead of having a fortunate outcome in the sense that the rape facilitates a marriage, it rather has the negative consequence of temporarily jeopardizing an already existing marriage and the future of the young victim, whose mother desperately begs Pamphilus on her knees to keep the rape and

---

23 For an outline of the pattern of the comic rape plots, see e.g. Duckworth 1994 [1952]; Leisner-Jensen 2002.

24 For an overview of all incidents of consummated rape in Greek and Roman comedy, see Leisner-Jensen 2002. The rape in the parent generation in Terence's *Phormio* is not included here. See also Konstan and Raval 2018, 55–62 for a recent treatment of rape of and violence towards citizen women in new comedy.

25 James 1998 argues that in these two plays Terence presents rape in the worst possible light, and thus breaks with the convention of new comedy.

the subsequent birth of a child a secret.[26] In the end, Bacchis saves the day by paying a visit to the raped girl's mother, who recognizes her daughter's ring on Bacchis' finger. After this, she contentedly states that she has secured many well-deserved commodities for her former lover Pamphilus (*quot commodas res attuli! quot autem ademi curas!* Ter. *Hec.* 817, 'How many blessings I've brought him, and how many worries I've removed!').

The most unconventional rape-marriage scene in Roman comedy, and hence the most widely discussed in modern research, is the rape of Pamphila in *Eunuchus*.[27] Here, the rape scene is situated in the middle of the play, at the centre of the action, and the rape is committed in daytime by a sober and apparently calculating perpetrator after the divine *exemplum* of Jupiter in disguise and his rape of Danae.[28] The perpetrator is the young man Chaerea, who sees the young girl Pamphila in the street, as she is about to be delivered to the *meretrix* Thais as a present from her soldier lover Thraso. He immediately falls in love with her and must have her, and reminds his slave Parmeno that he has promised to help him in such circumstances, and that Parmeno often used to say that 'if he ever found something to love', *aliquid inueni / modo quod ames* (Ter. *Eun.* 308–309), he would be of great use in this matter. Parmeno is for his part on his way to Thais as well, as he is supposed to deliver a eunuch bought for her by Phaedria, Chaerea's older brother, who also is in love with her. Chaerea envies the eunuch, who will be a slave in the same house as the beautiful girl, and Parmeno suggests that there is a way for Chaerea to enjoy the advantages that he thinks will be bestowed upon the eunuch: *tu illis fruare commodis quibu' tu illum dicebas modo: / cibum una capias, adsis tangas ludas propter dormias* (Ter. *Eun.* 372–373, 'You could enjoy the benefits which you were just saying would be his — eat with her, live with her, touch her, play with her, sleep next to her.'). The solution is that Chaerea should take the eunuch's outfit and go in his place. Chaerea does so, enters the house and rapes the girl, inspired by a painting

---

26 Even though in this case the rape does not directly facilitate a marriage, the fact that Pamphilus is the rapist ensures the conventional fortunate outcome of the genre, as Pamphilus is not forced to divorce the woman that he professes to love. A similar plot can be found in Menander's *Epitrepontes*. On the rape in *Hecyra*, see Rosivach 1998, 27–30; on the rape in *Epitrepontes*, 30–32.

27 E.g. Germany 2016; James 2016a; 1998; Christenson 2013, 263–269; Paraskeviotis 2013; Rosivach 1998, 46–50; Philippides 1995.

28 The young man Chaerea has most definitely planned out in detail how to gain access to the girl of his dreams. That sex/rape also was part of his initial plan is the most common view, but as discussed in Chapter One, Germany 2016 proposes that rape might not have been part of the original plan.

picturing Jupiter's rape of Danae, a deed he sees as a model for his own. Rather than being ashamed of his deed, he is afterwards exceedingly happy about it, and he praises his own luck and cannot wait to tell someone about it. Later in the action, we learn about the girl's reaction to the rape from the maid Pythias, who is infuriated on the raped girl's behalf and threatens to physically attack Chaerea. She describes the rape as particularly violent, as Chaerea had both torn the girl's clothes and pulled her hair *after* the rape, and the severity of the violence is underlined by the fact that the girl now is crying and silenced by fear. Both the time of the rape, the sequence of action and the description of the girl's reaction to the rape are unconventional features in the comedy genre, but the action takes a conventional turn again when Pamphila is discovered to be an Attic citizen, abducted and sold into slavery as a child. She is married off to Chaerea, who considers himself the luckiest man in the world for suddenly having been blessed by the gods with so many good things: *O populares, ecqui' me hodie uiuit fortunatior? | nemo hercle quisquam; nam in me plane di potestatem suam | omnem ostendere quoi tam subito tot congruerint commoda* (Ter. *Eun.* 1031–1033, 'Fellow countrymen, is there anyone alive today more fortunate than me? Nobody at all. The gods have clearly manifested all their powers in my case; so many blessings have been heaped upon me so unexpectedly.').

Against the background of the Roman marriage institution and its strong link between forced abduction, rape and marriage, the rape-marriage plots must have had an extra level of resonance in the Roman context of the new comic genre. In many ways, the comic rapes followed by marriage between rapist and victim mirror the origin of the Roman marriage. A rape in the parent generation that secures the citizenship and rights of the offspring and hence a happy outcome, as in *Phormio*, closely mirrors the thought behind and the justification for the Sabine rape, i.e. that the women would carry legitimate Roman children with citizen rights. The connection might have been especially evident in the plot in the *Eunuchus*, where the rape-marriage theme and the fortunate outcome of the rape for all parties is so greatly elaborated.[29] The rapes are what would have been considered illicit sexual conduct, as the girls turn out to be citizens, but this potentially problematic feature is eliminated by the fortunate outcome for all involved parties and for society, in the form of a marriage and its natural outcome, the birth of a legitimate child. In this manner, the comic genre is in the end perfectly in line with traditional Roman ideals and values, a feature that is most prominent in Terence. In light of this, as I will argue in the following, it

---

29 Philippides 1995 argues that elements from the Roman wedding ritual can be found in the rape of Pamphila in the *Eunuchus*.

is not a coincidence that Ovid, whose elegiac poetry persistently returns to the rusticity of these precise values and the *crimen* that is imminent in the aetiological history of Rome,[30] lets his portrayal of the mythological foundation of the marriage institution play itself out at the theatre.

An Ovidian rape-marriage plot: a paradox

As Ovid sets out to teach young men how to find a *puella* in the first book of his didactic treatise *Ars amatoria*, he uses the aetiological myth of the rape of the Sabine women to illustrate how the 'hunt' should be conducted, and how the theatre is the perfect place to find suitable women. This is an obvious paradox: the Sabine women were the first legal wives of Rome, sought to increase the Roman population, and the story makes up the mythological foundation for the Roman marriage institution. Even though Ovid aims to teach his students to find love that has the potential to last for a longer period, the goal is in no way for them to find a wife and have children. The Sabine women would be the symbol for the same type of women referred to in line 31–32, *este procul, uittae tenues, insigne pudoris, / quaeque tegis medios instita longa pedes* (Ov. *Ars am.* 1.31–32, 'Keep far away, you slender fillets, emblems of modesty, and the long skirt that hides the feet in its folds.'), who Ovid claims have no place in his poem, as this would be against the fairly recently enacted Augustan law, and his work will contain no *crimen* (*inque meo nullum carmine crimen erit*, Ov. *Ars am.* 1.34, 'And in my verse shall be no wrong-doing.'). On the contrary, he later explicitly claims that his only intended female audience is *meretrices* (*et procul a scripta solis meretricibus Arte / summouet ingenuas pagina prima manus*, Ov. *Tr.* 2.303–304, 'Far from the "Art", written for courtesans alone, its first page warns the hands of upright women.').[31]

Ovid introduces the interlude on the Sabine women by stating that he will demonstrate how the theatre is the place for loss of chastity (*ille locus casti damna pudoris habet* (Ov. *Ars am.* 1.100, 'to chastity that place is fatal.'). This notion is repeated at the end of the interlude, where he concludes that the thea-

---

30 E.g. at *Am.* 3.5.37–42.
31 However, the latter statement, written in exile and addressed directly to Augustus, cannot necessarily be taken at face value; *Amores* 3.4 strongly suggests otherwise, and in *Amores* 1.7 the *puella* is describes as having *ingenuas ... genas* ('free-born cheeks') at line 50, jf. *ingenuas ... manus* ('free-born hands') at *Tr.* 2.204. Also, there are several *matronae* present in the *Ars amatoria*, in e.g. the story of Venus' adulterous affair with Mars in Book Two (*Ars am.* 2.561–600), which, if read in the context of Ovid's Rome, would indeed be a *crimen*.

tre even today is a dangerous place for beautiful women, *scilicet ex illo sollemni more theatra / nunc quoque formosis insidiosa manent* (Ov. *Ars am.* 1.133–134, 'And, mark you, by hallowed custom from that time our theatres even now are fraught with danger to the fair.'). It creates a tension when Ovid links the Sabine women to beautiful women of his own day and age of the type that are likely to be pursued by the elegiac lover; the Sabine women stood as the ultimate symbol of good Roman wives and child-bearers, and most importantly, as symbols of the type of women that are not to be pursued with the help of *ars*. Ovid's description of the grabbing and abduction of the terrified Sabine women is also not in line with the elegiac notion of using *ars* and *exorare puellam* (Ov. *Ars am.* 1.37, 'to persuade the girl'), which works to underline the conflict between the mythological *exemplum* and what is really to be achieved by his students.

What is highlighted by Ovid's version of the story, however, with his focus on the beauty of the women (as opposed to Livy's version), is the ever-present danger that beautiful women must face. As was established in the *Amores*, chastity and beauty cannot be combined: *quo tibi formosam, si non nisi casta placebat? / non possunt ullis ista coire modis* (Ov. *Am.* 3.4.41–42, 'Why did you marry a beauty if none but a chaste woman would suit? Those two things can never in any wise combine.'). The more disturbing message that Ovid here demonstrates is the difficulty for a woman to stay both 'chaste' and beautiful even if she wanted to, as one would inevitably have to face the imminent danger of being raped. The same idea is manifested in the *Metamorphoses* in the myth of Daphne's rape by Apollo (and many other rapes), and how Daphne's wish to stay a virgin forever could not be fulfilled due to Apollo's admiration of her beauty: *sed te decor iste quod optas / esse uetat, uotoque tuo tua forma repugnat* (Ov. *Met.* 1.488–489, 'But that beauty of yours, Daphne, forbade the fulfilment of your desire, and your form fitted not with your prayer.').[32] As will be shown in this section, this disturbing aspect is further brought out by allusions to the shocking rape scene in Terence's *Eunuchus*, where the young Chaerea spots a girl in the street that is so beautiful that he decides that he must have her, no matter what (*ipsam hanc tu mihi uel ui uel clam uel precario / fac tradas: mea nil refert dum potiar modo*, Ter. *Eun.* 319–320, 'Now get her delivered to me, by force or stealth or entreaty. I don't mind how, so long as I get possession of her.').

In addition to its paradoxical deployment, Ovid's account of the Sabine rape also contains deliberate alterations of the aetiological history of Rome. Accord-

---

32 See also James 2016b, 160.

ing to the tradition,[33] the rape of the Sabine women took place at the first cele-
bration of the *Consualia* in honour of the god Consus, which is something of
which Ovid and his readers would be aware.[34] However, in the *Ars amatoria*, he
nevertheless lets the mythological event take place in a different setting, the
theatre. Ovid introduces the interlude on the mythological rape by stating that
the theatre is a suitable place to hunt for women, and that Romulus was the one
who introduced this manner of hunting:

> *sed tu praecipue curuis uenare theatris;*
> *haec loca sunt uoto fertiliora tuo.*
> *illic inuenies quod ames, quod ludere possis,*
> *quodque semel tangas, quodque tenere uelis.*
>
> Ov. *Ars am.* 1.89–92

> *primus sollicitos fecisti, Romule, ludos,*
> *cum iuuit uiduos rapta Sabina uiros.*
>
> Ov. *Ars am.* 1.101–102

But specially do your hunting in the round theatres: more bountifully do these repay your
vows. There will you find an object for passion or for deception, something to taste but
once, or to keep, if so you wish.

You first, Romulus, disturbed the games, when the rape of Sabine women consoled the
wifeless men.

This change of setting is one of several factors that separates Ovid's account of
the Sabine rape from Livy's, and it is both peculiar and easily noticed by the
reader.[35] The theatre as 'hunting ground' might also not have been the most
obvious choice in Ovid's day and age, as the seating arrangements had been
strictly regulated by law under Augustus so as to introduce order at the viewing
of performances.[36] Men and women would sit separately, as women were allowed to sit in the back rows only, and there were special seats reserved for
married men. Most notably, at the time when the *Ars amatoria* was written,

---

33 On the connection between the rape of the Sabine women and the Consualia, see e.g.
Ogilvie 1965, 66–70.
34 Ovid mentions this festival in *Fasti* 3.197–200, and states that he will treat it in the right
place, which would have been in the second part of the work. See Heyworth 2019, *ad loc*. See
also Labate 2006, 205–209.
35 On Livy and Ovid's accounts of the rape of the Sabine women, see Hemker 1985.
36 *spectandi confusissimum ac solutissimum morem correxit ordinauitque* (Suet. *Aug.* 44, 'he had
corrected and regulated the very disordered and careless way of watching the games').

caelibes might have been banned from the theatre altogether.[37] That the seating arrangement at the time of the rape is pictured as in Augustan Rome is also made clear from the text, as Romulus' men in line 109 look back at the women (*respiciunt*) during the performance.[38] However, I will argue that the interlude on the rape contains a number of allusions to Terence, which shed light on Ovid's highly conscious choice of scenery. As will be demonstrated in the following, it seems that Ovid, in changing the location for the rape of the Sabine women from the *Circus Maximus*, where the *Consualia* was celebrated, to the theatre, is referring to the theatre at a generic and textual level as well.

The phrase *inuenies quod ames* in line 91 quoted above bears a striking, almost verbatim, textual resemblance to line 308/309 in Terence's *Eunuchus*, where Chaerea reminds the slave Parmeno about his promise to aid him in securing a love relationship: *scis te mihi saepe pollicitum esse 'Chaerea, aliquid* **inueni**/ *modo* **quod ames***: in ea re utilitatem ego faciam ut cognoscas meam'* (Ter. *Eun.* 308–309, 'you often made me a promise: "Chaerea, just find someone to love, and I'll make you aware how useful I can be in that regard."').[39] Shortly after, Parmeno, as he is suggesting a way for Chaerea to gain access to the house where the girl is kept, lists the things that he will enjoy there: *tu illis fruare* **commodis** *quibu' tu illum dicebas modo*: / *cibum una capias, adsis* **tangas ludas** *propter dormias* (Ter. *Eun.* 372–373, 'You could enjoy the benefits which you were just saying would be his — eat with her, live with her, touch her, play with her, sleep next to her.'). Again, the similarity to Ovid's account of what type of women one can find at the theatre is striking. In the last lines of the interlude, the allusion is further underscored and rounded off by the echo of the *commodis* in Parmeno's speech: *Romule, militibus scisti dare* **commoda** *solus*: / *haec mihi si dederis* **commoda**, *miles ero* (Ov. *Ars am.* 1.131–132, 'Ah, Romulus, you only knew how to bestow benefit on your warriors; if you but bestow such benefits upon me, I will be a warrior.').

The goods provided by Parmeno and Romulus are the same, described in both texts as someone to love, play with and touch, i.e. an object of love. The

---

37 A *Lex Iulia theatralis* was probably introduced at some point between 22 and 17 BCE. The ban on *caelibes* might have been part of the *Lex Iulia de maritandis ordinibus*, and it was probably wildly unpopular and removed by the *Lex Papia Poppaea* in 8 CE at the latest, on which see Rawson 1987, 98. On the *Lex Iulia theatralis*, see Rawson 1987, 83–114 and Bollinger 1969. See also Beacham 2005, 163–164.

38 See also Hollis 2009 [1977] *ad loc.*

39 James 2016a sees the repeated use of the neuter pronoun to denote women in the *Ars amatoria* as a mark of resentment towards women of the *meretrix* class, which can be found in both texts.

situations in the *Eunuchus* and in *Ars amatoria* also parallel each other, as the purpose in both cases is to obtain women. Ovid casts Romulus in a role parallel to his own role as the *praeceptor amoris*, the one who secures the *commoda* of love for those following his lead. This mirrors the role of the slave Parmeno, who does the same for Chaerea, i.e. offers him a way to gain access to Pamphila.[40] Chaerea in return rewards Parmeno with the titles *mearum uoluptatum omnium | inuentor inceptor perfector* (Ter. *Eun.* 1034–1035, 'the deviser, the initiator, the perfector of all my delights'). The rhetorical triplet here is quite striking; as Barsby notes, none of these words occur elsewhere in Plautus and Terence,[41] and the connotation is virtually the same as *praeceptor amoris*.[42] This might also interestingly be compared to the role given to the *meretrix* Bacchis in *Hecyra*, who secures 'good things' (described as *commodas res* in the quote above) for Pamphilus by revealing the fact that he is Philumena's unknown rapist and thus saving his marriage and earning herself the title 'protectress' (*o mea Bacchi', servatrix mea!* Ter. *Hec.* 856, 'Oh Bacchis, oh my darling Bacchis, my salvation!').

Another notable detail in Ovid's elegiac account of the legendary rape is the way he lets each man pick the woman he desires the most. In Livy, it is chance that decides which girl each man ends up with, which highlights the more pragmatic aim of the rape.[43] The ultimate goal is to find women for marriage and procreation to secure the growth of the city, and not temporary, passionate love affairs, and the looks of and attraction to one specific woman are not of importance.[44] In Ovid's elegiac universe, attraction is of the utmost importance, and the primary aim of the relationships would not be marriage for the sake of procreation but rather obtaining an erotic relationship for its own sake, in line with the convention of the genre. The elegiac frame is mirrored in how the *topos* of staring at the *puella* is prominent in Ovid's description of the event, as each of the Romans singles out and stares at the most beautiful among the women: *respiciunt oculisque notant sibi quisque puellam | quam uelit, et tacito pectore multa mouent* (Ov. *Ars am.* 1.109–110, 'They look about them, and each note with his glance the girl he desires, and they brood much in their secret hearts.'), immediately before they, on Romulus' signal, jump up to grab their chosen

---

40 Parmeno in the role as *praeceptor* is treated also in Chapter Three and Chapter Four.

41 Barsby 1999 *ad loc.*

42 James also sees Parmeno as taking on the role as a *praeceptor*; see James 2016a, 87–88.

43 *magna pars forte, in quem quaeque inciderat, raptae* (Liv. 1.9.11, 'In most cases these were taken by the men in whose path they chanced to be.').

44 The exception in Livy is a few girls that were considered particularly attractive, and therefore handpicked for the leaders.

girls. This adaption of the story fits the elegiac genre and Ovid's scheme much better, as the individual love-soldier's successful hunt for the girl he lusts for is the aim of his teaching. This can also be traced back to the *Eunuchus*, and Chaerea's gaze prior to the rape on the *uirgo*, described by him as the most beautiful of all girls. He is first angry for having lost her from his sight, *neque uirgost usquam neque ego, qui illam e conspectu amisi meo* (Ter. *Eun* 293, 'The virgin's lost; and so am I, now I've lost sight of her.'). It becomes evident that he does not really known the girl, but has just seen her in the street (PA*: ubi uidisti?* CH*: in uia.* Ter. *Eun.* 322, 'PA: Where did you see her? CH: In the street.'). He then describes how he looked for her again after having been held up by an old family acquaintance, *quom huc respicio ad uirginem* (Ter. *Eun.* 342, 'When I looked this way for the virgin'). Most notably, after having disguised himself as a eunuch and been left alone to guard the girl, he steals a last glance at her from behind a fan that he is using to create a breeze for her to dry after a bath, imme-diately prior to his violent attack:[45] *ego limis specto / sic per flabellum clanculum* (Ter. *Eun.* 601–602, 'I looked at her sideways through the fan, like this.'). It is at this very moment, in the words of Chaerea himself, he sees his (very much hoped for) opportunity to the rape the girl, as he later tells his friend Antipho: CH. (…) *simul alia circumspecto, / satin explorata sint. uideo esse. pessulum ostio obdo. / AN. quid tum? CH. quid 'quid tum', fatue?* (Ter. *Eun.* 602–603, 'CH: At the same time I had a good look round to make sure that the coast was clear. I saw it was, and bolted the door. AN: What then? CH: How do you mean "What then," you idiot?'). Traces of this comic situation, and Chaerea's gaze upon the girl, from when he sees her for the first time up to the point when he is ready to at-tack/rape her, can be found in the description of Romulus' soldiers quoted above, looking around, planning their attack while waiting for the right moment to jump up and snatch the women.

Many scholars have treated Ovid's presentation of the Sabine rape. As Hemker points out, Ovid emphasises the suffering of the victims of rape in his account and 'exposes the tragedy inherent in any philosophy which espouses domination as a means of gratifying one's own desires'.[46] Similarly, James ar-gues that Ovid, through his allusive engagement with Terence, exposes male privilege and disturbing attitudes towards *meretrices*, often marked by the use of the neuter pronoun *quod* to refer to women in situations where they are seen

---

45 This scene is not shown on stage. Chaerea describes the situation to his friend Antipho after the rape. The scene and its possible connection to mime is treated in Chapter One.
46 Hemker 1985, 46.

as love objects.[47] Labate, on discussing the function of the interlude on mythological rape, stresses the point that the ultimate goal — to find women — is the
same for Romulus' soldiers and Ovid's pupils, and that they will frequent the
theatres to find women and single out the most attractive ones. He states that
the *aition* of the Sabine Rape presents an *exemplum* which acts as an anti-
exemplum, as Romulus' method is *sine arte* and more suited to the pre-civilized
world, too simplistic and direct for the more refined world of Augustan Rome.
Ovid's pupils will hunt for women in the theatres, but they will use not rape but
ars, and the 'artistic' procedure of *exorare*.[48]

On the basis of what I have demonstrated in this section, I would like to
draw attention to the paradox that lies in the fact that the goal for Romulus is
also starkly contrasted with the goal of Ovid's pupils. Romulus' ultimate objective is to find *uirgines* for purposes of marriage and procreation to secure the
growth of Rome, which has nothing to do with to the programme of the *Ars
amatoria* and what the elegiac lover seeks to achieve. This paradox, I would like
to argue, is further underscored by the use of allusions to the comedy genre,
which is the main genre for the portrayal of rape of *uirgines* leading to marriage,
a trait evident in Terence in particular in the Roman context. This represents a
stark contrast to the ultimate goal of the elegiac lover and his view of love as
presented in the *Amores*, but fits perfectly well with the goal both of Augustan
marital law and the comedy genre. The ultimate goal and conventional ending
of comic plots involving an *adulescens* and a *uirgo*, including the plot revolving
around Chaerea and Pamphila in the *Eunuchus*, is the young man's entrance
into adulthood and a respectable manner of life via marriage. This solves all the
problems that might have occurred during the action of the play, such as rape
and, in some cases, subsequent pregnancy.[49] Thus, the paradox of using the
Sabine rape as *exemplum*, where Romulus' real soldiers parallel Ovid's pupils or
'the soldiers of love' (as in e.g. *militat omnis amans*, Ov. *Am.* 1.9.1, 'every lover is
a soldier'), Romulus the *praeceptor*, and the Sabine *uirgines*, the first legal wives
of Rome, the elegiac *puellae*, is highlighted by the allusions to the Terentian
rape scene in the passage. The Terentian rape-marriage plot fits perfectly with
the account of the Sabine rape, the origin of the Roman marriage institution,

---

47 James 2016a, 100, 107–109.

48 Labate 2006, 193–215.

49 As Sharon L. James rightly has pointed out to me, this goes for social and legal problems;
the emotional and personal consequences remain unsolved. Such issues are very much highlighted in Terence, as e.g. in the violent rape descriptions in the *Eunuchus* and *Hecyra*, and in
the overall description of the hopeless situation faced by a young pregnant girl in the latter
play.

which was the only acceptable form of living a respectable life in Ovid's time. However, both stories represent a contrast to the notion of elegiac love and the almost militant anti-marriage agenda of the genre. The contrast is emphasised, as Labate also notes, by the use of violence,[50] and, as I argue, further highlighted by allusions to the most violent rape-marriage plot in the comedy corpus. I would like to argue that in Ovid this brings out the violent aspect inherent in the Roman marriage institution, and the danger faced by women within this tradition. As will be further discussed in the next section, the issue of status is crucial, as the girl Pamphila of the *Eunuchus*, the Sabine women, and marriageable Roman women are all defined as *uirgines*, which works to underscore their citizen status.

Marriage, rape and law: a question of identity and status

Within the tradition of new comedy as a form of 'comedy of errors', confusion or misapprehension regarding certain facts and the identity of certain characters constitutes the basis for many of the plots. Particularly, the status of young women is crucial in facilitating the conventional fortunate outcome of the genre, as only women of citizen status according to the convention are eligible for marriage.[51] In Ovid's elegiac poetry too, women's status is a recurring theme and of critical importance: It would be illegal for him to promote adultery and encourage extramarital relationships with Roman, freeborn women, as opposed to e.g. *meretrices* and slaves. The status of the elegiac *puella* is therefore of the utmost importance, a fact that manifests itself when Ovid claims that he was exiled from Rome, never to return, partially due to this very issue of women's status in the *Ars amatoria*. As this section aims to demonstrate, identity and status are key issues in Ovid's allusive play on Terence in the first book of *Ars amatoria*, where the boundaries between Roman high-status women and freedwomen and *meretrices* are deliberately blurred.[52] Furthermore, the same issues of rape and status are strongly present also in the *Heroides* and the *Amores*.

In Ovid's twist on the story of the origin of Roman marriage, the Sabine women, though standing in for the elegiac *puellae*, represent the type of women that it would be a *crimen* to pursue, according to traditional Roman values reinforced by the *Lex Julia de adulteriis*. To the Romans, they stood as the ultimate symbol of chaste women and wives, and sexual relations with such women

---

50 Labate 2006, 208–209.
51 On error and misapprehension in Roman comedy, see Duckworth 1994 [1952], 140–142.
52 Gibson argues for the blurred status of the *puella*, see Gibson 1998; 2003.

would be defined as *adulterium* or *stuprum*. *Adulterium* and *stuprum* were only possible among freeborn persons, and whereas *adulterium* would be something committed by (and with) married women, *stuprum* was the violation of *uirgines* and widows, and extra-marital sexual acts among unmarried, freeborn persons in general.[53] This makes Ovid's deployment of the legend problematic, given the fact that it is here used as an illustration of how to find and initiate a sexual relationship, letting the women of the legend stand in for elegiac *puellae*. Later, in the hindsight of the poet's exile, these women will be explicitly declared to be *meretrices* in *Tristia* 2.[54] It is my belief that Ovid further underscores this problematic feature rather than obscuring it when he alludes to the *Eunuchus*, so as to create a connection between that work's violent rape scene and his version of the Sabine rape. In Ovid's rape-marriage plot, the Sabine women occupy the same role in the narrative as the young citizen girl Pamphila does in the *Eunuchus*, and in both cases, violation of law, or a *crimen*, is avoided by rape/marriage.

In the comic genre, the status of the beloved object is usually revealed to the audience by the term used to denote her, and the *uirgo*, one of the stock characters of the genre, is in almost every case a young, respectable woman that turns out to be eligible for marriage, i.e. of citizen status. The comic *uirgines* are conventionally involved in plots where the *adulescens* professes to be in love with a young girl whose citizen status, and hence marriageability, is not revealed to the characters until towards the end of the play.[55] The victims of comic rapes are, in almost all cases, *uirgines*, and the plots are solved by the discovery of this and the subsequent marriage between the raped *uirgo* and the *adulescens*. Had it not been for the marriage, the *adulescens* would have been guilty of a severe crime, i.e. *stuprum*,[56] but this would not be an acceptable outcome within the genre.[57] That the term *uirgo* is connected to citizen status is mirrored in the rape-marriage plot in the *Eunuchus*, where Pamphila is indicat-

53 See Csillag 1976, 179–180. Married freedwomen seem to have been included in the law, whereas the sexual activities of unmarried freedwoman do not seem to have been regulated in the same way. See Treggiari 1991, 277–298, and discussion in Gibson 1998, 295–296.
54 Ov. *Tr.* 2.303.
55 Watson 1983 argues that the terms *puella* and *uirgo* are used far less frequently as synonyms in Latin literature than has been supposed. See 120–123 for the *uirgo* character in new comedy.
56 On *stuprum* as a crime in republican Rome, see Fantham 2011, 115–143. On sanctions on sexual assault in Greece, see Cole 1984.
57 Even though it is joked about. In the *Eunuchus*, the slave Parmeno is led to believe that Chaerea is about to be punished for being a *moechus*, i.e. a man who has had sex with a free woman dependent of another man. See Ter. *Eun.* 957 and Barsby 1999 *ad loc.*

ed by this term during the whole action of the play, e.g. in line 313, where Chaerea describes Pamphila to Parmeno after having seen her in the street for the first time without knowing who she is (*haud simili' uirgost uirginum nostrarum*, Ter. *Eun.* 313. 'This virgin is quite different from those local virgins'), and several times after the rape, e.g. in line 659 (*uirgo ipsa lacrumat*, Ter. *Eun.* 659, 'the virgin is crying'). It is evident that the term *uirgo* is not necessarily the same as a biologically 'chaste' woman. In Terence's *Adelphoe*, in a conversation between the *senes* Demea and Micio, we are even told that a *uirgo* has given birth (DE. *puer natust.* MI. *di bene uortant!* DE. *uirgo nil habet.* Ter. *Ad.* 728, 'DE: "A baby's been born." MI: "Good luck to it!" DE: "The virgin is penniless."').[58] The term has to do with the girl's perceived moral state, as the comic *uirgo* never voluntarily involves herself in sexual relationships outside of marriage and always marries her rapist; the term *uirgo* mostly denotes her citizen status to the audience. As a character she stands in opposition to the *meretrix*, who is never raped, and never marries. In fact, it might not have made much sense to talk about rape and marriage when it came to slaves and *meretrices*, at least with regards to the law.[59]

Similarly, in the *Ars amatoria*, the Sabine women are referred to as *uirgines*, at the instance when the Romans leap up to grab them: *protinus exiliunt animum clamore fatentes, | uirginibus cupidas iniciuntque manus* (Ov. *Ars am.* 1.115–116, 'Straightway they leap forth, by their shouts betraying their eagerness, and lay lustful hand upon the virgins.').[60] Over the three books that constitute the didactic poem, Ovid deploys the term *uirgo* eight times (in addition to one in-

---

58 See also Watson 1983, 122.

59 What defines rape in this context, i.e. illicit *stuprum*, to 'spoil' a young woman for marriage, is avoided by the marriage between rapist and victim. When marriage is not possible due to the status of the woman, this would not be an issue. One would never talk about the rape of e.g. one's own slave, and women living in concubinage and prostitutes by profession were not included among the women who could be involved in *stuprum*, see Csillag 1976, 181. It is not all clear how freedwomen prostitutes stood with regards to freeborn women's rights to freedom from rape, but there is little surviving legal or literary evidence for the prosecution of rape of a Roman prostitute, even if she were to fall under the definition 'free'. See Strong 2016, 15 and McGinn 1998, 326–337 for discussion.

60 It is worth noting that an additional Terentian flavour might also be detected here: In the next couplet, Ovid describes the scene as lambs fleeing from wolfs (*utque fugit uisos agna nouella lupos*, Ov. *Ars am.* 1.118, 'as the young lamb flees the watching wolves'), a rapist-victim image also deployed by Terence (*scelesta, ouem lupo commisti*, Ter. *Eun.* 832, 'wicked woman, you put the lamb together with the wolf'). As Barsby 1999 *ad loc.* notes, the expression is proverbial, but in the context of the striking presence of Terence in this section, it is hard not to see it in context of the Terentian line.

stance of the adjective *uirgineus*), the first being the mention of the Sabine women in 1.116. The next occurrence is in line 1.261, here as a reference to the virgin goddess Diana (*illa, quod est uirgo, quod tela Cupidinis odit, / multa dedit populo uulnera, multa dabit*, Ov. *Ars am.* 1.261–262, 'because she is a virgin and hates the darts of Cupid, she has given and will give to our people many a wound.'). Next, in 1.624, it is stated that even chaste women care about their looks (*delectant etiam castas praeconia formae; / uirginibus curae grataque forma sua est*, Ov. *Ars am.* 1.623–624, 'Even honest girls love to hear their charms extolled; even to virgins their beauty is a care and a delight.'). Then, towards the end of book one, we find another rape of a *uirgo*, in the story of Achilles' rape of Deidamia (*forte erat in thalamo uirgo regalis eodem*, Ov. *Ars am.* 1.697, 'It chanced that in the same chamber was the royal virgin.'). In 2.55 there is a reference to the *uirgo Tegeaea*, i.e. Callisto, and in 3.75 the term is used to denote a certain age (*a uirgine*, 'since maidenhood'). Lastly, the aqueduct Virgo is mentioned in 3.385 (*gelidissima Virgo*), and the constellation of Virgo in 3.388 (*Virginis aetheriis … equis*). As Watson points out, Ovid is 'the first writer to make extensive use of *uirgo* in the technical sense "virgin"'.[61] However, as is evident in the examples above, the term is also inseparably connected to citizen status. In 1.623–624, the meaning of *etiam castas* and *uirginibus* works to separate these types of girls from others, in a way that not only refers to age and 'virginity' but also implies 'respectability' (e.g. the lover should not fail to praise his mistress' looks, as this is something that *even* a chaste girl would have enjoyed), and that they are not the kind of girls that normally could be (openly) pursued by the elegiac lover. High status is obviously also implied in the case of Deidamia, a *uirgo regalis*, and in the case of the Sabine women, who stand as ideals for all chaste Roman women and wives. In addition, as is made apparent by the *exemplum* of Diana, a *uirgo* is one who does not involve herself in elegiac love, here symbolised by the arrows of Cupid.

The situation in the *Ars amatoria* that comes closest to resembling the rape of the Sabine *uirgines*, and which fittingly also shares several prominent traits with the rape of the *uirgo* in *Eunuchus*, is the rape of the *uirgo regalis* Deidamia by Achilles, dressed up as a woman and hidden amongst the daughters of the king of Skyros Lycomedes. James argues for several resemblances between the *Eunuchus* and the mythological illustration and states that 'although Deidamia and Achilles are a mythical princess and hero, and thus formally inapposite models for a Roman lover and his courtesan *puella*, their encounter maps on to

---

61 Watson 1983, 129.

that of Chaerea and Pamphila quite well.'[62] Ovid's is the only surviving treatment of the rape prior to Statius' *Achilleid*,[63] and he uses the rape as an *exemplum* of how women actually enjoy force when it comes to love and sex (*uim
licet appelles: grata est uis ista puellis; / quod iuuat, inuitae saepe dedisse uolunt*,
Ov. *Ars am.* 1.673, 'You may use force; girls like you to use it; they often wish to
give unwillingly what they like to give.'). The situation bears several striking
parallels to the one in the *Eunuchus*, where Chaerea, just as Achilles gains access to the women's quarters dressed as a woman, dresses up as a eunuch and
thus gains access to the women's quarters of Thais' house. There, he is left alone
with the girl, as he is seen as harmless and fit to be trusted with the important
task of guarding her while Thais herself is away, so that she can be securely
returned to her high-class citizen brother. In both cases, the men reveal their
true identities by rape.

To highlight the presence of the Terentian play in Ovid, I would here like to
point out an additional connection on the textual level as well. In the *Eunuchus*,
as the raped girl, in line with convention, has no lines (and in addition is si-
lenced by fear by the violence conducted towards her), Thais finds out that her
eunuch is not a eunuch after all from the maid Pythias, who has discovered his
true identity as a consequence of the rape of the girl:

> PY. *quid tibi ego dicam misera? illum eunuchum negant
> fuisse. TH. quis fuit igitur? PY. iste Chaerea.*
> TH. *qui Chaerea? PY. iste ephebu' frater Phaedriae.*
> TH. *quid ais, uenefica? PY. atqui certe **comperi**.*
>
> Ter. *Eun.* 822–825

> PY: Oh dear, what can I say? They say it wasn't the eunuch. TH: Who was it then? PY: That
> Chaerea. TH: Which Chaerea? PY: That brother of Phaedria's, the ephebe. TH: What are
> you saying, you poisonous wretch? PY: Well, it's true. I've checked.

In a similar manner, Deidamia discovers Achilles' true identity, and that he is
not really a woman, by rape in the Ovidian account: *haec illum stupro **comperit**
esse uirum* (Ov. *Ars am.* 1.698, 'by her rape she found him to be a man.'). As
Barsby notes, that Pythias has 'found out for certain' (*comperi*) might refer to
her and Phaedria's questioning of the real eunuch, whereupon he reveals that it

---

62 James 2016a, 98. I would argue that the repeated use of *uirgines* as *exempla* in the *Ars amatoria* combined with the presence of the comic *uirgo* Pamphila also points to a complex play
with the issue of status.
63 After the loss of Euripides' *Skyrians* and most of the epithalamium ascribed to Bion. Heslin
2005, 267.

was Chaerea who took his clothes. However, it might also refer to the whole situation; Pythias is shocked and outraged after finding Pamphila raped by a person she thought incapable of rape, and to whom she had entrusted the girl's safety. It is at this point clear to her that the so-called eunuch has raped the girl, and she describes the event in explicit detail to Phaedria before they go on to question the real eunuch, who then discloses Chaerea's scheme.

Again, there is a clear tension between the notion of *exorare puellam* and 'that girls really enjoy force', and the use of actual force to rape a *uirgo*. This tension becomes especially evident when seen in the light of Ovid's treatment of rape and use of force against women elsewhere, e.g. in the *Metamorphoses*, and the focus he dedicates to the emotional and physical reactions of the victims.[64] This is the case concerning the Sabine rape in the *Ars amatoria* as well, as Hemker also relates:

> If this 'game' were as innocent as the narrator suggests, the women would not be as frightened as they are. As when Ovid relates the inner terror of sexually abused virgins in the early books of the *Metamorphoses*, this eight line description (117–24) dwells on and emphasizes the victimized women's response.[65]

The *exemplum* of Achilles and Deidamia is as puzzling in the context as the Sabine rape is in the opening of the book, and as Hemker points out, that women would enjoy force 'contradicts the evidence presented in the Sabine episode'.[66] What is more, Ovid denotes the action as *stuprum* twice, in 1.698 (quoted above) and again shortly after, *uis ubi nunc illa est? quid blanda uoce moraris / auctorem stupri, Deidamia, tui?* (Ov. *Ars am.* 1.703–704, 'Where is that violence now? Why with coaxing words, Deidamia, do you delay the author of your rape?'). This brings attention to the legal aspect of the situation; the term *stuprum* represents a criminal offence, and it is closely connected to Deidamia's status, also denoted by the use of the term *uirgo*; *stuprum* was a legal crime according to the *Lex Iulia de adulteriis*, defined as the sexual activity of freeborn unmarried 'virgins'. Committing *stuprum*, as will be shown in the following, would be a hazardous occupation for both the man and woman involved, and

---

64 See Richlin 1992b.

65 Hemker 1985, 45.

66 Hemker 1985, 46. As will be further discussed in Chapter Five, contradictions might be explained by a shift of perspective, i.e. the perspective of the victims in the Sabine episode and Deidamia's perspective in her situation, vs. a pure male perspective, presented as e.g. here in the statement *uim licet appelles*. The contradiction creates tension in the text, and problematizes the male perspective by representing the devastating effect it might have on women, who are generally in a more vulnerable position.

what is more, it is exactly the type of *crimen* that Ovid promises the reader will *not* be taught in his *Ars amatoria* already in his disclaimer in the opening of the book, where he implicitly states that nothing will be taught that breaks the *Lex Iulia de adulteriis*.

In the comedy genre, *stuprum* is always avoided by the conventional fortunate outcome of illicit extramarital affairs, i.e. the eventual marriage between raped *uirgines*, who turn out to be of citizen status, and their rapists. In other words, if a rape is followed by a marriage, no criminal action has taken place. This is well demonstrated in the *Eunuchus*, where Pythias tricks Parmeno into believing that Chaerea is about to be punished for being a *moechus*, or sexual offender, as it has been discovered that the girl he has raped is not a slave, but a citizen girl. In reality, he is not to be punished, as they are to be married. This notion is reflected in the story of the Sabine rape, where the fortunate outcome, i.e. the marriage between the Romans and the Sabine women, and the promise of citizen rights and legitimate children, prevents the act from being defined as illicit *raptus* in the eyes of the Romans. In Ovid's account of the legendary event, this aspect is further highlighted through allusions to Terence and the most memorable rape-marriage plot in the comedy corpus. Deidamia's status as *uirgo* puts her in the same category as both Pamphila in the *Eunuchus* and the Sabine women, and what makes this very similar case of rape a criminal offence must be the lack of a fortunate ending, i.e. a marriage union.[67] What is on the surface a demonstration of how women supposedly enjoy force from a male point of view, then, is a woman begging her rapist to stay, to secure a fortunate outcome, i.e. marriage, and to avoid the consequences and shame of involvement in a crime, i.e. *stuprum*.[68]

When a man used force to rape a woman, she was innocent before the law for having extramarital sexual relations.[69] Consequently, when the legend of Achilles and Deidamia is placed in Ovid's Roman context, Achilles, or the Roman man that he is meant to illustrate, is the only one that faces criminal charg-

---

67 As James points out, the *Iliad* gives no indication that Achilles thinks about Deidamia as his wife. James 2016a, n. 22. However, in Statius' later version of the myth, Achilles and Deidamia marry, which is evident from e.g. that Lycomedes, when their affair (and child) is discovered, states that he is not opposed to bind himself to a *gener* as great as Achilles (*nec tamen abnuerit genero se iungere tali*, Stat. *Achil.* 917, 'and after all he would not refuse to join himself to such a son-in-law.'). Marriage is also implied by the title of the fragmented *Epithalamium of Achilles and Deidamia*, attributed to Bion, which was probably Ovid's immediate source for the story. See Hollis 2009 [1977], commentary on lines 1.681–704. My text for Statius is Bailey 2003.
68 See also James 2016a, 98.
69 Treggiari 1991, 279.

es in this case of *stuprum*. This might offer an explanation of why force, according to the *praeceptor,* is pleasing to women, as there are according to law two ways for freeborn women to have sex without suffering legal consequences, either by force or within the bounds of marriage. However, if we look to the Roman aetiological history, a part of which introduced the *Ars amatoria*, the better alternative to living with the shame that followed from a rape was, for an honourable woman, if not marriage, death. This is clearly demonstrated by the story of Lucretia, who after her rape by Sextus Tarquinius, the son of the last king, kills herself as a sign of her nobility, even though she was seen as free from any blame by both her father and her husband on account of the violence with which the crime was conducted.[70] Ovid demonstrates the same point in his account of an event further back in Rome's legendary past, in the way he relates the faith of the Vestal Virgin Rhea Silvia, who according to the legend was raped by Mars and subsequently gave birth to Romulus and Remus. According to Ovid's account in *Amores* 3.6, she wanders the banks of the river Anio while she mourns the loss of her virginity and fears how she will be scorned by the people as an *adultera*, or sexual offender (Ov. *Am.* 3.6.77). *Adultera* is yet another legal term, and is connected to the *crimen* Ovid hints at when he shortly before in *Amores* 3.4 says that Romulus and Remus was born *non sine crimine* (*Am.* 3.4.39, 'not without a crime').[71] In the end, the best solution she can think of is to give in to the river and throw herself into the water, an event described as both a rape/marriage and possibly a suicide. Thus, to be involved in what were considered sex crimes could also prove to be fatal, as death was to be preferred for a noble woman over living with the shame of having had a part in an illicit sexual union. By focusing on the legal aspect in the story of Deidamia and Achilles, I argue, Ovid demonstrates the potential risks of love, especially for a woman, who might be in real danger if she should choose to participate in elegiac love, or even if she is raped.

The technical legal terms *stuprum* and *adulter/adultera* are rare in Roman love elegy and for the most part avoided.[72] *Stuprum* is only used elsewhere by Ovid in his elegies in *Heroides* 5,[73] where Oenone describes her rape by Apollo as

---

70 The rape of Lucretia is treated in Ovid at *Fast.* 2.685–852.
71 This must have been a shocking statement to the contemporary audience and in the light of the poetic context, as Ovid in *Amores* 3.4 demonstrates that a husband should accept his wife's adultery, which was a punishable offence according to the Augustan law on *lenocinium*.
72 *Adulter/adultera* is avoided by Propertius and Tibullus, the only occurrence being at Prop. 2.34.7. In contrast, it occurs on multiple occasions in Ovid in all of his elegiac works (adultery is also famously the theme of *Amores* 3.4). On legal language in Ovid in general, see Ziogas 2016.
73 The fourth and last occurrence of *stuprum* in Ovid is at *Met.* 2.529.

stuprum at line 143: *nec pretium stupri gemmas aurumque poposci: / turpiter ingenuum munera corpus emunt.* (Ov. *Her.* 5.143–144, 'I did not ask for precious stones and gold as price for my rape: it is shameful to purchase a freeborn body.').[74] Even though the lines describing the rape are controversial and deleted by several editors,[75] it seems to me that Oenone's description of her rape fits perfectly with other Ovidian rapes and the rape descriptions in the *Ars amatoria*: by defining her rape as *stuprum*, a criminal offence according to Roman law, Oenone draws attention to her high status, which is also highlighted by her statement that she did not ask for anything in return. like a *meretrix* would.[76] This fits well with her overall focus on her high status as a nymph and a worthy wife of Paris, in contrast to the unworthy and unfaithful Helen. The notion of Apollo taking her virginity as spoil, *spolium uirginitatis* at line 140, might also be compared to *Ars am.* 1.125, where the Sabine women are described as *genialis praeda*, spoil for the marriage-bed, both being images of *militia amoris*.[77] Furthermore, the passage describing the rape is strongly connected to Ovid's treatment of rape in the first book of the *Ars amatoria* through the repetition of the first half of line 131, *uim licet appelles et culpam nomine uelles; / quae totiens rapta est, praebuit ipsa rapi* (Ov. *Her.* 5.131–132, 'You may call it violence, and veil the fault in the word; yet she who has been so often stolen has surely lent herself to theft.') at *Ars am.* 1.673 (quoted above), right before the only additional occurrences of the term *stuprum* within his elegies, in the Deidamia-Achilles narrative at *Ars am.* 1.698 and 1.704. The intention of Oenone's rape story seems to be to separate her from the faithless Helen, and to prove her own fidelity to Paris; even if Helen might claim to have been raped by Theseus, according to Oenone, she surely must have exposed herself to it, as it happened to her so many times. Furthermore, Helen is an *adultera* (Ov. *Her.* 5.125), yet another legal term, for having let herself be taken away from her husband by Paris. Oenone herself, on the other hand, has remained chaste (*casta* at Ov. *Her.* 5.133) to her

---

74 My text for *Heroides* is Knox 1995. Lines 140–145 of Ovid's *Heroides* 5 are not included in the Loeb edition; the translation is my own.
75 Palmer follows Merkel in condemning Oenone's graphic description of her rape by Apollo, and many editors have followed in deeming these disturbing lines as spurious. Knox 1995 keeps the lines due to the unsatisfactory couplet 139/46 resulting from such a deletion. Jacobson also argues for the authenticity of the lines; see Jacobson 1974, 185–187.
76 Knox 1995 *ad loc.* compares line 144 with the Plautine line *amator meretricis mores sibi emit auro et purpura* (Plaut. *Mostell.* 286, 'Yes, a lover buys a prostitute's favours with jewelry and purple-dyed clothes.').
77 I treat *militia amoris* in Chapter Five.

husband, even if she was pursued by would-be lovers and even raped; her rape was *stuprum*, and the only apparent reason for her remaining *casta* is that she was forced, i.e. she fought back, and therefore is free from blame, in contrast to the adulterous Helen.[78] However, Oenone's appeal to Paris as an elegiac character through the narration of her rape fails.[79]

None of these legal concerns would apply to the elegiac *puellae* of the *Ars amatoria* if they really were, as Ovid claims, *meretrices*, who would neither be eligible for marriage nor included in the Augustan laws regulating *stuprum* and *adulterium*, as these were aimed at Roman *matronae* and *uirgines*. In the cases cited above, Ovid makes sure that the term *uirgo* never stands in for an actual elegiac *puella*, even though the opposite is quite common. The identity and status of the *puella* of the *Ars amatoria* is never clearly defined,[80] and as Gibson states in his treatment of the status of the *puella* of book three, to take Ovid's statement that the addressees are low-status women only literally might seem naïve, 'in view of the spirit of the earlier *Amores* and the way that Ovid's disclaimers serve to draw attention to issues of status rather than to resolve them'.[81] Similarly, it is problematic to straightforwardly see the 'real' audience behind the *meretrices* as *matronae*.[82] The third book of the *Ars amatoria*, Gibson argues, in contrast to the polarity between *meretrix* and *matrona* expressed by Augustan law, 'through corresponding to no known stereotype, [...] blurs the boundaries of these two traditional worlds in a uniquely potent manner'.[83] Whereas the *puella* remains blurred, the term *uirgo* is much more clear; in one way she is the diametrical opposite of the *puella*, as one who would not involve herself in elegiac love, but it is also a legal term, as a definition of a type of woman that is 'off limits' for extramarital relationships and for reciprocal love in general, as the only exception would be situations involving rape. This, I would argue, is highlighted by Ovid's allusive play with Terence; in Terence, as in the New Comic genre in general, the *uirgo* never voluntarily has extramarital sex.

---

78 As Knox points out, Oenone's aim is to play upon any suspicion that Paris might have about Helen's character. See Knox 1995 on *Her.* 5.133–146.
79 Lindheim sees Oenone as a character belonging in pastoral, unable to enter into Paris' elegiac world. See Lindheim 2004, 83–101. Another explanation for Oenone's ultimate failure to win Paris back, as not only a manipulator of pastoral and elegy, but also of epic, is offered by Drinkwater 2015.
80 Except for his explicit claim in *Tristia* 2.
81 Gibson 1998, 302.
82 Gibson 1998, 296.
83 Gibson 2003, 34. See also Gibson 2006, 121–142.

She is, on the other hand, often raped, an aspect that is highlighted in Terence and presented in the worst possible light, with his particular representation of the devastating effect of an often violent rape on the victim. As the comic convention dictates, raped *uirgines* almost always marry their rapists, which eliminates the dangerous and illegal aspect of the situation for both parties. This of course stands in stark contrast to the ideal of love presented in the elegiac genre, and the more obvious choice of *exemplum* from the comic world might therefore seem to be the *meretrix*, who never marries (and she too is present in the elegiac genre). However, Ovid's elegiac *puella* is not defined by such clearly defined roles as the *uirgo* and the *meretrix* represent in the comic universe, and features such as her status and social rank — and by extension the legal implications that would follow — remain undefined. Thus, the unsafe aspects of love are never really eliminated.

Conclusion

As I have aimed to show in this chapter, Ovid exploits Terence's most violent and shocking rape-marriage plot in the first book of the *Ars amatoria* through a number of allusions to the *Eunuchus* in his interlude on the rape of the Sabine women, the legendary origin of the institution of Roman marriage, to demonstrate how the elegiac lover should hunt for a *puella*. This constitutes a paradox, as both the Sabine women and the comic rape victim represent Roman wives, and thus allegedly the opposite of the type of women the elegiac *puella* represents. The closely narrated fear and terror of the women is also far from the elegiac notion of *exorare puellam*. This creates a tension in the text between Roman traditional values and the elegiac ideal, which, as I argue, highlights problematic and violent aspects of the Roman tradition, newly reinforced by moral laws mandated by Augustus. This is also closely linked to the issue of status; for certain classes of women, matters concerning sexuality are regulated by strict norms and laws, and to break these might have severe social consequences, as is demonstrated in several of Ovid's elegiac rape descriptions. This point is well demonstrated in the comic genre, where women of citizen status never have sexual relationships except by rape and are in the end married off to their rapists to avoid any problematic and illegal issues, after the disclosure of their true identities as citizen daughters. The rape-marriage plot is a stock feature of new comedy that gains particular attention in Terentian comedy, where insight into the emotional reactions of rape victims is offered through the narrative of other female characters. That this theme is so elaborate in Terence makes him an apt source for allusions in

Ovid. The identity and status of Ovid's *puella*, on the other hand, remain blurred; this proved to be so problematic that it was ultimately perceived as breaking with the Augustan law, and may have been (part of) the explanation for the poet's exile. This is also highlighted by the allusion to the same shocking rape scene in the opening of his exilic *Tristia* 2, addressed directly to the emperor, treated in Chapter One.

3 Love as disease: the love cure

Introduction

The literary image of love as a disease, though addressed and applied in multiple genres,[1] is generally seen as a stock trait of love elegy, the primary genre for love and lament.[2] Though prominent in all of the Latin elegiac poets, this image is most developed by and culminates with Ovid,[3] who makes it the key objective of his erotodidactic sequel to the *Ars amatoria*, the *Remedia amoris*, where he offers a cure to the illness that is love.[4] As Henderson points out, the title of the *Remedia amoris* indicates that the subject to be treated is a type of love different from the one in the *Ars amatoria*, and love is here described as an illness in terms such as *uitium*, *morbus* and *uulnus*;[5] it is the unhappy lovers, those who suffer under a cruel mistress (or master, as the advice, according to the *praeceptor*, can also be used by women)[6] to such a degree that they might kill themselves, who are the target audience for the love cure. Here, still through the voice of the *praeceptor amoris* or *Naso magister*, Ovid instructs unhappy lovers on how to fall out of love, and thus put an end to their miseries.

When Ovid wrote the *Remedia amoris*, there was already an established tradition that used terms of disease and cure to depict different categories of turmoil, such as emotional, moral and political,[7] and Propertius, Tibullus and probably Gallus had deployed the image of love as a sickness and its subse-

---

1 On love as illness in ancient literature in general, see Funke 1990. On Hellenistic use of the image, see e.g. Griffiths 1990 (on the image of love as disease in the love songs of Ancient Egypt and their influence on the later tradition); Rynearson 2009; Faraone 2006 (on Theocritus *Idyll* 11).

2 See e.g. Maltby 2006, 153–156. On love as disease in philosophy (Cicero and Lucretius) and Roman love elegy and the relationship between the genres, Caston 2006.

3 Cf. e.g. Hejduk 2011.

4 On the other hand, as one of Ovid's remedies is to replace the *puella* with a new one, which refers the reader back to the *Ars amatoria*, he also creates a never-ending circle of love and lament. On the incurability of elegiac love and that the advice of the *Remedia amoris* is not really opposed to that given in the *Ars amatoria*, but that the two texts pull 'their reader into an inescapable circle of elegiac love', see Fulkerson 2004. A cure for love within the bonds of traditional love elegy is in fact impossible, as the suffering of love is a necessary condition for love elegy; see Conte 1989 (on the *Remedia amoris* as both the fullest culmination of the elegiac genre and its end). On the *Remedia amoris* as a suicide strategy for the love poet, see also Thorsen 2014.

5 Henderson 1979, xii.

6 Ref. Ov. *Rem. am.* 49 and 813–814.

7 See Fantham 1972, 14–18.

https://doi.org/10.1515/9783111308036-003

quent terminology in their elegies.[8] As Henderson points out, *Remedia amoris* is not simply a reversal of the *Ars amatoria*; rather 'its inspiration came from the same sources as its companion's had, the native elegiac and the Hellenistic didactic tradition'.[9] It is seen as a reply to the metaphor of unreciprocated love as a *dolor immedicabilis*,[10] and notably to Propertius' appeal for help in his hopeless obsession with Cynthia in his elegies 1.1. and 2.1,[11] as nobody within the didactic tradition seems to have thought of writing a cure-poem for this particular illness before.[12] Furthermore, the inspiration from Callimachean poetry has been treated by several scholars; Henderson points to influence from the *Iambi*, and that Ovid in his deployment of them in the *Remedia amoris* is 'simultaneously acknowledging the influence of the Master, Callimachus, and setting the seal (discreetly) on his own achievement as the Master's Roman successor in this sphere.'[13] Henderson recognises the program for the *Remedia amoris* as possibly suggested by Propertius 1.1, which addresses several themes that become important in the Ovidan poem, such as e.g. the danger of too much *oti-*

---

8 Caston 2006. On Propertius, Maltby 2006, 153–156.

9 Henderson 1979, xiii.

10 A common metaphor throughout Greek literature (found in Euripidean tragedy and Hellenistic epigram in particular), found in Latin in Catullus (76. 19–16), before Gallus and the elegists. Henderson 1979, xiii.

11 *et uos, qui sero lapsum reuocatis, amici, / quaerite non sani pectoris auxilia* (Prop. 1.1.25–26, 'Else you, my friends, who too late call back the fallen, seek medicines for a heart that is sick') and *hoc si quis uitium poterit mihi demere, solus / Tantaleae poterit tradere poma manu* (Prop. 2.1.65–66, 'Only a man who can rid me of this failing will be able to put fruit in Tantalus' hand.').

12 As Henderson points out, the cure-poem 'had a niche to itself' among the didactic verse of the metaphrasts of the Hellenistic era, of which Nicander's *Alexipharmaca* (on poisons and antidotes) and *Theriaca* (on remedies for snake-bites) survive. Yet nobody seems to have thought of writing on the cure for love, despite the metaphor being widespread in literature. See Henderson, xiv.

13 Henderson 1979, xv. Henderson points to references in the *Remedia amoris* (at 82 and 117–118, and probably 75) to the fifth of the *Iambi*, which offers advice to a school-teacher (a certain Cleon or Apollonius) on curbing his lust for boys. Henderson also recognises the contribution of comedy and mime, but regards it as of minimal significance with regards to the *ego-praeceptor*. Of motifs that complement the explicit erotodidaxis, he mentions the comic *lena* as advisor. See Henderson 1979, xii–xvii for his full discussion of the sources for the *Remedia amoris*. On Ovid and Callimachus, see also Acosta-Huges 2009, 236–251, and on the assessment of Callimachus in the *Remedia amoris*, 239–241. Boyd 2009, 104–119, taking the poem on its own terms as a correction to the tendency in scholarship to look at the *Remedia amoris* as nothing more that an appendage to the *Ars amatoria*, also provides an introduction to work on the poem. On genre(s), see pages 115–118.

um,[14] and that e.g. Propertius' antithesis of *consilium* and *furor* reappears in the preface of the *Remedia amoris*. For the cures, Ovid's own *Ars amatoria*, the fourth book of Lucretius' *De rerum natura* and Cicero's *Tusculanae disputationes* are mentioned as the main sources from which Ovid draws.[15]

The specific imagery that associates the sickness of love with *morbus* and potential cures is evident from the beginning of Roman literary production in Plautus. The example that is perhaps most relevant in the present context is found in his Menander-based play *Cistellaria* in a conversation between the *meretrices* Selenium (who is not really a *meretrix*, but a freeborn citizen) and Gymnasium, after it has been discovered that the father of Alcesimarchus, Selenium's lover who has promised to marry her, has decided that he will rather marry a distant relative:[16]

> SEL: *eho an amare occipere amarum est, opsecro?*
> GY: *namque ecastor Amor et melle et felle est fecundissumus;*
> *gustui dat dulce, amarum ad satietatem usque oggerit.*
> SEL: *ad istam faciem est morbus qui me, mea Gymnasium, macerat.*
> GY: *perfidiosus est Amor.* SEL: *ergo in me peculatum facit.*
> GYM: *bono animo es, erit isti morbo melius.* SEL: *confidam fore,*
> *si medicus ueniat qui huic morbo facere medicinam potest.*
>
> Plaut. *Cist.* 69–74

> SEL: What! Falling in love isn't bitter, is it?
> GY: To be sure, Love abounds in honey as well as in gall; if you taste him, he gives you sweetness, but then he piles you up with bitterness till you're full.
> SEL: The illness that's tormenting me is of that sort, my dear Gymnasium.
> GY: Love is treacherous.
> SEL: Yes, he's embezzling all I have.
> GY: Take heart, that illness will get better.
> SEL: I trust it will, if the doctor comes who can cure this illness.

To this might be added two examples of medical language that can be related to love in the *Mercator* in a conversation between the *adulescentes* Charinus and Eutychus, though the implication here seems to be insanity: EV: *sanus es?* CH: *pol sanus si sim, non te medicum mi expetam* (Plaut. *Merc.* 489, 'EV: Are you in your right mind? CH: If I were, I wouldn't seek you as my doctor') and EV: *hic homo non sanust.* CH: *medicari amicus quin properas mihi?* (Plaut. *Merc.* 951,

---

14 The same thing is mentioned in Catull. 51. I am indebted to Sharon L. James for pointing this out to me.
15 See Henderson 1979, xv–xvii.
16 Plaut. *Cist.* 68–70 alludes to Sappho's fragment 130; see Ingleheart 2019, 212 and n. 28.

'EV: This chap isn't in his right mind. CH: why don't you as a friend heal me quickly?'). However, as Fantham points out, even though the link between love and illness can be detected in Plautus through these passages, 'what is exceptional in Plautus (...), is very common in Terence'.[17] In Terence, as I aim to show in this chapter, pathological love is more fully incorporated as a consistent image.

As I argue in the following, the *Remedia amoris*, in addition to its roots in the Greek literary tradition and its interaction with its Latin predecessors within the elegiac genre and authors such as Cicero and Lucretius, exploits the allusive potential that lies in the Roman tradition of literary deployments of the metaphor of love as an illness and different cures for love, in which Terence plays a large part. As I aim to show, the Terentian slave Parmeno in the *Eunuchus* casts himself in a role very similar to that of the *praeceptor amoris*, and parts of the Ovidian programme in the *Remedia amoris*, as well as many of the specific notions of lovesickness proposed by the *praeceptor*, are inspired by notions that can be traced to the Terentian comedies, the *Eunuchus* and *Andria* in particular.

First, however, I will point out some Terentian echoes that can be found in the *Remedia amoris* which partake in Ovid's larger allusive network and latch onto the allusions deployed in the *Ars amatoria*, treated in Chapter Two. At the same time, these echoes point forward to the Terentian allusions and in a way foreshadow the explicit mention of Terence in *Tristia* 2, treated in Chapter One. As was shown in Chapter Two, the *Ars amatoria* displays a close connection to Terentian rape descriptions, and particularly the *Eunuchus*, where the *adulescens* Chaerea's rape of the *uirgo* Pamphila was mirrored in rapes used as *exempla* in the first book of Ovid's poem. Furthermore, as demonstrated in Chapter One, the very same play was deployed in the poet's defence for the *Ars amatoria* in *Tristia* 2, where an explicit reference to Terence and his *conuiuae* characters also appears as part of a defence for the poet and for poetic productions as something separate from the poet's private person. As I argue, Ovid's claim that 'Thais is in his art' in the middle of the *Remedia amoris* as part of his defence for his work as a poet must be seen in the context of his later ironic deployment of Terence in his letter to Augustus and defence of art and the artist in exile. Additionally, a Terentian allusion in the *Remedia amoris* that evokes the opening of the first book of the *Ars amatoria*, and is later revisited in the double *Heroides*, brings out aspects of harmful and sick love.

---

17 Fantham 1972, 18.

Terentian connections in the *Remedia amoris*

In the middle of the *Remedia amoris*, over lines 357–436, there is a section discussing different measures to take to repel excessive passion and how one should focus on one's beloved's off-putting features as part of the love cure. However, after a few lines the discourse is interrupted by an over 30-line defence of the poet's literary choices and the *Ars amatoria*, addressed to *quidam*, or 'certain people', at line 361 (cf. also *unus et alter* at 364 and *quicumque es* at 371), who apparently have criticised it for being obscene or immoral: *nuper enim nostros quidam carpsere libellos, / quorum censura Musa proterua mea est* (Ov. *Rem. am.* 361–362, 'for certain folk of late have found fault with my writings, and brand my Muse as a wanton.'). What follows is a defence of poetry and how it should be understood within the frames of its own genre. Henderson notes that it seems evident that Ovid does not fear his critics at this point and that he finds the accusations unjustified, and that if Augustus had been offended by the poem, Ovid has not yet been made aware of this.[18] Still, however, it looks as though Ovid revisits this passage in exile, and links it to his more elaborate defence for the *Ars amatoria* in *Tristia* 2, where the poet alludes to line 362 quoted above with the phrase *uita uerecunda est, Musa iocosa mea* (Ov. *Tr.* 2.354, 'my life is seemly, my Muse playful').[19] This allusion in *Tristia* 2 also simultaneously brings the point from line 387 into play, where the poet states that *si mea materiae respondet Musa iocosae, / uicimus et falsi criminis acta rea est* (Ov. *Rem. am.* 387–388, 'if my Muse meets the charge of mirthful themes, I have won, and she is accused on a false charge'), i.e. that his poetry cannot be criticised for simply being appropriate to its genre.

As was demonstrated in Chapter One, the defence of art is a point of connection between Terence and Ovid in exile; this connection can be detected also here, in the *Remedia amoris*, and one can easily see the parallel between Ovid's defence for his poetry against the anonymous *quidam*, who find faults with it at 361, and Terence's prologues, directed against a certain *poeta uetus* and other unnamed critics of his plays. In his unique prologues, Terence does a very similar thing to what Ovid is doing in the *Remedia amoris*, i.e. claims that he is doing only what there already is precedent for within his genre:

> id isti uituperant factum atque in eo disputant
> contaminari non decere fabulas.
> faciuntne intellegendo ut nil intellegant?

---

18 Henderson 1979, *ad loc.*
19 See also Henderson 1979, 87.

> qui quom hunc accusant, Naeuium Plautum Ennium
> accusant, quos hic noster auctores habet,
> quorum aemulari exoptat neglegentiam
> potius quam istorum obscuram diligentiam.
>
> Ter. *An.* 15–21

His critics abuse him for doing this, arguing that it is not right to contaminate plays in this way. But isn't their cleverness making them obtuse? In criticising our author, they are actually criticising Naevius, Plautus, and Ennius, whom he takes as his models, preferring to imitate their carelessness in this respect rather than the critics' own dreary pedantry.

Very similar defences are also evident in the *Eunuchus, Heautontimoroumenos, Phormio* and *Adelphoe,* and must be said to be a stock trait of the Terentian prologue. Ovid deploys the same tactic in the *Remedia amoris* and again more prominently in *Tristia* 2, when he states that he is the successor of Gallus, Tibullus and Propertius, none of whom has been punished for writing content proper to their genre:

> his ego successi, quoniam praestantia candor
>   nomina uiuorum dissimulare iubet.
> non timui, fateor, ne, qua tot iere carinae,
>   naufraga seruatis omnibus una foret.
>
> Ov. *Tr.* 2.467–470

I was successor to these — since goodwill orders me to cover up the outstanding names of the living. I did not fear, I confess, that where so many ships had sailed, and all had been saved, one would be shipwrecked.

In *Tristia* 2, Ovid deploys Terence as he demonstrates the point quoted above, i.e. that even though the content of his poetry might be *iocosa*, this cannot be taken as a testimony to the poet's private life. In this context, he uses Terence and the tragic playwright Accius as ironic examples of other poets that cannot be seen as representatives for their characters and the content of their genres. The point is an elaboration of the argument made in the *Remedia amoris,* i.e. that he writes what is proper for his genre, that there is a division between art and life, and apparently that the female audience and the women targeted in his *Ars amatoria* are *meretrices*, here represented by the comic *meretrix* Thais:

> quis ferat Andromaches peragentem Thaida partes?
>   peccet, in Andromache Thaida quisquis agat.
> Thais in arte mea est: lasciuia libera nostra est;
>   nil mihi cum uitta; Thais in arte mea est.
>
> Ov. *Rem. am.* 383–386

> Who could endure Thais playing Andromache's part? She would err, who in Andromache played the part of Thais. Thais is the subject of my art; unfettered is my love-making: nothing have I to do with fillets; Thais is the subject of my art.

Henderson states here that Ovid has in mind two specific plays, the *Andromache* of Euripides and the *Thais* of Menander, of which only minimal fragments remain,[20] whereas Traill argues that Ovid's allusion here is to Thais at a level of genre, rather than to be associated with the specific play only, i.e. that Thais in the *Remedia amoris* invokes the typical comic *meretrix* character known from multiple plays within the genre.[21] It is, however, worth taking into consideration here that both Andromache and Thais as characters carry with them a specific and rich Roman tradition, which inevitably comes into play in the allusion here for the educated Roman reader. Andromache is featured in the tragedies of e.g. Ennius and Accius,[22] and Thais is a prominent and memorable character in Terence's *Eunuchus* — a play with a particularly rich reception in the Roman tradition — where she is curiously portrayed in a way that differs from the conventional comic *meretrix*.[23] Ovid himself must also have been aware of the allusive effect of the Roman tradition of such characters, especially given that he later specifically mentions Accius and Terence and the dramatic types of their genres when he later alludes to this very section of the *Remedia amoris* in *Tristia* 2.

A second connection that has a certain Terentian flavour can be found in the opening of the poem. The apparent goal of the *Remedia amoris* is to offer young men (and women) affected by the sickness-called-love a cure and a way out of the miserable state that they are in. To initiate the cure, Ovid states, one should — if one is not already gravely infected — not initiate a more long-term relationship, which will be hurtful in the future; the first thing that must be done is to identify the object of love, and then step back, out of the situation: *quale sit **id quod amas**, celeri circumspice mente, / et tua **laesuro** subtrahe colla iugo* (Ov. *Rem. am.* 89–90, 'Consider in swift thought what kind of thing it is you love, and withdraw your neck from a yoke that may one day gall'.). This phrase, with the curious use of the neuter pronoun for the *puella* — which also repeats the opening of the poem where the happy lover is excluded from the target audience for the cure, ***si quis amat quod amare iuuat**, feliciter ardens / gaudeat* (Ov. *Rem. am.* 13–14, 'If any lover has delight in his love, let him rejoice in his

---

20 Henderson 1979, *ad loc.*

21 Traill 2001, 300.

22 E.g. Ennius' *Andromacha* and Accius' *Astyanax*.

23 The name Thais is not taken from Menander's *Eunuchus*, where the *meretrix* is named Chrysis. On the portrayal of Thais in the *Eunuchus*, see Duckworth 1994 [1952], 259–261.

happy passion') — takes the reader back to the opening of the *Ars amatoria*. As was demonstrated there, identifying the object of love is also the first step to take when wishing to find a mistress, *principio, **quod amare uelis**, reperire labora* (Ov. *Ars am.* 1.35, 'First, strive to find an object for your love'), a phrase repeated shortly later as part of the demonstration that the theatre is the perfect place to begin the search, *illic **inuenies quod ames**, quod ludere possis / quodque semel tangas, quodque tenere uelis* (Ov. *Ars am.* 1.91–92, 'There will you find an object for passion or for deception, something to taste but once, or to keep, if so you wish.'). This section on the theatre and the subsequent interlude on the rape of the Sabine women, here curiously located at the theatre, is part of an allusive network that connects the work to Terence's *Eunuchus*, which contains a strikingly similar phrase, in addition to the use of the neuter pronoun for the object of love, in a notably parallel situation, as demonstrated in Chapter Two. This network of allusions and its connection to Terence is here, by the allusion in the opening of the *Remedia amoris*, further extended.[24]

As shown in Chapter Two, when Ovid uses the rape of the Sabine women as an *exemplum* for how to find a *puella*, this constitutes a paradox, as the Sabine women were the first Roman wives, and must be seen as a symbol for those wearing the married women's *uitta*, i.e. the women that he claims have no place in his poetry. The paradox is further highlighted by the allusive play with the rape of a comic *uirgo* in Terence's *Eunuchus*, and the fact that such comic rapes always facilitate a proper marriage between a young man and woman of citizen status. This same double meaning can be detected in the extension of the allusive network at *Remedia amoris* line 90, where being under the yoke, in addition to being an image linked to *seruitium amoris*,[25] is also an image of marriage as *coniugium*, literally two that are joined or pulling together. The *praeceptor*'s advice here could then also be read to suggest that one should avoid entering into marriage, which will be hurtful or cause injury in the future, while one still can. This is ironic, seeing that avoiding marriage actually facilitates love in Ovid's anti-marital elegiac universe, and thus entering into marriage should be the perfect cure for elegiac love. However, this would mean Ovid's breaking with his genre. Instead, and in compliance with his genre, Ovid's advice is to replace one elegiac love relationship with another, and thus he refers the reader back to the *Ars amatoria* (something that arguably makes the Ovidian intention of curing love seem less than genuine). Notably, as will be demonstrated in the

---

24 Henderson points out that the combination of *amare* with a neuter pronoun as object is an Ovidian formula earlier found in Terence and Lucretius. See Henderson 1979, 31–32.
25 Henderson 1979, *ad loc.*

following section of this chapter, in Terence, entering into a proper marriage is suggested as the obvious medicine for the lovesick mind of a young man.

The idea that love/marriage can cause harm, *laedere*, reappears in combination with the use of the neuter pronoun for the beloved later in Ovid's works, in *Heroides* 20 and 21, in the letters of Acontius and Cydippe. In his letter, Acontius states that *si noceo **quod amo**, fateor sine fine nocebo* (Ov. *Her.* 20.35, 'if I harm that which I love, I confess I shall harm endlessly'),[26] whereupon Cydippe's reply reads *dic mihi nunc solitoque tibi ne depice more: | quid facies odio, sic ubi amore noces? | si **laedis quod amas**, hostem sapienter amabis* (Ov. *Her.* 21.57, 'Come, tell me, and deceive me not in your usual way: what will you do from hate, when you harm me so from love? If you injure one you love, it will be wise to love your foe.'). Here, however, it is the object of love, expressed by *quod*, that is afflicted by illness, rather than the lover himself, and Cydippe's illness is very real and deadly, due to Acontius' wish to marry her: according to the story, Acontius sees Cydippe during a religious festival on Delos, immediately falls in love with her and tricks her into swearing in the temple of Diana that she will marry him. Due to this, when Cydippe later tries to marry her original fiancé, she falls ill and almost dies, and has no choice but to marry Acontius.

As becomes clear from Cydippe's reply, if this is what one calls love, one should rather love one's enemies; maybe, in other words, if you harm the one you love, love is not really love. It is interesting to trace this allusion back through the *Remedia amoris*, *Ars amatoria* and the *Eunuchus*; that love can harm is doubtlessly an idea also present in Ovid's account of the Sabine rape and the rape of Pamphila in the *Eunuchus*. Both cases graphically describe the victims' suffering due to men's wish to possess/marry them, in both cases described as love (cf. *illic inuenies quod ames*, Ov. *Ars am.* 91 and *aliquid inueni | modo quod ames*, Ter. *Eun.* 308–309). It is interesting to notice that the story of Acontius and Cydippe also carries traits reminiscent of many New Comic rape-marriage plots, which often start with a young man seeing a girl at a religious festival, whereupon he falls in love, decides that he must have her, and in the end marries her. Neither the comic *uirgines* nor Cydippe has any real say or choice.[27] Such play with double meanings and layers in the text is a familiar trait in Ovid's elegiac poems. The allusion in the *Remedia amoris* at 89–90 which

---

26 I borrow this translation from Thorsen 2021, who treats the Ovidian version of the story with a specific focus on the concepts of love, disease, and marriage. My text for the double *Heroides* is Kenney 1996.

27 I am grateful to Thea Selliaas Thorsen for pointing this out to me and for pointing me in the direction of the Acontius-Cydippe letters.

invokes the opening of the *Ars amatoria*, and in the extension of this the Terentian rape-marriage plot, brings out the double meaning of withdrawing one's neck from the yoke and the violence that is inherent in the Roman marriage institution. This is further enhanced when read in light of the passage in the *Heroides* 21, which plays with a similar image of harmful or even sick love.

What kind of a disease is this? Terentian lovesickness

Whereas Ovid dedicates himself to writing a poem grounded on the concept of love as a disease, the concept of love as an illness and the idea of curing love is not the main thread *per se* within any of the Terentian comedies, as these notions occur more as scattered literary images. Still, as I aim to demonstrate in this section, a clear and coherent concept of love as a sickness that manifests itself in young lovers in different ways can be detected in Terence, and it is followed up by the ideas and vocabulary of possible cures. In the Terentian corpus, young men are on multiple occasions described as infected with some kind of disease as they haplessly yearn for the object of their love, and the metaphor is prominently and coherently present already in the playwright's first production, the Menander-based play *Andria*.

In *Andria*, the *senex* Simo discusses with his slave the future of his son, the *adulescens amans* Pamphilus, and reflects on the idea that a bad teacher might have a bad influence on the youth's already love-sick mind: *tum siquis magistrum cepit ad eam rem inprobum, / ipsum animum aegrotum ad deteriorem partem plerumque adplicat* (Ter. *An.* 192–193, 'what's more, if any of them have a reprobate for a teacher, he tends to steer their lovesick hearts in the wrong direction.') The adjective *aegrotus*, or diseased, is also used in the same manner by the same character later in the same work, *priu' quam harum scelera et lacrumae confictae dolis / redducunt animum aegrotum ad misericordiam, / uxorem demu'* (Ter. *An.* 558–560, 'before those women's wicked ways and cunningly contrived tears can work on his lovesick mind and reduce him to pity, let's give him a wife.'). The other young man of the play, Charinus, describes himself in a similar manner, as he is asked by his slave Byrria to expel love from his mind to avoid inflaming his desire for no reason:

> BY: *ah!*
> *quanto satiust te id dare operam qui istum amorem ex animo amoueas [tuo],*
> *quam id loqui quo mage lubido frustra incendatur tua!*
> CH: *facile omnes quom ualemus recta consilia aegrotis damus.*
>
> Ter. *An.* 306–309

BY: Oh! How much better to set about banishing that love from your heart than to say things which only inflame your desire to no purpose!
CH: We can all readily give good advice to the sick when we're well.

Similarly, in the *Heautontimoroumenos*, the *senex* Menedemus laments the fact that he has driven his son Clinia away, as he treated him and his (love)sick mind too harshly when he first discovered that he was having a love affair: *ubi rem resciui, coepi non humanitus / neque ut animum decuit aegrotum adulescentuli / tractare, sed ui et uia peruolgata patrum* (Ter. *Haut.* 99–101, 'When I found out, I didn't handle him humanely and with due regard to the feelings of a lovesick lad, but harshly, as is the common way of fathers.'). In all these cases, *aegrotus* is used to describe the mind as infected by love, with a focus on how this infection manifests itself; the lovesick mind of a young man can be easily affected in a negative manner and he can be led down the wrong path in life, if not treated correctly and swiftly.[28]

In *Andria*, the notion that love is a disease with a cure is clear, and the cure proposed by the *senex* Simo is to settle down in a respectable marriage. This is perfectly in line with the comic convention and the negative view of love normally displayed by the parent generation within the genre, and traditional Roman values in general: marriage is a duty and the proper way to live, and thus the right thing to do for the young man. As opposed to love, marriage is not a matter of passion or lust, and married life in the parent generation is generally not described in a distinctly positive manner within the genre.[29] At 192–193, Simo is afraid that his son, due to his lovesick mind, will let himself be led down the wrong path by his slave, who might come up with some trick to prevent him from getting married, i.e. prevent his mind from getting cured. Similarly, at 558–560 he is eager to get his son settled in a proper marriage so that he is not tricked by prostitutes, as he follows up with *spero consuetudine et / coniugio liberali deuinctum, Chreme, / de(h)inc facile ex illis sese emersurum malis.* (Ter. *An.* 560–562, 'I expect that, once he is tied down by a respectable marriage, Chremes, he will easily extricate himself from the other situation.').

However, as explained in the opening of Chapter Two, a happy marriage within the Roman tradition would generally be seen as facilitating a good and stable union, which becomes clear also in the reaction of the father of the proposed wife, Chremes, who is furious about the fact that Simo is asking him to

---

28 These passages represent all the instances of *aegrotus* in Terence. In addition, *aegrotam* is used of a young woman who has just given birth to describe the condition she is in at 922 in the *Adelphoe*.

29 On the portrayal of married life in new comedy, see Duckworth 1994 [1952], 282–285.

promise his daughter to a young man who is in love with someone else and not at all interested in marriage:

> (...) at rogitas? perpulisti me ut homini adulescentulo
> in alio occupato amore, abhorrenti ab re uxoria,
> filiam ut darem in seditionem atque in incertas nuptias,
> eiu' labore atque eiu' dolore gnato ut medicarer tuo.
>
> Ter. An. 828–831

A fine question! You persuaded me to promise my daughter to a young lad involved in another love affair who had no intention of taking a wife, condemning her to squabbling and an unstable marriage, all so that your son could be cured through her pain and her suffering.

Here, too, it is explicitly clear that Pamphilus' love is a sickness, and Chremes is not interested in being the one to heal him by letting his daughter be exploited as mere medicine (with *medicarer* at 831). Later in the play at 944 this verb is used again by Pamphilus himself, when it is discovered that the girl that he is in love with is actually a daughter of Chremes, and that he is in the possession of the last piece of the puzzle, i.e. the girl's real name, before a marriage between them can be organised: *egon huiu' memoriam patiar meae / uoluptati obstare, quom ego possim in hac re medicari mihi?* (Ter. *An.* 943–944, 'Shall I allow my happiness to be spoiled by his forgetfulness, when the remedy is in my own hands?'). Interestingly, for Pamphilus here to heal means to preserve his own happy state of mind by revealing the real name of his dream girl and getting to marry her. Though in a somewhat different way, this also means to prevent lovesickness or unhappy love by marriage, as Pamphilus now will be able to continue his relationship with the beloved, but within the bounds of marriage.

One of the prominent aspects of the effects of Terentian lovesickness is the notion that the diseased mind of the young man easily can be corrupted, as seen in the case of Pamphilus in the *Andria*. His father is afraid that he might be affected by e.g. fake tears, which he sees as a symptom that might be exploited by prostitutes to gain sympathy when needed. This notion is also present in the *Eunuchus*, where the slave Parmeno warns his young master Pamphilus that his beloved, the *meretrix* Thais, might deploy fake tears to soften his anger after having shut him out of her house for the benefit of his rival the day before (lines 67–80). That Parmeno sees Pamphilus' love for Thais as a form of *morbus*, sickness, and his subsequent behaviour as its symptoms, becomes evident not long after: *di boni, quid hoc morbist? adeon homines inmutarier / ex amore ut non cognoscas eundem esse! hoc nemo fuit / minus ineptu', magis seueru' quisquam nec magis continens* (Ter. *Eun.* 225–227, 'Good gods, what kind of a disease is this? To think that people can be so changed by love that you wouldn't recognise them as the same person! Nobody was less irresponsible than Phaedria or more serious or more sober-minded.'). The point here seems to be that the sickness that is love has affected the young man, and the symptoms represent deviance from what can be recognized as the ideal picture of a male citizen as responsible, serious, and sober-minded.

Notably, the noun *remedium* occurs seven times in the Terentian corpus on various occasions, and it is one of the author's preferred metaphors and one that does not occur in Plautus. However, as Fantham points out, the medical origin of the word is at this point forgotten, and the figurative sense has become the normal usage of it; as in Cicero, it is not associated with *morbus*, but rather with misfortunes and grief.[30] It is, however, on two occasion associated with curing negative aspects of unhappy love; in *Phormio*, the *adulescens* Antipho is contemplating over how the other *adulescens* of the play, Phaedria, has been able to cure (*mederi*) his love troubles after acquiring money to buy the music girl that he was in love with, whereas there is no remedy for his own tricky situation, i.e. that he has married a poor woman that he loves, without his father's consent:

> *quam scitumst ei(u)s modi in animo parare cupiditates*
> *quas, quom res aduorsae sient, paullo mederi possis!*
> *hic simul argentum repperit, cura sese expediuit;*
> *ego nullo possum remedio me euolvere ex his turbis (...).*
>
> Ter. *Phorm.* 821–824

How wise it is to entertain desires that can easily be cured when things go wrong! He escaped from his worries as soon as he acquired the money, whereas I have no way of extricating myself from my troubles.

In the *Eunuchus*, the flatterer Gnatho works as the love advisor for the rival of the play, Thraso, and talks of the only remedy for preventing jealousy by making Thais jealous instead: *GN: rogas? / scin, si quando illa mentionem Phaedria / facit aut si laudat, te ut male urat? TH: sentio. GN: id ut ne fiat haec res solast remedio* (Ter. *Eun.* 436–439, 'GN: Need you ask? You know how, if ever she mentions Phaedria or praises him, it pains you terribly? TH: And I feel it. GN: There's only one way to prevent this happening.'). Similarly, but with different vocabulary, the slave Parmeno at line 940 of the play professes to have brought *salus*, or health, to the young man Chaerea by making prostitutes seem off-putting to him.

---

30 Fantham 1972, 18.

Thus, there is in Terence a clear and developed, though scattered, notion of love as an illness, explicitly expressed as *morbus*, with symptoms, such as change of personality, *rabies* (madness or frenzy, used by Parmeno about Chaerea's love for Pamphila at Ter. *Eun.* 301), and corruptibility (by e.g. fake tears). It is also one that has a cure, such as revealing and seeing the true and corrupting ways of prostitutes, and entering into a proper marriage, explicitly expressed by the use of *medicari*. To compare, Ovid's *Remedia amoris* is fully dealing with love as a disease (*morbus*, e.g. *semina morbi* at line 81) or wound, and how to cure it, and this can be said to be the utmost development of this image. Due to genre, the ultimate cure that will put a definite end to the illness differs between Terence and Ovid; in Terence, all problems are wiped out when the societal order is re-established and the young man (in most cases) married. Marriage is not an option in Ovid's erotodidactic elegies, and maybe love is an illness that is not meant to be cured permanently at all. However, as I argue in the following sections of this chapter, there are specific traits in the Terentian comedies that point forward to Ovid's elaborate and systematised love-cure, which might indicate that he has picked up on the early Roman development of the *topos* in Terence, where it is arguably more elaborated than in his predecessor Plautus.

A love-cure in the *Eunuchus*: a programmatic connection?

As pointed out in the introduction to this chapter, Henderson suggests that the outline or programme for the *Remedia amoris* might stem from Propertius 1.1. One of the arguments for this is that Ovid repeats Propertius' antithesis of *consilium* and *furor* in the opening at line 10:

> *tum mihi constantis deiecit lumina fastus*
>   *et caput impositis pressit Amor pedibus,*
> *donec me docuit castas odisse puellas*
>   *improbus et nullo uiuere consilio.*
> *ei mihi, iam toto **furor** hic non deficit anno,*
>   *cum tamen aduersos cogor habere deos.*
>
> Prop. 1.1.3–8

It was then that Love made me lower my looks of stubborn pride and trod my head beneath his feet, until the villain taught me to avoid decent girls and to lead the life of a ne'er-do-well. Poor me, for a whole year now this frenzy has not abated, while I am compelled to endure the frown of heaven.

Cf.

> quin etiam docui qua possis arte parari,
>   et, quod nunc **ratio** est, **impetus** ante fuit.
>
> Ov. Rem. am. 9–10

In fact, I have taught by what skill you might be gained, and what was impulse then is science now.

As Henderson points out, Ovid's *ratio,* translated to 'skill' or 'method', is more or less synonymous with *ars* or *consilium* (cf. Ov. *Rem. am.* 703, *consilium est, quodcumque cano*) and *impetus,* translated 'impulse' or 'madness', with *furor* (cf. *dum furor in cursu est, currenti cede furore: | difficiles aditus impetus omnis habet,* Ov. *Rem. Am.* 119–120, 'while its fury is at full speed, give way to its furious speeding; impetuous force is ever hard to face.'). In addition, according to Henderson, the terms in combination in Ovid also recall the technical language of Stoic ethics, and the virtue of subordinating animal instincts and appetites (*impetus, appetitiones;* ὁρμαί) to reason (*ratio;* λόγος).[31]

A similar antithesis between reason (*consilium/ratio*) and madness (*furor/ impetus*) can also be recognised in the opening of the *Eunuchus,* in its famous opening scene involving the disillusioned and shut-out Phaedria and his slave Parmeno, and the slave's answer to Phaedria's lament:

> ere, quae res in se neque **consilium** neque **modum**
> habet ullum, eam consilio regere non potes.
> in amore haec omnia insunt uitia: iniuriae,
> suspiciones, inimicitiae, indutiae,
> bellum, pax rursum: **incerta** haec si postules
> **ratione certa** facere, nihilo plus agas
> quam si des operam ut cum **ratione insanias**.
>
> Ter. *Eun.* 57–63

Master, when a thing has no logic to it and no means of control, you can't rule it by logic. A love affair has all these symptoms: wrongs, suspicions, quarrels, truces, war, peace again. If you try to impose certainty on uncertainty by reason, you'd achieve no more than if you set about going insane by reason.

Here, Parmeno contrasts love that has no *consilium* or *modum* and thus cannot be controlled by *consilium,* and which contains a number of uncertainties, *incerta,* with that which is *certa* and controllable by *ratio.* The contrast is highlighted

---

31 See full discussion at Henderson 1979, *ad loc.*

at line 63, with the oxymoron 'going insane rationally'. As Barsby points out, *consilium* here has connotations of 'judgement', 'sense' and 'reason', *modus* of 'moderation', 'restraint' or 'control',[32] and *ratio* is more or less a synonym of both. The Terentian vocabulary is represented in both the Propertian and the Ovidian text, and 'to go mad/insane', *insanire* is represented by *furor*, madness and *impetus*, impulse or fury.

Notably, it has been shown that this Terentian scene can be interpreted within the same philosophical sphere as that onto which Ovid takes hold; it has a particularly rich reception in later Roman literature, and Barsby notes that the philosophical implications of the scene are exploited by Horace (and later by Persius at 5.161–175), who also recognises the antithesis present in the text. Here, the scene is deployed to contrast the lover's madness and enslavement with the Stoic wise man, who is sane and free.[33]

> *'sume, catelle!' negat : si non des, optet: amator*
> *exclusus qui distat, agit ubi secum, eat an non,*
> *quo rediturus erat non arcessitus, et haeret*
> *invisis foribus? 'nec nunc, cum me uocet ultro,*
> *accedam? an potius mediter finire dolores?*
> *exclusit; reuocat: redeam? non, si obsecret.' ecce*
> *seruus non paulo sapientior: 'o ere, quae res*
> *nec modum habet neque consilium, ratione modoque*
> *tractari non uult. in amore haec sunt mala, bellum,*
> *pax rursum: haec si quis tempestatis prope ritu*
> *mobilia et caeca fluitantia sorte laboret*
> *reddere certa sibi, nihilo plus explicet ac si*
> *insanire paret certa ratione modoque.'*
>
> <div align="right">Hor. <i>Sat.</i> 2.3.259–271</div>

'Take them, pet.' He says, 'No.' Were you not to offer them, he would crave them. How differs the lover who, when shut out, debates with himself whether to go or not to where, though not invited, he meant to return, and hangs about the hated doors? 'Shall I not go even now, when she invites me of her own accord? Or rather, shall I think of putting an end to my affliction? She shut me out. She calls me back. Shall I return? No — not if she implores me.' Now listen to the slave, wiser by far of the two: 'My master, a thing that admits of neither method nor sense cannot be handled by rule and method. In love inhere these evils — first war, then peace: things almost as fickle as the weather, shifting about by blind chance, and if one were to try to reduce them to fixed rule for himself, he would no more set them right than if he aimed at going mad by fixed rule and method.'

---

32 Barsby 1999, *ad loc.*
33 However, as Barsby points out, Parmeno does not really reflect the philosophical wise man, as he is rather a cynical realist. See Barsby 1999, 91 for full discussion.

Furthermore, the notion of a love advisor or teacher character of superior knowledge is prominent in both Ovid and Terence. As will be further discussed in the next chapter, the Ovidian *praeceptor* or *magister* (cf. *Naso magister* at 2.744 and 3.812 of the *Ars amatoria*) takes on a role that in many ways is paralleled by e.g. the comic slave character (but also the comic flatterer, cf. e.g. Gnatho, who offers advice to Phaedria's soldier rival), who is one of the characters that offers advice to the young men of the plays in matters of love.[34] In the present context it is sufficient to note that the comic slave advisor offers advice in both situations: first, where young men wish to initiate a relationship, as e.g. in the Eunuchus, where Parmeno offers Chaerea advice on how to secure access to his beloved, or Davos in *Andria*, who is accused of being a wicked teacher (*magistrum ... inprobum*, Ter. *An.* 192, quoted above) and who might lead one of the lovesick young men in the play down the wrong path; also, when it comes to getting the upper hand in a shifting relationship or falling out of love, as he takes on the voice of reason as opposed to the lovesick and in some cases 'insane' young man. The first type of advisor or *magister* is paralleled by the *praeceptor* in the Ars amatoria (and being a *magister improbus* here is effectively what Ovid was eventually accused of), whereas the latter task is similar to the one that the *praeceptor* takes on in the *Remedia amoris*.

Notably in the present context, being 'the voice of reason' or helping young men fall out of love is also in several cases in Terence connected in some way or another to the concept of sickness and/or cure. One example of a slave advising a young man to stop loving is Byrria in *Andria* at lines 306–309, quoted above, whereupon the young man Charinus responds that it is easy for one that is healthy to give such advice to one that is sick; another example is Gnatho, who offers Thraso a 'remedy' for jealousy at *Eunuchus* line 439. The most prominent example is, however, Parmeno of the same play, who brags at length about having taught Chaerea how to forever hate *meretrices* by showing him how they act when they are alone with no men present. To know such things, Parmeno claims, brings *salus* to young men, which in addition to salvation also might bear the meaning of health or wellbeing as opposed to illness, which would also be in line with Parmeno's earlier comment on love as both sickness and madness:

---

34 Fulkerson suggests that the *seruus callidus* of comedy makes a transition into elegy as an aspect of the lover; Parker 1989 suggests that the comic lover is split into the *adulescens amator* and the *seruus callidus*, whereas Fulkerson argues that this splitting is undone in the elegiac lover. See Fulkerson 2013, 190–193 and Parker 1989, 242–243. I will treat the relationship between Ovid's *praeceptor* and the Terentian slave character further in Chapter Four.

reuiso quidnam Chaerea hic rerum gerat.
quod si astu rem tractauit, di uostram fidem,
quantam et quam ueram laudem capiet Parmeno!
nam ut omittam quod ei amorem difficillumum et
carissumum, a meretrice auara uirginem
quam amabat, eam confeci sine molestia
sine sumptu et sine dispendio: tum hoc alterum,
id uerost quod ego mi puto palmarium,
me repperisse quo modo adulescentulus
meretricum ingenia et mores posset noscere
mature, ut quom cognorit perpetuo oderit.
quae dum foris sunt nil uidetur mundius
nec magis compositum quicquam nec magis elegans
quae cum amatore quom cenant ligurriunt.
harum uidere inluuiem sordes inopiam,
quam inhonestae solae sint domi atque auidae cibi,
quo pacto ex iure hesterno panem atrum uorent,
nosse omnia haec salus est adulescentulis.

Ter. Eun. 923–940

I'm returning to see how Chaerea is getting on. If he's handled the situation cleverly, heaven help us, how much praise will Parmeno receive today and how deservedly! Not to mention that I've secured for him without trouble and without cost or outlay a very difficult and very expensive love affair, since the girl he loved belonged to a greedy courtesan; there's the other point — and I reckon this to be my master stroke — that I've found a way for a young lad to discover the character and habits of courtesans in good time, so that having discovered them he will hate them forever. So long as they're out in public, there's nothing more refined, more composed, more elegant, as they pick daintily at their food while dining with a lover. But to see their filth, squalor, and poverty, and how repulsive they are when they are alone at home and how greedy they are for food, how they devour stale bread dipped in yesterday's soup — to know all this is the salvation of young lads.

This scene demonstrates the slave's likeness to the *praeceptor* as love doctor in the *Remedia amoris* particularly well, and Parmeno's efforts to bring good health to the lovesick Chaerea might be thought of as an erotodidactic love cure in miniature: he is celebrating his successful lesson in the crooked ways of prostitutes, which he imagines he must have given the young man, and that he with this lesson has caused him to hate such women forever and thus brought him *salus*. Furthermore, it becomes clear at line 940 that he considers his brilliant lesson a potentially beneficial for *all* young men in the same situation, and thus gives the impression of elevating himself to the position of general love advisor of universal knowledge. The slave's role in this scene can easily be paralleled with the role of Ovid's love doctor, who offers advice with a very similar aim, i.e. to put the lover off of the beloved.

Furthermore, the overall idea in this section also overlaps with the Ovidian notion that, by taking on 'the role of pander',[35] one can simultaneously provide healing:

> *et quisquam praecepta potest mea dura uocare?*
>   *en, etiam partes conciliantis ago.*
> *nam quoniam uariant animi, uariabimus artes;*
>   *mille mali species, mille salutis erunt.*
>
> Ov. Rem. am. 523–526

And can anyone call my precepts hard? lo! I even play the reconciler. For since natures vary, I will vary my arts; the disease has a thousand forms, I have a thousand remedies.

This is effectively the same thing with which Parmeno credits himself, i.e. that he has secured an affair for his young master and through this also let him see his beloved for what she really is and put him off her (and prostitutes in general).[36] And here too, the aim is to bring *salus* (ref. *salutis* at 526). Rather than turning love into hate by letting the lovesick see the disgusting habits of his beloved, the advice that follows in the Ovidian text is to overindulge, that is to take every opportunity to be with the beloved up until the point where her very house feels distasteful and it gives no pleasure to spend time there:

> *i, fruere usque tua nullo prohibente puella;*
>   *illa tibi noctes auferat, illa dies.*
> *taedia quaere mali: faciunt et taedia finem;*
>   *iam quoque, cum credes posse carere, mane,*
> *dum bene te cumules et copia tollat amorem*
>   *et fastidita non iuuet esse domo.*
>
> Ov. Rem. am. 537–542

Continue, unchecked, to enjoy your girl; let hers be your nights, and hers your days. Seek to be sated with your complaint: satiety too can make an end. Still remain, even when you think you could do without, until you have all your fill, and plenty destroys passion, and her house, grown distasteful, causes you no delight.

In both of these passages, the aim is to get the lover to loathe the object of love by spending time with her, and in both cases, this is facilitated by the advisor, who is the one pulling the threads. It has been noted of Parmeno, with regards to this scene and elsewhere, that there are several references that indicate that

---

35 I borrow this translation of *partes conciliantis* from Henderson 1979, *ad loc.*
36 Even though he first claimed that his suggestion that Chaerea should let himself be taken to Thais' house dressed as the eunuch was a joke.

he is presented as if he were a poet or playwright, and that he takes on the role as author of the 'play within a play', that is the scheme to sneak Chaerea into Thais' house dressed as a eunuch. The *palmarium* at 930 probably refers to the prize for dramatic competitions, as he is celebrating the success of his plot.[37] In this metatheatrical sense then, Parmeno is the author of a play (cf. also Phaedria's comment on Chaerea's scheme at 689 as a *fabula*, a possible metatheatrical reference)[38] in his role as slave advisor. It is interesting to compare this notion with the fact that Ovid the *praeceptor* here is depicting himself as taking on a role within a plot with the metaphor *partes conciliantis ago*, which can bear the meaning of acting out a role in the theatrical sense.[39] The *partes conciliantis*, or role as the one who brings forth a union or 'matchmaker', might also be compared to the role of the slave advisor, like Parmeno, who takes credit for having facilitated Chaerea's affair in his own 'play within a play', and is later celebrated by Chaerea himself for having been the one who gave the advice that led to the successful union (*illumne qui mihi dedit consilium ut facerem*, Ter. *Eun.* 1045, 'The one who suggested the plan of action').[40]

The steps to recovery: Terentian remedies in *Remedia amoris*

In addition to Terentian echoes playing a part in a larger allusive network and traits in the *Eunuchus* that point forward to Ovid's elegiac love cure as a possible source of inspiration, I would lastly like to highlight some specific instructions found in the *Remedia amoris* that can be traced back to similar pieces of advice and notions in Terence. The idea of an unworthy mistress using e.g. fake tears to get her way, which, as demonstrated above, is prominently present in Terence, is frequently revisited by Ovid. The same is true of the notion that too much *otium* is bad for the lover who wants to stay away from his mistress; the fact is that many of the Terentian *adulescentes* seem to be the target candidates for an Ovidian love cure. As shown above, just as the young men of *Andria* are described as sick or as having a sick mind, the same goes for Clinia of

---

37 See Barsby 1999, *ad* line 930 and Frangoulidos 1994, 125 n. 11. See Fantham 1972, 33–34 for the metaphor.

38 See Barsby 1999, *ad loc.* and Frangoulidos 1994, 125 n. 10.

39 *OLD*, *ago*, 25 b.

40 And probably also the matchmaker characters of comedy in general. The term *conciliatrix* is used with this meaning of a female slave character at Pl. *Mil.* 1410, and as Henderson 1979 *ad loc.* notes, it was also the title of a *fabula togata* by C. Quinctius Atta.

the *Heautontimoroumenos*. The most prominent example, however, is found in the *Eunuchus* and the lovesick Phaedria.

Phaedria in the opening of the play is the young man in the New Comic corpus that might come closest to suffering under what Ovid terms *indignae regna puellae* (Ov. *Rem. am.* 15, 'the tyranny of an unworthy girl'), as he expresses his anger over his mistress' behaviour towards him: *o indignum facinu'! Nunc ego / et illam scelestam esse et me miserum sentio: / et taedet et amore ardeo* (Ter. *Eun.* 70–72, 'What an outrageous way to behave! Now I realise that she's a scoundrel and I'm in misery. I'm fed up with her, but I'm on fire with love.'). In many cases in new comedy, it is not actually the mistress herself that causes the lover's misery by refusing him, but other factors and so-called blocking characters, who conventionally stand in the way of the love affair, e.g. the *senex*, which is the case in both *Andria* and *Heautontimoroumenos*, or the typical comic pimp or *lena*. Another plot variation that recurs frequently in elegy is where the lover has to compete for his mistress' attention with a wealthy rival.[41] This is the case for Phaedria; his beloved Thais falls into the sub-category of the independent *meretrix*, whose stock traits within the genre are greed and mercenariness.[42] Thus, he places the blame for his misery mostly with Thais herself, who has refused to accept him into her house for the benefit of his richer soldier rival.[43]

As Barsby notes on this passage, Phaedria foreshadows the Catullan lover with his mixed emotions of love and hate; this character might thus have had a direct influence upon the later Roman tradition, even though the motif itself can be traced to Greek origins.[44] Furthermore, *miser* 'becomes the stock epithet for the tormented lover in Roman elegy',[45] and notably, the conventional comic expression *me miserum*, here deployed by Phaedria in a situation of erotic lament, becomes a favourite idiom for Ovid, in the *Amores* in particular, whereas it is not found in Tibullus and only twice in Propertius.[46]

---

41 James 2012, 256.

42 Barsby 1999, 100.

43 She does, however, reveal her true and more honourable intentions in a monologue, and it is thus clear to the audience or reader that she does not belong solely to the mercenary type.

44 Barsby 1999, And, as Konstan 1986 demonstrates, seeing in the *Eunuchus* an anticipation of elegiac subjectivity, he generally comes very close to the elegiac lover.

45 Barsby 1999, *ad* line 71.

46 See e.g. McKeown 1989 *ad Am.* 1.1.25. As he points out, the exclamation is fairly common in comedy and rhetorical prose. In *Am.* 1.1.25., he suggests that Ovid perhaps is echoing Prop. 1.1.1 *Cynthia prima suis miserum me cepit ocellis* ('Cynthia first with her eyes ensnared me, poor wretch'). The exclamation occurs a number of times in both Plautus and Terence in different contexts.

Phaedria's emotional state in the opening of the *Eunuchus* might also be compared to a similar notion later in the Ovidian text, as the *praeceptor* treats miserable lovers who want to learn how not to love, but cannot:

> tu mihi, qui, quod amas, aegre dediscis amare
> nec potes et uelles posse, docendus eris.
> saepe refer tecum sceleratae facta puellae
> et pone ante oculos omnia damna tuos
>
> Ov. *Rem. am.* 297–300

> But you who love and with pain unlearn your loving, who cannot and yet wish you could, you must be taught by me. Bring often to your mind what your cursed girl has done, and set all your loss before your eyes.

Phaedria's outburst as he realises how badly Thais is behaving, *indignum facinus* at line 70, and his subsequent description of Thais as *scelestam* in line 71, might here be compared to the *sceleratae facta puellae* at line 299 of the Ovidian text. In general, Phaedria fits well with the image of a lover who cannot unlearn the impulse to love, but wishes he could, as becomes evident in the opening lines 46–56, where he considers whether he should stop tolerating the insults (*contumelias* at line 48) of *meretrices* and whether he should go back to Thais after having been shut out for the benefit of his rival Thraso the day before: *exclusit; reuocat: redeam? non si me obsecret. / siquidem hercle possis, nil prius neque fortius*, Ter. *Eun.* 49–50, ('She shut me out, she calls me back: shall I go? No, not if she implores me. If only you could, by god, this would be the best course, and the bravest.').[47] The best would be not to put up with her behaviour, he concludes, but he is afraid that he might not be able to go through with the plan, and ensures himself that he must think the matter through while he still can.

Also for the Ovidian lovers, being shut out for the benefit of another is one of the things one should keep in mind when trying to stop loving:

> sic mihi iurauit, sic me iurata fefellit,
> ante suas quotiens passa iacere fores!
> diligit ipsa alios, a me fastidit amari:
> institor heu noctes, quas mihi non dat, habet.
>
> Ov. *Rem. am.* 303–306

---

47 The OCT-edition (Kauer, Lindsay and Skutsch 1965 [1926]) gives lines 50–56 to Parmeno, and thus lets his speech go from 50 to 70. I here and elsewhere follow Barsby 1999 in letting Phaedria's speech go to line 56, and let Parmeno's speech begin at 57, introduced by the vocative *ere*. See Barsby 1999, 90 for full discussion.

> Thus did she swear to me, and swearing played me false; how often did she suffer me to lie before her door! She cares for others herself, but scorns my love: a pedlar (curse him!) enjoys the nights she refuses to me.

According to Parmeno, staying angry at Thais for being excluded in favor of his rival would be advisable for Phaedria in his miserable state, but as he warns him, he must be aware that his anger might easily be quenched by a single false tear. Thais could then take this opportunity to turn the attack back on him instead:

> *et quod nunc tute tecum iratus cogitas*
> *'egon illam, quae illum, quae me, quae non..! sine modo,*
> *mori me malim : sentiet qui uir siem' :*
> *haec uerba una mehercle falsa lacrimula*
> *quam oculos terendo misere uix ui expresserit,*
> *restinguet, et te ultro accusabit, et dabis*
> *ultro supplicium.*
>
> Ter. Eun. 64–70

> And as for your present angry thoughts — 'I — her? when she — him? when she — me? when she won't –? Just let it be, I'd prefer to die, she shall realise what sort of man I am' — god knows she'll quell that sort of talk with one tiny little false tear, which she's just managed to squeeze out by rubbing her eyes all pathetically; and she'll turn the accusation back on you, and you'll be the one who pays the penalty.

This notion is also evident in *Andria* at 558–560, quoted above; the lovesick mind can easily be driven to pity for the object of love by her false tears. That women (and men) might use tears to affect a lover is a concept repeatedly revisited in Ovid. A situation very similar to the one in the *Eunuchus*, as also noted by McKeown,[48] is pictured in *Amores* 1.8., where women are instructed by a *lena* called 'Dipsas', (Gr. 'thirsty'), to make love last by e.g. excluding the lover from her house, meeting his accusations with new accusations, and learning how to fake tears to soften his anger:

> *surda sit oranti tua ianua, laxa ferenti;*
> *   audiat exclusi uerba receptus amans;*
> *et quasi laesa prior nonnumquam irascere laeso:*
> *   uanescit culpa culpa repensa tua.*
> *sed numquam dederis spatiosum tempus in iram:*
> *   saepe simultates ira morata facit.*

---

48 'The train of thought in this passage is clearly illustrated by a comparison with Ter. *Eun.* 64ff', McKeown 1989, 242.

quin etiam discant oculi lacrimare coacti,
  et faciant udas illa uel ille genas

                                          Ov. *Am.* 1.8.77–84

Let your portal be deaf to prayers, but wide to the giver; let the lover you welcome over-
hear the words of the one you have locked out; sometimes, too, when you have injured
him, be angry, as if injured first-charge met by counter-charge will vanish. But never give
to anger long range of time; anger that lingers long oft causes breach. Nay, even let your
eyes learn to drop tears at command, and let mistress or slave-boy cause you wet cheeks;

This topic is revisited in the *Remedia amoris*, where the unhappy lovers are
warned about the same trick, in a manner similar to how Phaedria was warned
by Parmeno:

neue puellarum lacrimis moueare, caueto:
  ut flerent, oculos erudiere suos.
artibus innumeris mens oppugnatur amantum,
  ut lapis aequoreis undique pulsus aquis.

                                          Ov. *Rem. am.* 689–692

And take care not to be moved by girls' tears: they have taught their eyes to weep. By in-
numerable arts are lovers' feelings assailed, as the rock is beaten by waves on every side.

The idea that one might fake tears to obtain something from one's lover is by no
means unique to Terence and Ovid, and *puellarum lacrimis moueare* at line 689
and *artibus aequoris* at 692 might be seen in connection with Propertius' *nil*
moueor lacrimis*; ista sum captus ab* **arte**(Prop. 3.25.5, 'Your tears move me not:
it was that trick which ensnared me'), in his renouncement of Cynthia.[49] Also in
Propertius, the image of having been ill, or wounded, and becoming healthy
again and thereafter not as easily affected is present shortly before: *nunc demum*
uasto fessi resipiscimus aestu, / uulneraque ad sanum nunc coiere mea (Prop.
3.24.17–18, 'Now at last, weary from the wild surge, I have recovered my sanity,
and my wounds have now closed up and healed.'). It is worth noting, however,
that the particular link between the imagery of lovesickness and being suscepti-
ble to corruption, by fake tears in particular, is present in both Terence's *Andria*
and his *Eunuchus*. This idea, especially in light of the connection between the
latter play and the elegiac genre, might have had an influence on the later Roman tradition.

When the lover is *medicabilis* (Ov. *Rem. am.* 135), or ready to be treated, the
praeceptor's first piece of advice is to stay busy, as free time inevitably will

---

49 See also Henderson 1979 *ad loc.*

cause the 'pleasant evil' that is love: *res age, tutus eris* (Ov. *Rem. am.* 144, 'be busy, and you will be safe.'). The same idea can be re-found in the *Eunuchus*, where it is deployed by Phaedria as he plans to depart to the countryside to exhaust himself, though not to fall out of love, but to be able to stay out of his mistress' way for a couple of days to allow her to secure the girl Pamphila, who is in the possession of his rival: *rus ibo: ibi hoc me macerabo biduom* (Ter. *Eun.* 187, 'I'll go to the farm and stew in misery there for two days') and *ego rus ibo atque ibi manebo* (Ter. *Eun.* 216, 'I'll go to the farm and stay there.'). Going to the countryside is also one of the alternatives mentioned by Ovid's *praeceptor*, *rura quoque oblectant animum studiumque colendi* (Ov. *Rem. am.* 169, 'The country also delights the mind, and the pursuit of husbandry.').

As Henderson notes, a comparison can be made with a similar notion in Plautus' *Mercator*, where the young man Charinus decides to go into exile in despair after having been unable to secure himself access to the slave girl Pasicompsa, and his friend Eutychus suggests the countryside as an alternative: *quanto te satiust rus aliqio abire, ibi esse, ibi uiuere, / adeo dum illius te cupiditas atque amor missum facit?* (Plaut. *Merc.* 656–657, 'how much better is it for you to go somewhere in the country, remain there, and live there until your desire and love for her lets go of you?'). The idea here is that Charinus should stay in the countryside until he falls out of love, which is essentially the same as the goal for Ovid's target audience. However, there is still an interesting link to the Terentian play here, as the concept of keeping busy to be able to stay away from the beloved and, notably, the issue of wearing oneself out to be able to sleep properly are each present in both Terence and Ovid:

> PH: *censen posse me offirmare et*
> *perpeti ne redeam interea? PA: tene? non hercle arbitror;*
> *nam aut iam reuortere aut mox noctu te adiget horsum insomnia.*
> PH: *opu' faciam, ut **defetiger** usque, ingratiis ut dormiam.*
> Ter. Eun. 217–220, ''

> PH: Do you suppose I can be resolute and hold out without coming back meanwhile?
> PA: You? No, I don't, for god's sake. Either you'll return at once, or presently when night comes insomnia will drive you back.
> PH: I'll work on the farm until I'm so utterly exhausted that I sleep in spite of myself.

Cf.

> *nocte **fatigatum** somnus, non cura puellae,*
> *excipit et pingui membra quiete leuat.*
> Ov. Rem. am. 205–206

Tired out, at nightfall sleep, not thoughts of a girl, will await you, and refresh your limbs with healthy repose.

In these passages, both the idea and the general vocabulary overlap.[50] As the discussion between Phaedria and Parmeno in the Terentian quote leads straight to Parmeno's introduction of the concept of the illness with his rhetorical question *quid hoc morbist?* at 225, this fits the context of the *Remedia amoris* particularly well. Again, even if the idea of going to the countryside to distract oneself from love is not unique to Terence and Ovid, and though Ovid might not have had Terence exclusively in mind, there are several points of connection, ideas that occur and are combined in both authors, which, in addition to similarities in vocabulary, suggest that Terence played a role in the development of this Ovidian motif. The fact that the *Remedia amoris* also contains a defence of Ovid's *ars* articulated in manner that is similar to his *Tristia 2*, where Terence is explicitly mentioned and, as has been argued in Chapter One, plays such a prominent role, adds to the impression of a Terentian soundboard of Ovid's complex *Cures for love*.

Conclusion

As I have aimed to demonstrate in this chapter, there are several allusions to Terence in the *Remedia amoris* that, when read as part of a larger allusive network, connect the poem to the author's previous works but also foreshadow later allusive play in the exile poetry and Ovid's defence for his poetic production; in this, I would argue that he also exploits the style of the unique Terentian prologue. In the same manner as demonstrated in Chapter One and Chapter Two, Ovid deploys Terence also in the *Remedia amoris* so as to address current societal issues, conservative morals and the status of art and the artist. Additionally, I hope to have shown that the seeds of some of Ovid's erotodidactic notions can be traced to Terence, also when it comes to the downsides of love and the negative imagery that is connected with it; the Terentian slave character plays a central role here as a temporary representative of reason, as opposed to the madness and illness of the lover; as I touched upon, the slave is cast in a role similar to that of a *magister* or *praeceptor*, which will be more exhaustively treated in the next chapter. There is in Terence a clear and consistent, though scattered, image of love as a sickness with a cure; though this is not a Terentian

---

50 Not necessarily verbatim, as this would not be allowed by the meter.

invention, I would argue that it is deployed by him in a manner that foreshadows the elegists' use of the image and its culmination in Ovid's *Remedia amoris*. However, this simultaneously works to highlight the generic conditions that separate the genres. Marriage, the conventional outcome of the comic plots, effectively puts an end to the young men's sufferings, as is the case for both the young men in *Andria* and for Chaerea in the *Eunuchus*; it is the ultimate cure for love in Terence, and at the same time secures the reinstatement of proper social order. The reciprocity that is so central to the image of successful elegiac love is left out of the picture, however, and the (often raped) citizen girls often have no lines in the play. Eventually, the headstrong *meretrix* Thais in the *Eunuchus* suffers a similar fate; the lovesick Phaedria successfully regains control over himself and his life and is thus 'cured' from his disease at the end of the play, as he makes a deal with his rival to share Thais, as long as the rival foots the bill for them both. As Phaedria regains control, Thais loses it; she is at this point no longer present on stage and has no say in the matter. Ovid's love cure, on the other hand, can never effectively put an end to the lover's misery; the real remedies would not be possible within the bounds of his genre.

4 Genre and conditions: slaves, lovers and the slavery of love

Introduction

Seruitium amoris or the metaphorical slavery of love is for the Roman love elegists the primary image used to describe the state in which the lover finds himself when he has given up control, surrendered to love and is in the power of the
puella, who now becomes the *domina*. It is usually read as an ironic reversal of
status, but as Fulkerson notes, 'it might also be the best way to express a desire
for equality'.[1] Copley defines it as 'an expression of the lover's humility and
abasement, of his willingness in the name of love to undergo punishments and
to undertake duties which in real life were felt to be peculiar to the slave alone,
and entirely unworthy of a free man',[2] and states that it 'is an idea which seems
constantly in the mind of the elegists; in fact with them *seruitium* virtually becomes a synonym for *amor*.'[3] The *topos* of *seruitium amoris* then, might be said
to be a generic marker of the elegiac genre, and thus also for Ovid's works, but,
as I hope to demonstrate in this chapter, with some twists to the image; as I aim
to show in the following, prominent examples of *seruitium amoris* in Ovid display surprising connections to the comic genre and some of Terence's presentations of both slavish young lovers and actual slave characters.

In the present context it is interesting to notice that, in the words of Fulkerson, 'actual *seruitium amoris* does not appear as such in Roman comedy', even
though references to young lovers behaving in a slavish or powerless manner
due to love occurs on some occasions.[4] Copley states that the single instance of
seruitium amoris is found in the *Eunuchus*, but that it shows no evidence of ro-
mantic-sentimental development, which becomes characteristic for the later

---

[1] Fulkerson 2013, 192, also 188–190; James 2003, 12. In addition to Fulkerson 2013, significant
studies on the *seruitium amoris* of the Roman love elegists are Copley 1947, Lyne 1979, and
Murgatroyd 1981.
[2] Copley 1947, 285.
[3] Copley 1947, 291. Copley 1947 argues for the originality of the Roman elegists in their deployment of *seruitium amoris*, ultimately deriving from common speech. See also Lyne 1979, for
the view that the elegiac poets, and more particular Propertius, invented this motif. Murgatroyd 1981 argues that previous examinations of the metaphor contain a number of omis-
sions and inaccuracies, and that the motif was more common in Hellenistic literature than
acknowledged.
[4] Fulkerson 2013, 190.

https://doi.org/10.1515/9783111308036-004

writers.[5] It seems then, that the extended use of *seruitium amoris* and the image of the beloved as a *domina*, such a prominent *topos* in the elegiac writers, is a factor that distinguishes the genres of new comedy and Roman love elegy.

This might be explained by the nature of the two genres themselves: As Fulkerson states, the elegists write about the ups and downs of a single erotic relationship, and the downs tend to be what is the most interesting, as a 'happily ever after' outcome to the relationship would effectively put an end to the story.[6] In contrast, this is the very aim and expected outcome of the comic genre, which focuses on the young man's road to the fortunate final event that is marriage, surely with an appropriate number of comic hindrances along the way, but not anything that would make the audience doubt that everything would turn out as it should in the end. Another factor that makes the metaphor of being a slave to the beloved so effective in elegy is the issue of the status of the *puella*, which remains (deliberately) blurred;[7] the issue of status present in the genre and otherwise in society could in this way lay the foundation for interesting dynamics relating to who is under whose dominance. Such a play on dominance and status might not have had the same effect within the strict social boundaries of Roman comedy; while it is true that in the comedy genre, status is an issue of crucial importance to conventional misapprehension plots, and the revelation of a young girl's true status as a citizen facilitates a marriage at the end of the action in several of the extant plays, the characters are still much more clearly defined, and the audience would conventionally already know their background from the beginning, even though temporary mix-ups would be expected to occur on stage.

Still, as this chapter will argue, Ovid deploys features of several of Terence's unconventional characters in his development of the elegiac *topos* and related subjects. As research has already established, the Terentian *adulescens* is the comic lover that comes closest to the elegiac type,[8] and especially the image of the disillusioned, jealous and shut-out Phaedria in the first act of the *Eunuchus*, after finding that his gifts have not had the hoped for effect and that he does not

5 Copley 1947, 290.
6 Fulkerson 2013, 182.
7 As I argued in Chapter Two, Ovid exploits the blurred status of the *puella* in his treatment of the Sabine rape. As Fulkerson also notes, many have suggested that the status of the beloved in elegy is deliberately blurred, maybe as a reaction to Augustus' attempt to clarify such issues, alternatively just to leave open narrative possibilities, or due to the genre's lack of such detailed information. See Fulkerson 2013, n. 2. See also Gibson 1998, and 2003, 25–37 on the status of the Ovidian *puella*.
8 E.g. Konstan 1986; Barsby 1999, 90–91, 100–101.

hold the primary position with his mistress. Phaedria thus finds particular resonance with the elegiac image of the metaphorical enslavement of the lover. I believe that Ovid too deploys this scene, in the *Ars amatoria* in particular, where being shut out by one's mistress is represented as something that inevitably will occur in an elegiac relationship, and thus should be handled in the right manner. Furthermore, it will be argued that Terentian lovers acting in a slave-like manner can be linked to the concept of *seruitium amoris* as it is represented by Ovid in the *Ars amatoria*, often in an act where a role is assumed so as to gain physical access to the *puella* or *domina*. In both Terence and Ovid, this builds on the notion that slaves would have direct access to their mistress, which is something that the elegiac lover would often lack.

In addition to the relationship between the slave-like comic *adulescens* and the Ovidian lover, actual slave characters will be of relevance in the present discussion; considering that Rome was a slave-owning society and that Roman comedy and love elegy are rooted in social practice, slave characters are understandably conspicuous within both genres.[9] Research has already established a link between the comic *seruus* and the elegiac lover, as it has been noted that the *adulescens amator* and the *seruus callidus* are combined in the figure found in the elegiac writers.[10] In this chapter, I will treat a passage from *Heroides* 20, Acontius' letter to Cydippe, that I believe demonstrates this principle particularly well, being at the same time connected to Ovid's network of Terentian allusion. This poem also contains one of the most noticed accounts of traditional *seruitium amoris* in Ovid. As I will argue, Acontius is represented in a manner that comes close to the description of a stock comic slave. Lastly, I will argue for a connection between the Terentian slave, Parmeno in the *Eunuchus* in particular, and Ovid's *praeceptor amoris*, as they assume roles as advisors in love, and that this connection also brings out important differences between Ovid's elegiac poetry and the comic genre.

---

9 On the presence of slavery in Roman literature, see Fitzgerald 2000. On slaves and Roman comedy, see Fitzgerald 2019. On slaves in Terence, see McCarthy 2004. On Roman republican theatre as 'slave theatre', see Richlin 2017 (on Plautus).
10 On the relationship between the *adulescens* and the *seruus* in Roman comedy, see Parker 1989, 242–243. On the role of the comic slave in Roman love elegy, see Fulkerson 2013, 190–193.

Terence's powerless lovers

Fulkerson, commenting on the connection between elegiac *seruitium* and the Roman Comic genre in general, mentions two instances of young men acting in a slavish manner (Plaut. *Curc.* 1–11 and *Poen.* 447–448); the young lover Phaedromus of the *Curculio* who in a servile fashion obeys Venus and Cupid, and the lover of the *Poenulus*, whom Amor induces to obey his own slave. Neither of them is pictured as a slave of the beloved. In addition, several instances of powerless behaviour are mentioned, including two from Terence.[11] The first Terentian example is found at lines 223–228 of the *Heautontimorumenos* and the young man Clitipho's monologue; he complains about his strict father, explains that he is excited by *amicae dicta* (*Haut.* 223, 'what my mistress says') — that is her commands to give and bring her gifts (described by Clitipho as her *'da mihi'* and *'adfer mihi'* at line 223) — as he describes her as *potens procax magnifica sumptuosa nobilis* (*Haut.* 227, 'strong-willed, demanding, arrogant, expensive, high and mighty creature.'). The mistress here is the greedy *meretrix* Bacchis, and as is Fulkerson's point, the focus is on the feeling of being powerless, as there is no way for Clitipho to give her what she demands.[12] However, the repetition of the mistress' imperatives might also indicate that the relationship is characterised by her giving him orders, i.e. that he behaves in a slavelike manner around her.

The second example of a powerless lover in Terence mentioned by Fulkerson is the much-discussed opening scene of the *Eunuchus*, treated also in the previous chapter, where the *adulescens* Phaedria finds himself in emotional turmoil, as he has been summoned to Thais' house after having been shut out the day before to make way for his rival, the soldier Thraso. He ponders back and forth, as he wants to stand up for himself and not put up with her harassment but is at the same time not sure whether he will be able to keep himself from going there later, at which point he might not be wanted at all. What Phaedria fears is, as Fulkerson points out, loss of control over his own emotions, and that he then will end up in a situation where he is in the control of his mistress. However, this scene (lines 46–80) includes notions that can be linked more directly to imagery involving slavery as well; Phaedria is afraid to be defeated and fears that Thais then will end up toying with him: *eludet ubi te uictum senserit.* (Ter. *Eun.* 55, 'she'll taunt you once she sees you beaten.'). The image strongly calls up lack of power and being under someone else's domi-

---

11 Fulkerson 2013, 190, n. 30.
12 Fulkerson 2013, 190, n. 30.

nance, and Donatus suggests in his commentary that the metaphor of is from gladiatorial combat.[13] The association with a gladiator losing a match involves in itself comparison with a type of slave (a gladiator), and Phaedria's slavish position is also highlighted by his own slave's suggestion that he should buy his own freedom back (*quid agas? nisi ut redimas captum quam queas / minimo*, Ter. *Eun.* 74–75, 'What to do? What else but ransom yourself from your captivity at the lowest possible price?').[14]

The opening scene of the *Eunuchus* displays similarities with the *paraclau-sithyron*. This motif, associated with both Greek and Roman love poetry,[15] has also been recognised in comedy, and the earliest example in Latin literature can be found in Plautus' *Curculio*.[16] In this Plautine play, Copley identifies specific Roman traits of the *paraclausithyron* such as the personification of the door, the theme of *furtiuus amor* and the girl's *custos*, and most significantly, that the girl is placed in an entirely new position, as she is not the one responsible for the denied access, in contrast to the Greek *paraclausithyra*, where it is the girls themselves who are to blame.[17] The Terentian scene does not include any of the listed features that Copley sees as specifically Roman, nor does it contain a song in front of the door.[18] It seems to be closer to the Greek tradition, as it is the girl herself that is responsible for the exclusion, and it is Thais herself who has denied Phaedria access to her house at the agreed time.[19] However, the exclusion

---

13 *Eludere proprie gladiatorum est cum uincerint*, quoted by Barsby 1999, *ad loc.* See also Fantham 1972, 31.

14 However, as Barsby 1999, *ad loc.* notes, the image seems to be that of buying back prisoners of war. Fulkerson also points out that the comic examples of the powerless behaviour of lovers primarily use metaphors of hunting and military defeat. I will treat this and other military metaphors in Chapter Five.

15 An important study on the development of the Greek and Roman *paraclausithyron* is Copley 1956. On *paraclausithyron* in the Roman elegists, see also Yardley 1978.

16 Duckworth 1994 [1952], 116.

17 Copley 1956, 28–42. Frangoulidis 2013 discusses how the opening scene of Plautus' Curcu-lio draws on *paraclausithyron* by altering all its key features.

18 Phaedria is, however, standing close to Thais' door when he delivers his opening speech, something which becomes evident when Thais exits her house, hears Phaedria and his slave's conversation and asks him why he is not coming inside (*quis hic loquitur? ehem tun hic eras, mi Phaedria? / quid hic stabas? quor non recta intro ibas?* Ter. *Eun.* 86–87, 'Who's that speaking? Oh hello! It's you, my dear Phaedria! Why are you waiting here? Why don't you come straight inside?'). The comic stage conventionally shows a street and the front of tree houses. Thais' house is next to Phaedria's, and in the opening scene he and Parmeno either exited his house or entered the stage from one of the sides.

19 As Copley notes, 'the *Eunuchus* shows, if anything, a regression from the type established by Plautus to the earlier Hellenistic pattern.' Copley 1956, 43.

of Phaedria is due to a richer rival, a figure that will emerge later in the Roman elegies and in the *paraclausithyron* as the *diues amator*.[20]

What is most conspicuous about the Terentian *paraclausithyron*, and which also points forward to the later tradition of the motif, is the deployment of what becomes the standard term for shutting out the lover, *excludere*, throughout the play;[21] *exclusit; reuocat: redeam?* (Ter. *Eun.* 49, 'She shut me out, she calls me back: shall I go?'). The incidence is referred to several times by the slave Parmeno shortly after, first as he imitates Phaedria, *'egon illam, quae illum, quae me, quae non ..!'* (Ter. *Eun.* 65, 'Am I to (forgive) her, who (preferred) him, who (excluded) me, who does not (repay my love) ...?'),[22] then *ceterum de exclusione uerbum nullum?* (Ter. *Eun.* 87–88, 'Not a word about shutting him out!'), and *credo, ut fit, misera prae amore exclusti hunc foras* (Ter. *Eun.* 98, 'I suppose you shut him out through love, poor woman. It does happen.'). Later in the play, Parmeno refers to Phaedria as one who would not have Thais shut out other lovers for his sake: *atque haec qui misit non sibi soli postulat / te uiuere et sua causa excludi ceteros* (Ter. *Eun.* 480–481, 'And moreover, the man who sent these presents doesn't demand that you live for him alone and shut out all others for his sake.'). The term is used with the same meaning in *Andria* (*ut ab illa excludar, hoc concludar*, Ter. *An.* 386, 'I'll be shut out from her and shut in here') and *Adelphoe* (*amat: dabitur a me argentum dum erit commodum; / ubi non erit fortasse excludetur foras*. Ter. *Ad.* 118–119, 'He's in love: I'll keep him in funds as long as it suits me; when it doesn't, maybe he'll be thrown out.'), but not with the same frequency as in the *Eunuchus*.[23]

The *paraclausithyron* famously occurs again in Lucretius, in his description of what became the definition of the *exclusus amator*, who later becomes a stock figure in Roman elegy, in book four:

---

20 Copley notes that rivalry between rich and poor lovers is a commonplace of erotic poetry, comedy (Aristophanes, Plautus and Terence are mentioned as examples) being the richest source for the tradition. However, he states, Horace in *Epode* 11 is the first to bring the rich rival into clear focus in a paraclausithyron, and that this element is now added (by Horace or a preceding source that he is imitating) 'to the circle of embellishments and refinements which have been growing up around the paraclausithyron', something which 'greatly increased its erotic, psychological, and dramatic interest'. Copley 1956, 52–54. I would like to argue that Terence and the *Eunuchus* also has played a part in this particularly Roman development.

21 See Barsby 1999, *ad* line 49. See also Hanses 2020, 286–293.

22 I borrow this suggested translation from Barsby 1999, *ad loc.*, with the meaning of the words omitted in Parmeno's line in brackets.

23 There is a second scene in the *Eunuchus* that can be related to the *paraclausithyron* motif, that is the soldier Thraso's attempt to besiege Thais' house. This is, however, closer to the concept of *militia amoris*, and will be treated in Chapter Five.

at lacrimans exclusus amator limina saepe
floribus et sertis operit postisque superbos
unguit amaracino et foribus miser oscula figit;

Lucr. 4.1177–1179

But the lover shut out, weeping, often covers the threshold with flowers and wreaths, anoints the proud doorposts with oil of marjoram, presses his love-sick kisses upon the door;

Copley concludes that Lucretius in his description must have found inspiration in contemporary now lost *paraclausithyra*, which again represented a development of the Roman version closer to the one found in Plautus' *Curculio* than Terence's more Greek inspired version.[24] However, the repetition of *excludere/exclusio* in the *Eunuchus* in particular strongly indicates that the play's opening scene should not be overlooked in the Roman development of the motif and the definition of the *exclusus amator*, and the final form of the Roman *paraclausithyron* as it was developed by Tibullus, Propertius and Ovid.

I will not go further in discussing the general development of the Roman *para-clausithyron* and the role of Terence in the present context,[25] but rather will point out what I believe is a connection between the situation in the opening scene in the *Eunuchus* and Ovid's particular treatment of the motif in the *Ars amatoria*. In the second book of the *Ars amatoria*, Ovid treats the issue of being locked out from one's mistress's house, in a passage that includes elements of *seruitium amoris* at 511–534, and thus links the *paraclausithyron* to the image. Here, the *praeceptor* advises the lover to be prepared to face the problems of love, one of them being the possibility of being shut out by one's mistress on the promised night:

dicta erit isse foras, quam tu fortasse uidebis:
    isse foras et te falsa uidere puta.
clausa tibi fuerit promissa ianua nocte:
    prefer et inmunda ponere corpus humo.
forsitan et uultu mendax ancilla superbo
    dicet 'quid nostras obsidet iste fores?'
postibus et durae supplex blandire puellae
    et capiti demptas in fore pone rosas.
cum uolet, accedes; cum te uitabit, abibis:
    dedecet ingenuos taedia ferre sui.
'effugere hunc non est' quare tibi possit amica

---

24 Copley 1956, 43–47 (on *paraclausithyron* in Lucretius).
25 For the development of the motif in Catullus and Horace, see Copley 1956, 47–69, for Roman elegy, see 70–140.

dicere? non omni tempore †sensus obest.†
nec maledicta puta nec uerbera ferre puellae
turpe nec ad teneros oscula ferre pedes.

Ov. *Ars am.* 2.521–534

She will be said to have gone out, though maybe you can see her inside: believe she has gone, and that your eyes deceive you. On the promised night her door will be shut against you: endure to lay your body even on unclean ground. Perhaps some lying, proud-faced maid will say, 'Why does this fellow besiege our door?' Supplicate and coax both door and cruel girl, take the roses from your head and hang them on the doorpost. When she is willing, go to her; when she shuns you, depart; the freeborn man should not bear to become a bore. Why should your mistress be able to say, 'I cannot escape from this fellow'? Discretion is not always a bad thing. Think it not shameful to endure a girl's abuse or blows, nor to give kisses to her tender feet.

As Copley points out, Ovid presents here the standard view on being shut out, i.e. that it is one of the situations that the lover should expect and should prepare for, except for the fact that he presents it as something that is almost to be welcomed, rather than something inevitable that must be endured.[26] In the end, being shut out is just another mechanism of the relationship, and should be met in good spirit; it is in this context that the *praeceptor* offers advice. At this point, I believe, Ovid invokes the image of Phaedria in the *Eunuchus*. It is worth noting that Phaedria is in a position of seeking advice (and the advice that he gets will be treated later in the present chapter), whereas Ovid's *praeceptor* is offering advice in an identical situation. Phaedria was shut out for the benefit of his rival on the day before, i.e. he met a *clausa ianua*; this is highlighted also by his advisor Parmeno at line 98, as they confront Thais about the incident (*exclusti ... foras*).

Phaedria's main issue in the opening is that he has been asked by his mistress to return, and is unsure whether he should. In the Ovidian text, the answer to lovers in this situation is given in line 529: go to her when she wants you to, depart when she shuns you. The point is that the lover should not be wearisome to his mistress and make her feel like she cannot evade him (lines 530–532). Interestingly, Ovid's advice here is in perfect line with the way Parmeno later describes Phaedria as a lover to Thais, when he delivers his gifts to her and tries to present his master in the best possible light in comparison to his soldier rival:

atque haec qui misit non sibi soli postulat
te uiuere et sua causa excludi ceteros,
neque pugnas narrat neque cicatrices suas
ostentat neque tibi obstat, quod quidam facit;

---

26 Copley 1956, 84–85.

uerum ubi molestum non erit, ubi tu uoles,
ubi tempu' tibi erit, sat habet si tum recipitur.

Ter. *Eun.* 480–485

And moreover, the man who sent these presents doesn't demand that you live for him alone and shut out all others for his sake. He doesn't narrate his battles or parade his scars, or get in your way, as a certain person does. He's content to be invited in when it's convenient, when it suits you, when you have the time.

Parmeno here describes Phaedria as unjealous, and happy to visit only when it would suit Thais. This might not be perfectly in line with the impression the audience would have of Phaedria based on the opening of the play, and how he there handled being shut out, but it is the image of the perfect lover according to the Ovidian standard: he is content to be accepted only when the mistress wishes it so (*ubi tu uoles* at line 484 cf. *cum uolet accedes* at 2.529 in Ovid), and when it is not a nuisance (*molestum* at 484 cf. *taedia* at 2.530 in Ovid).

According to the *Ars amatoria*, one should not be afraid to assume the role of the powerless lover, who acts on the whim of his mistress, and who does not mind taking on the role as her slave (as will be further discussed in the next section of this chapter), as these are all steps on the way to getting what one wants, i.e. to be with one's beloved. In the end, the lover is not really powerless, as he would do these things voluntarily and intentionally, following the advice of the *praeceptor*, to give a certain impression, much like the impression Parmeno tries to give of Phaedria. On the other hand, the Ovidian lover would then actually have to accept being shut out from time to time and not being in full control, as this is in the nature of the elegiac relationship. Phaedria, however, in the end of the play, gains full control: he manages to maintain his relationship with Thais, but now without having to pay her, as he accepts the soldier Thraso as a continuing rival as long as he pays for them both. Now, it is no longer Thais who decides when to accept which lover, but rather Phaedria himself, as the flatterer Gantho, the mind behind the unconventional deal, explains to him: *facile pellas ubi uelis* (Ter. *Eun.* 1080, 'You can easily throw him out when you want to.'). Thais, who is not the typical greedy courtesan and only wished to maintain the relationship with the soldier until she was able to secure the girl Pamphila from him, and who also professes that she really loves Phaedria, never consents to this arrangement.[27] It now seems like the social order has been re-established, which is in line with the convention of the genre, as Phaedria no longer appears to be in the uncontrolled, powerless state that he occupied at the

---

27 On the surprising conclusion to the *Eunuchus*, see Barsby 1999, 280–283.

beginning of the play. The initially powerless Clitipho at the end of the *Heauton-timorumenos* even more clearly moves on to lead a conventional Roman adult life, as he agrees to give up his *meretrix* mistress to marry a citizen girl.[28]

Seruitium amoris? Acting the slave

To Fulkerson's two instances of Terentian lovers acting in a powerless manner one may add two examples related to *seruitium amoris* mentioned by Murgatroyd. One is the soldier Thraso in the *Eunuchus*, who, in accordance with the mythological example of Hercules and Omphale, decides to act as a servant for the *meretrix* Thais (Ter. *Eun.* 1025–1028), this being the first occurrence of a mythological *exemplum* in connection with *seruitium amoris*.[29] The myth of Omphale and Hercules is also deployed in elegy at Prop. 3.11.17–20, Ov. *Her.* 9.73–118, and Ov. *Ars am.* 2.217–220. The other example is Phaedria in *Phormio*, who acts as an attendant slave, *paedagogus*, for an actual slave, a lyre-playing girl or *citharistria* with whom he is in love (Ter. *Phorm.* 144–145).

The idea of the lover performing servile duties for the beloved in a non-mythological context, as found for the first time in Terence's *Phormio*, is picked up again by Ovid in the second book of the *Ars amatoria* and is identified as an aspect of his deployment of the image *seruitium amoris*:[30]

> ipse tene distenta suis umbracula uirgis,
>   ipse fac in turba, qua uenit illa, locum.
> nec dubita tereti scamnum producere lecto,
>   et tenero soleam deme uel adde pedi.
> saepe etiam dominae, quamuis horrebis et ipse,
>   algenti manus est calfacienda sinu.
> nec tibi turpe puta (quamuis sit turpe, placebit)
>   ingenua speculum sustinuisse manu.
> ille, fatigata praebendo monstra nouerca
>   qui meruit caelum quod prior ipse tulit,
> inter Ioniadas calathum tenuisse puellas
>   creditur et lanas excoluisse rudes.
> paruit imperio dominae Tirynthius heros:
>   i nunc et dubita ferre, quod ille tulit.
> iussus adesse foro iussa maturius hora
>   fac semper uenias nec nisi serus abi.

28 Ter. *Haut.* 1045–1068.
29 Murgatroyd 1981, 594.
30 See Murgatroyd 1981, 594 and 599. Cf. also Tib. 1.5.61–66 and 1.9.42.

occurras aliquo tibi dixerit: omnia differ;
  curre, nec inceptum turba moretur iter.
nocte domum repetens epulis perfuncta redibit:
  tum quoque pro seruo, si uocat illa, ueni.
rure erit, et dicet 'uenias': Amor odit inertes:
  si rota defuerit, tu pede carpe uiam.
nec graue te tempus sitiensque Canicula tardet
  nec uia per iactas candida facta niues.

Ov. Ars am. 2.209–232

Do you yourself hold her parasol outstretched upon its rods, yourself make room for her in the crowd, where she is coming. Nor hesitate to place the footstool for her trim couch; take off her slipper from her dainty foot, or put it on. Often too when she is cold, though you are shivering too, you must warm your lady's hand in your own lap. Nor think it base (though base, it will give pleasure) to hold a mirror in your free born hand. He who won the heaven which first he bore himself, when his step-mother was wearied of sending monsters, is believed to have held a basket among Ionian girls, and to have spun fine the unworked wool. The Tirynthian hero obeyed a mistress' command: go, shrink from enduring what he endured! Bidden meet her at the Forum, go earlier than the hour of bidding, nor leave till it be late. She has told you to join her somewhere: put off everything, run! let not the crowd delay your passage. At night she will return to her house, the banquet finished: then too come in the slave's stead, if she calls. You are in the country, and she says 'Come!' Love hates the sluggish: if wheels fail, make the journey on foot. Let neither the fatal heat and the thirsty Dogstar delay you, nor a road made white by fallen snow.

As Fulkerson points out, one of the functions of *seruitium amoris* in the elegiac genre might be inspired by the fact that the slaves in elegy are in constant contact with the *puella*, as they attend upon her bodily wants and needs (as was a main task of domestic slaves in general), and that *seruitium amoris* thus expresses the poets' desire for access to the *puella* and the possibility of being close to her; even though the tasks they imagine performing might be degrading, they also require physical closeness.[31] This idea is well illustrated by the example from *Phormio*, and the section in Ovid expands on this idea, as Murgatroyd notes, and includes new tasks such as farm-labour and taking on the role as doorkeeper and guard,[32] which can all easily be compared with Phaedria performing the duties of the *paedagogus* to be near his beloved.

The point illustrated by these examples is that it is slaves, after all, who have direct access to the beloved object of the young lovers of both comedy and elegy, something which they themselves often initially lack. This is addressed again by Ovid shortly after, though from a slightly different angle. Here, the

---

31 See Fulkerson 2013, 189–190.
32 Murgatroyd 1981, 599.

point is that one should not think it unworthy to be on good terms with slaves, as this would be highly beneficial due to their proximity to the *puella* and the possibility of securing their help:

> *nec pudor ancillas, ut quaeque erit ordine prima,*
> *nec tibi sit seruos demeruisse pudor.*
> *nomine quemque suo (nulla est iactura) saluta,*
> *iunge tuis humiles ambitiose manus.*
> *sed tamen et seruo (leuis est impensa) roganti*
> *porrige Fortunae munera parua die;*
> *porrige et ancillae, qua poenas luce pependit*
> *lusa maritali Gallica ueste manus.*
> *fac plebem, mihi crede, tuam; sit semper in illa*
> *ianitor et thalami qui iacet ante fores.*
>
> Ov. *Ars am.* 2.251–260

Blush not to win over handmaids, as each stands first in rank, nor blush to win over slaves. Salute each one by name: you lose nothing thereby; clasp low-born hands, ambitious one, in yours. Ay, even to a slave, should he ask you (the cost is trivial), offer some small gift on the day of Fortune; offer it to a handmaid also, on the day that the Gallic band paid penalty, tricked by the marriage-robe. Believe me, make the humble folk your own; let the gatekeeper ever be one of them, and him who lies before her chamber-door.

The same idea is conspicuous throughout the *Amores*, where slaves are addressed by the *poeta amator* several times, often by name, to allow him access to his *puella*. In 1.6, he tries to persuade a *ianitor* to let him in to his beloved, in 1.11 he tries to persuade the hairdresser Nape to deliver a letter to Corinna, and in 2.2 and 3 he addresses the eunuch Bagoas, who is *custos* for his mistress; these would all be the type of *ancillae* and *serui* mentioned in the passage from book 2 of *Ars amatoria*.[33] The use of slave names and the frequent use of the terms *seruus* and *ancilla*, rarely used in Augustan poetry in general,[34] I would like to argue, marks the importance of slaves or the slave role for the lover in Ovid. The eunuch would stand in a special position as *custos*, meaning literally the one who takes care of (or guards or protects) the nuptial chamber in Greek, cf. Ov. *Ars am.* 2.260, the one who guards the *thalamus*.[35] For a lover to have this type of slave on one's side would be very beneficial.

---

33 Cf. also Cypassis in *Am.* 2.7 and 2.8, though the situation there is a different one.

34 Ovid's use of these words has been recognised as a sign of influence from the comic genre. See Janka 1997, 213 *ad Ars am.* 2.251–252 and McKeown 1989, 247 *ad Am.* 1.8.87–88.

35 The woman in 2.2/3 has a husband and, as McKeown notes, Ovid might be alluding to the *Lex Iulia de adulteriis coercendis* on *lenocinium* at *Am.* 2.2.47–62. McKeown 1989, 48 *ad loc.* To

I would like to suggest that the enviable proximity (from the point of view of the lover) of slaves in general and the eunuch in particular to their mistress or other household females, and simultaneously how acting the slave and perform slave duties might secure access to the beloved, is perhaps most clearly illustrated within the comic genre by the event that gives name to Terence's *Eunuchus*. That is, the younger brother Chaerea's scheme as he dresses himself in the eunuch Dorus' clothes to gain access to the girl Pamphila, following the advice of his slave Parmeno. Both Parmeno (though he shortly after claims that he was only joking) and the young Chaerea recognise the favourable role that the eunuch would possess, as he would have direct access to the girl as her fellow slave (cf. Ovid's Bagoas in *Am.* 2.2/3).

The eunuch is introduced first at line 167 of the Terentian play; Phaedria, in a heated argument, reminds Thais that it is not only his rival who provides her with expensive gifts, and that he is in possession of an Ethiopian slave girl and a eunuch servant that he has bought for her for 20 minas, a sum that makes for an expensive gift.[36] When Parmeno shortly after is about to deliver the slaves to Thais' house, he encounters Chaerea, who expresses his jealousy of the eunuch slave, in perfect accordance with the notion that Fulkerson describes: he is jealous that the eunuch slave will get to spend time with the girl Pamphila, who is kept in the house of Thais, on a daily basis:

> CH: *o fortunatum istum eunuchum quiquidem in hanc detur domum!*
> PA: *quid ita?* CH: *rogitas? summa forma semper conseruam domi*
> *uidebit conloquetur aderit una in unis aedibus,*
> *cibum non numquam capiet cum ea, interdum propter dormiet.*
>
> Ter. *Eun.* 365–368

> CH: Oh the lucky eunuch, to be taken into that house as a gift!
> PA: How do you mean?
> CH: You ask? He'll have this gorgeous fellow slave at home all the time to look at and talk to. He'll live together in the same house, he'll sometimes eat with her, and from time to time he'll sleep next to her.

The same notion becomes evident again later in the play, as Chaerea explains his scheme to his friend Antipho:

---

have a eunuch slave would indicate a high-status household; see McKeown 1989, 28. In Terence's *Eunuchus*, it is stated that Thais had wished for a eunuch, as only wealthy women (*reginae*) have such slaves. See Barsby 1999, *ad* line 168. This also adds to the controversy concerning the status of the *puella* in the *Ars amatoria*.
36 See Barsby 1999, *ad* line 169.

> CH: *primam dices, scio, si uideris.*
> *quid multa uerba? amare coepi. forte fortuna domi*
> *erat quidam eunuchu' quem mercatu' fuerat frater Thaidi,*
> *neque is deductus etiamdum ad eam. submonuit me Parmeno*
> *ibi seruo' quod ego arripui.* AN: *quid id est?* CH: *tacitu' citius audies:*
> *ut uestem cum illo mutem et pro illo iubeam me illoc ducier.*
> AN: *pro eunuchon?* CH: *sic est.* AN: *quid ex ea re tandem ut caperes commodi?*
> CH: *rogas? uiderem audirem essem una quacum cupiebam, Antipho.*
>
> Ter. *Eun.* 567–574

CH: You'll give her top marks, if you see her, I'm sure. To put it briefly, I fell in love. By a lucky chance there was a eunuch at home whom my brother had bought for Thais, and he hadn't yet been delivered to her house. At this point our slave Parmeno dropped me a suggestion which I snatched up.
AN: What was that?
CH: You'll hear all the quicker if you keep quiet. To exchange clothes with him and have myself taken there in his place.
AN: In place of the eunuch?
CH: That's right.
AN: And what would you achieve by that, if I may ask?
CH: What a question! I would look at, listen to, and live together with the girl I wanted, Antipho.

We also learn how he was set to perform typical slave duties after having been put in charge of caring for the girl, for example using a fan to make a breeze for her after a bath.

> CH: ...
> *dum haec mecum reputo, accersitur lauatum interea uirgo:*
> *iit lauit rediit; deinde eam in lecto illae conlocarunt.*
> *sto exspectans siquid mi imperent. uenit una. 'heus tu' inquit 'Dore,*
> *cape hoc flabellum, uentulum huic sic facito, dum lauamur;*
> *ubi nos lauerimu', si uoles, lauato.' accipio tristis.*
> AN: *tum equidem istuc os tuom inpudens uidere nimium uellem,*
> *qui esset status, flabell[ul]um tenere te asinum tantum.*
> CH: *uix elocutast hoc, foras simul omnes proruont se,*
> *abeunt lauatum, perstrepunt, ita ut fit domini ubi absunt.*
> *interea somnu' uirginem opprimit. ego limis specto*
> *sic per flabellum clanculum; simul alia circumspecto,*
> *satin explorata sint. uideo ese, pessulum ostio obdo.*
> AN: *quid tum?* CH: *quid 'quid tum,' fatue?* AN: *fateor.* CH: *an ego occasionem*
> *mi ostentam, tantam, tam breuem, tam optatam, tam insperatam*
> *amitterem? tum pol ego is essem uero qui simulabar.*
>
> Ter. *Eun.* 592–606

CH: (...) While I was thinking over all this, the virgin was summoned to take her bath. She went, bathed, returned. Then the maids laid her down on the bed. I stood waiting to see if they had any orders for me. One of them came up and said, 'Hey you, Dorus, take this fan and make a nice little breeze for her, like this, while we take a bath. When we've done so, if you like, you can take one.' I accepted the fan with a scowl.

AN: How I wish I had seen your impudent expression, and your posturing, and you holding your little fan, you great ass.

CH: She had scarcely uttered these words and they all rushed out of the room to take their baths, chattering away, as happens when the master is absent. Meanwhile the virgin fell asleep. I looked at her sideways through the fan, like this (posturing), and at the same time had a good look round to make sure that the coast was clear. I saw it was, and bolted the door.

AN What then?

CH: How do you mean 'What then,' you idiot?

AN: Sorry.

CH: Was I going to let slip the opportunity when it was offered to me, so great, so fleeting, so desired, so unexpected? If I had, I would actually have been what I pretended to be, for heaven's sake.

Even though this must surely have been seen as a degrading task, which also becomes evident from Antipho's reply as he makes fun of him for holding a little fan, it lets him get close to the girl of his dreams, and he ends up raping and eventually marrying her. The plot can be said to mirror Ovid's advice to take on the role of a slave and perform tasks that requires proximity to the *puella*, as e.g. removing her slippers or holding up a mirror for her.

At the end of his narrative, Chaerea makes the joke that if he had not taken this opportunity to rape the girl, he would actually have been what he pretended to be, that is, as Barsby notes, a eunuch,[37] and thus not capable of raping the girl. However, I would like to suggest that the joke might also be interpreted as playing on the idea that he, as a freeborn man, has taken on and acted out the role of a slave, a notion that would be closely linked with the elegiac *seruitium* and the particular Ovidian *praeceptor*'s notion that one might have to temporarily degrade oneself by assuming the role of a slave to get what one wants. This is highlighted by the fact that Chaerea is desperate not to be seen in his eunuch outfit by fellow citizens, and we learn how he, as he had no place to change out of his costume without being discovered after it had served its purpose, had to run from alley to alley to avoid being recognised (Ter. *Eun.* 840–849). He also faces the risk of being punished by Thais, now that he is dressed as a *fugitiuus*, a run-away slave, who has committed a terrible crime. This is made a point as Chaerea, still dressed as Dorus, encounters Thais and her servant Pythias:

---

37 Barsby 1999, *ad loc.*

CH: (...)
sed estne haec Thai' quam uideo? ipsast. haereo
quid faciam. quid mea autem? quid faciet mihi?
TH: *adeamu'. bone uir Dore, salue: dic mihi,*
aufugistin? CH: *era, factum.* TH: *satin id tibi placet?*
CH: *non.* TH: *credin te inpune habiturum?* CH: *unam hanc noxiam*
amitte: si aliam admisero umquam, occidito.
TH: *num meam saeuitiam ueritus es?* CH: *non.* TH: *quid igitur?*
CH: *hanc metui ne me criminaretur tibi.*
TH: *quid feceras?* CH: *paullum quiddam.* PY: *eho, 'paullum', inpudens?*
an paullum hoc esse tibi uidetur, uirginem
uitiare ciuem? CH: *conseruam esse credidi.*
PY: *conseruam! uix me contineo quin inuolem in*
capillum, monstrum: etiam ultro derisum aduenit.
TH: *abin hinc, insana?* PY: *quid ita? uero debeam,*
credo, isti quicquam furcifero si id fecerim;
praesertim quom se seruom fateatur tuom.

Ter. Eun. 848–863

CH: (...) But is that Thais I see? It is. I'm stuck what to do. What's it matter, though? What can she do to me?
TH: (to Pythias) Let's go up to him. (to Chaerea) Good day, Dorus, my good man. Tell me, did you run away?
CH: Yes, madam, I did.
TH: Are you happy with your conduct?
CH: No.
TH: Do you suppose you'll get away with this?
CH: (wheedling) Forgive this one offence. If I ever commit another, you can put me to death.
TH: Were you afraid that I would be a cruel mistress?
CH: No.
TH: What, then?
CH: I was afraid that she (indicating Pythias) would tell tales on me.
TH: What had you done?
CH: Nothing very much.
PY: Hey, nothing very much, you shameless creature? Does it seem to you nothing very much to rape a citizen virgin?
CH: I thought she was a fellow slave.
PY: A fellow slave! I can scarcely restrain myself from flying at your hair, you monster! (to Thais) On top of it all he comes here to mock us.
TH: (to Pythias) Come off it! You're crazy!
PY: What do you mean? I'm scarcely going to be held liable if I do anything to this rascal, especially as he's claiming to be your slave.

This reading, i.e. that Chaerea has degraded himself as a citizen by taking on the role as slave (note also that he calls Thais *era*, and uses the term *conseruam*), is supported by what I argue is an allusion to *Eun.* line 606 (*tum pol ego is essem uero qui simulabar*) in Horace's satire 2.7, where the slave Davus, based on the Stoic paradox that 'all fools are slaves', aims to prove that his master, Horace, is really a fellow slave:[38]

> tu cum proiectis insignibus, anulo equestri
> Romanoque habitu, prodis ex iudice Dama
> Turpis, odoratum caput obscurante lacerna,
> **non es quod simulas**? metuens induceris atque
> altercante libidinibus tremis ossa pauore.
> quid refert, uri uirgis ferroque necari
> auctoratus eas, an turpi clausus in arca,
> quo te demisit peccati conscia erilis,
> contractum genibus tangas caput? (...)
>
> Hor. Sat. 2.7.53–61

You, when you have cast aside your badges, the ring of knighthood and your Roman dress, and step forth, no longer a judge, but a low Dama, with a cape hiding your perfumed head, are you not what you pretend to be? Full of fear, you are let into the house, and you tremble with a terror that clashes with your passions. What matters it, whether you go off in bondage, to be scourged and slain with the sword, or whether, shut up in a shameful chest, where the maid, conscious of her mistress's sin, has stowed you away, you touch your crouching head with your knees?

Davus' point here is, in the words of Muecke, 'that the condition of slavery that Horace assumes as a disguise is shown to be a spiritual slavery to the passions of fear and lust'.[39] In the section quoted above, the slave Davus casts Horace in a stock scene from adultery mime,[40] where he is dressed as a slave and smuggled into his mistress' house. This stock scene from mime bears a striking resemblance to the scheme that gives name to the *Eunuchus,* and, I argue, Horace simultaneously invokes this particular scene and the lengths to which the young citizen Chaerea is willing to go to gain access to a girl, i.e. dressing up as a eunuch and being ordered around by a *meretrix* and her servants to perform the typical duties of a eunuch slave.[41] The degrading aspect is also highlighted by the fact that

---

38 On the argumentation in *Sat.* 2.7, see Muecke 1993, 212–214. See also Fitzgerald 2000, 18–27. As Muecke points out, *Sat.* 2.7 is very similar to *Sat.* 2.3 in structure and idea, though 2.3 on a much larger scale. *Sat.* 2.3 contains multiple verbal echoes of the opening scene of Terence's *Eunuchus.* See Muecke 1993, 131 and 161, and Hanses 2020, 234–237.

39 Muecke 1993, *ad* 2.7.56.

40 Muecke 1993, *ad* 2.7.59.

41 Satire 2.7 is in general inspired by new comedy, see Muecke 1993, 212–213, Fitzgerald 2000, 18–27. Germany argues that the rape scene in the *Eunuchus* invokes a scene from mime; see Germany 2016, 120–156.

Chaerea, without realising it, is apparently being made fun of by the actual slave Parmeno, with comments such as e.g. *praeterea forma et aetas ipsast facile ut pro eunucho probes* (Ter. *Eun.* 375, 'besides, you're so young and good-looking, you could easily pass as a eunuch'), implying that the citizen man could easily be mistaken for a eunuch slave due to his young age and perhaps 'unmanly' looks.

Chaerea is knowingly and deliberately acting in the role as slave; he lets himself be delivered to Thais as one by his own actual slave, performs slave duties in her home while being ordered around by her other slaves, all to gain access to the girl of his dreams, a scheme in which he ultimately succeeds. The scene also has similarities with a stock theme from mime, making a joke out of this exact scenario, that is a male citizen acting the slave so to gain access to his mistress, a similarity that Horace picks up on by alluding to it in his satire 2.7. For Chaerea, the scheme is an act, and it works as a 'play within the play'. The point is the same for Ovid's version of the *seruitium amoris* as it is presented in the *Ars amatoria*: the lover is not turned into a helpless slave to his mistress due to his love for her, but is rather, just like Chaerea, advised to take on the role of slave to secure access for himself (*fac modo, quas partes illa iubebit, agas.* Ov. *Ars am.* 2.198, 'only play the part she bids you play'. Cf. also *curre* at *Ars am.* 2.206, which might be a nod to the comic *seruus currens*). It is all an act to gain something, i.e. access, and this is the very point; Chaerea is pretending (cf. *simulabar* at 606), he is led to Thais' house *pro eunucho* (cf. Parmeno's line at 375), that is 'in place of a eunuch', just as the lover, according to the praeceptor of the second book of the *Ars amatoria*, should answer his mistress' call *pro seruo* (cf. line 228), 'in place of the slave'.[42] This is also the point that Horace had made fun of in his satire; is not the man who is willing to degrade himself by acting the role of the slave really a slave after all? For Chaerea, this state where he is degraded is only temporary, and the order of the world is re-established as he rapes the girl, who then turns out to be a citizen and a proper marriage between them is arranged. How the poet-lover and the young readers of the *Ars amatoria* are to regain their proper societal positions after this act remains an open question.

---

42 The focus on acting in both Ovid and Terence, I would argue, highlights the fact that the *seruitium* is pretended and temporarily. This differs somewhat from the notion of the *pauper* in Tib. 1.5.61–66.

Ovidian *seruitium*: the cunning lover

Research on Latin love elegy has already pointed to a connection between the comic slave and the elegiac lover.[43] Suggesting that the comic slave, in addition to the *adulescens*, makes his way into elegy, Fulkerson argues that the dividing of the lover into an *adulescens* and a scheming slave acting on behalf of the *adulescens* effected in the comic genre is undone in the elegiac lover,[44] who is simultaneously haplessly in love and plotting to get what he wants.[45] In the following, I will give an example from the *Heroides*, Acontius' letter to Cydippe, that I believe demonstrates this point particularly well. *Heroides* 20 contains one of the chief examples of *seruitium amoris* in Ovid, and, as I would like to argue, is connected to Ovid's Terentian allusions treated throughout the previous chapters.

As Fulkerson points out, certain traits of the comic slave can be detected in some of the lovers in the elegiac genre, and in the words of Conte, 'Ovid, in the *Amores*, tries to be both wise slave and young master in love at the same time'.[46] The following passage, I believe, from Ovid's *Heroides* 20, Acontius' letter to Cydippe, demonstrates this principle particularly well. Here, Acontius admits that he might have used tricks to get Cydippe to promise to marry him, but that his reason for this was love:

> deceptam dicas nostra te **fraude** licebit,
>   dum **fraudis** nostrae causa feratur amor.
> fraus mea quid petiit, nisi uti tibi iungerer uni?
>   id te, quod quereris, conciliare potest.
> non ego natura nec sum tam **callidus** usu:
>   sollertem tu me, crede, puella, facis.
> te mihi compositis (si quid tamen egimus) a se
>   astrinxit uerbis ingeniosus Amor.
> dictatis ab eo feci sponsalia uerbis
>   consultoque fui iuris Amore **uafer**.
> sit fraus huic facto nomen dicarque **dolosus**,
>   si tamen est quod ames uelle tenere **dolus**.
>
> Ov. *Her.* 20.21–32

I will give you leave to say you were deceived, and by wiles of mine, if only of those wiles my love be counted cause. What was the object of my wiles but the one thing — to be unit-

---

43 See Fulkerson 2013, 190–192.
44 Parker 1989, 242–243 argues for such a splitting.
45 Fulkerson 2013, 191–192.
46 Conte 1989, 453.

ed with you? The thing you complain of has power to join you to me. Neither by nature nor by practice am I so cunning; believe me, girl, it is you who make me skilful. It was ingenious Love who bound you to me, with words — if I, indeed, have gained aught — that I myself drew up. In words dictated by him I made our betrothal bond; Love was the lawyer that taught me knavery. Let wiles be the name you give my deed, and let me be called crafty — if only the wish to possess what one loves be craft!

As demonstrated in the previous chapter, the Acontius-Cydippe story has several traits in common with a stock New Comic plot in general, that is a young man spotting a young woman during a festival,[47] whereupon he decides that he must have her; the aim of the story is marriage, which is also what Acontius desires, and a series of complications, e.g. the presence of a rival, intervene before the union can be secured. In such marriage plots, the young *uirgines* of the comic genre have no say in the matter; neither has Cydippe, who in her reply letter to Acontius describes herself as a *uirgo* who has been deceived (*elusa uirgine* at Ov. *Her.* 21.116).

Preparing tricks so that the *adulescens amator* can win the beloved is the role of the comic slave, who acts on behalf of his young master. Acontius, on the other hand, plays the role of both lover and trickster combined; he is simultaneously the one who burns with love (*meus ... ardor* at 20.17 and 42)[48] and the one who cheats and is *callidus* and *dolosus*, standard epithets for trickster slaves in the comic plays, also associated with the use of *fraus*.[49] Of particular interest here is that these are combined with *uafer*, or cunning, in line 30, which is also used by Ovid to describe the actual stock comic slave in *Ars amatoria* 3.332: *cuiue pater uafri luditur arte Getae* ('or he whose father is deceived by the crafty Geta's cunning').[50]

---

47 For the story of Acontius and Cydippe, see Callim. *Aet.* Book 3, fr. 67–75 (Pfeiffer), Ov. *Her.* 20/21, Aristaenetus 1.10 (Bing and Höschele).

48 = *ego ardens*, see Kenney 1996 *ad* 20.17. Terence provides the earliest examples of the direct metaphor *ardeo* in the meaning of burning of love, see e.g. Barsby 1999. *ad Eun.* 72.

49 E.g. *serua erum, caue tu idem faxis alii quod serui solent, / qui ad eri fraudationem callidum ingenium gerunt* (Plaut. *Asin.* 256–257, 'Save your master, don't do the same as other slaves do, who have cunning ways only in order to cheat master') and (the maid Pythias to the slave Parmeno) *at etiam primo callidum et disertum credidi hominem* (Ter. *Eun.* 1011, 'Yet once I even believed you a clever capable sort of a fellow.'). See also Barsby 1999, *ad loc.*, on how Terence here plays with the stock character.

50 As Gibson 2003 *ad loc.* points out, it is not entirely clear which author Ovid is referring to here. The context is a list of writers, so far Greek, but the *seruus fallax* is a feature more conspicuous in a Roman context than in Greek new comedy. I discuss the possibility of a Terentian presence in this line in Chapter One, note 1. Fantham 1984, 303 n. 14 argues that Ovid might have inserted the name to give specificity to a general allusion. Geta is a slave's name in sever-

At the end of the quoted passage we can see the recurrent combination of *quod* and *amo* with *quod ames* in line 32; it takes the reader back to the opening of the first book of the *Ars amatoria* and Romulus' scheme to abduct the Sabine women. As discussed in Chapter Two, this scene contains rich allusions to the *Eunuchus*, and Chaerea's trick to sneak into the house of Thais to get to the girl Pamphila, following the divine *exemplum* of Jupiter. As has been argued by James, there are several allusions to the play throughout the book, and that *fallite fallentes*, deceive the deceivers, at line 645 echoes *Eunuchus* 385, *nunc referam gratiam atque eas itidem fallam, ut ab is fallimur?* (Ter. *Eun.* 385, 'Now I will return the favour and cheat them in the same way that they cheat us?'), spoken by the young man Chaerea as he justifies his plan. As James then points out, 'the collocation marks a nexus of linguistic and thematic significance to both texts and raises an unexpected question: when does "deceive" (*ludere, fallere*) mean merely "to fool", and when does it mean "to commit rape?".'[51] Drawn into this nexus is also the Acontius and Cydippe story, which is also mentioned in the first book of the *Ars amatoria*; *littera Cydippen pomo perlata fefellit, / insciaque est uerbis capta puella suis* (Ov. *Ars am.* 1.457–458, 'A letter carried in an apple betrayed Cydippe, and the girl was deceived unawares by her own words.'), and in her reply to Acontius at *Her.* 21.116, where she refers to herself with the words *elusa uirgine* in reference to the same incident; in both cases the point is that she has been deceived into promising to marry Acontius, which, as was demonstrated in Chapter Two, is strongly associated with rape in both Terence and Ovid.[52] Cydippe is disturbingly close to being raped after she has been 'played'/'deceived' by Acontius' letter.

Acontius' letter is one of the Ovidian cases of what has been identified as *seruitium amoris*, due to his willingness 'to undergo servile punishment for tricking Cydippe',[53] whom he asks to act as his *domina*:

---

al comedies of Menander (e.g. *Heros* and *Perinthia*) and in two of the six plays of Terence (*Phormio* and *Adelphoe*).

51 James 2016a, 86.

52 As I argue in Chapter Five, Ovid alludes to Ter. *Eun.* 942 (*ego pol te pro istis dictis et factis, scelus, / ulciscar, ut ne **inpune** in nos **inluseris.** Ter. *Eun.* 941–942, 'I'll punish you, by heaven, you villain, for those words and deeds of yours; you won't get away with making fools of us.') in the first book of the *Ars amatoria* at line 643: (*ludite, si sapitis, **solas impune puellas*** Ov. *Ars am.* 1.643, 'If you are wise, cheat women only, and avoid trouble'). The Terentian line is spoken by the maid Pythias, and the *scelus* who she claims has deceived the household by facilitating the young man Chaerea's rape of the *uirgo* Pamphila is the slave Parmeno.

53 Murgatroyd 1981, 603. See also Kenney 1996, 194 *ad* lines 75–90.

> *ante tuos liceat flentem consistere uultus*
>   *et liceat lacrimis addere uerba suis,*
> *utque solent famuli, cum uerbera saeua uerentur,*
>   *tendere submissas ad tua crura manus.*
> *ignoras tua iura: uoca; cur arguor absens?*
>   *iamdudum dominae more uenire iube.*
> *ipsa meos scindas licet imperiosa capillos,*
>   *oraque sint digitis liuida facta tuis.*
> *omnia perpetiar; tantum fortasse timebo*
>   *corpore laedatur ne manus ista meo.*
>
> Ov. Her. 20.75–84

Let me have leave to stand weeping before your face, and have leave to add words which suit the tears; and let me, like a slave in fear of bitter stripes, stretch out submissive hands to touch your feet! You know not your own right; call me! Why am I accused in absence? Bid me come, immediately, after the manner of a mistress. With your own imperious hand you may tear my hair, and make my face livid with your fingers. I will endure all; my only fear perhaps will be lest that hand of yours be bruised on me.

I suggest that the combination of *callidus* and *uafer* to describe Acontius earlier in the poem adds to the image of Acontius as slavelike, and that Ovid also links this image to the comic slave character, who also constantly faces the threat of punishment for the tricks that he comes up with on behalf of the young lover of the play.[54] The use of *callidus* to describe a lover does not occur in Tibullus and Propertius, whereas Ovid uses the term on several occasion, e.g. of Jupiter, described as a *callidus ... adulter* at *Am.* 1.10.4,[55] and at *Ars am.* 2.262, where the lover is advised to be *callidus* when choosing gifts for his mistress: *nec dominam iubeo pretioso munere dones; / parua, sed e paruis callidus apta dato* (Ov. *Ars am.* 2.261–262, 'Nor do I bid you give your mistress costly gifts: let them be small, but choose your small gifts cunningly and well.'). In the latter case, the use of *domina* for the *puella* links the passage to *seruitium amoris*, whereas the term *callidus* simultaneously links the lover as slave to the trickster slave of comedy.

---

54 Parker 1989 investigates jokes and threats about torturing slaves in Plautus. An example from Terence is Parmeno in the *Eunuchus*, who fears that he will be punished by the father of the young men of the play: *dicam hercle, etsi mihi magnum malum scio paratum* (Ter. *Eun.* 968, 'Shall I tell him or not tell him? I'll tell him, by god, even though I know it'll mean a thrashing for me.'). However, the slaves in literature usually escape actual punishment; see also Duckworth 1994 [1952], 288–289.

55 Jupiter as chief trickster and adulterer in Ovid and Terence was treated in Chapter One.

However, though linked to the image of *seruitium*, the *callidus* aspect of the lover seems to have little to do with passionate elegiac love. Jupiter the trickster and 'rapist in disguise' has not much to do with the elegiac lover, and Acontius's feelings towards Cydippe are in fact the opposite of the conventional description of elegiac love; he is not motivated by the hope of a mutual love relationship, but rather wishes to possess Cydippe in marriage, regardless of her feelings about the matter. This is much closer to the comic rape-marriage plot than the elegiac, non-marital love affair. Cydippe is in the end forced to marry Acontius, not because she learns to love him, but to save her own life. It seems to me that what is proved, if anything, by the story of Acontius and Cydippe, is that whereas you can trick someone into marrying you, you cannot trick someone into loving you. That Acontius presents himself as a slave to Cydippe is nothing more than a mock *seruitium*, and it becomes evident shortly after that he really sees himself as her *dominus*: *elige de uacuis quam non sibi uindicet alter: / si nescis, dominum res habet ista suum* (Ov. Her. 20.149–150, 'Choose from those who are free one whom another does not claim; if you do not know, those goods have a master of their own.').[56] It might seem strange then, that the *praeceptor* would advise the lover to be *callidus* when choosing gifts, but it might be interpreted as a nod to the comic, ever-calculating slave character, and the slavelike role the lover will often assume to get to the girl of his dreams.

The *praeceptor amoris* and the Terentian slave

In this last section of this chapter, I would like to point to a connection in elegy to the comic slave type in elegiac didactic, which is most developed in Ovid in his *Ars amatoria* and *Remedia amoris*, and that in some sections, aspects of the Terentian slave are included in the construction of the Ovidian *praeceptor*. There are several general traits that can be seen as shared by the *praeceptor* and the typical comic slave, as both function as advisors and instructors for young men in matters concerning love and relationships. Furthermore, the comic slave is also generally the role that can most closely be associated with the playwright himself.[57] As was mentioned in Chapter Three, Davus in the *Andria* is described as a *magister inprobus* by the *senex* Simo, who is afraid that the slave might lead his son Pamphilus down the wrong path in matters of love; this notion of the

---

56 Thorsen 2019 and 2021 explore these and other aspects of the Acontius-Cydippe letters. See the latter for the point that Acontius sees himself as Cydippe's *dominus*.
57 See Sharrock 2009, 131–140 (on Plautus), and 140–156 (on Terence).

slave as a *magister* of love can easily be compared to *Naso magister* of the *Ars amatoria*.[58] Previous research has already recognised the similarity of the role of the *praeceptor* and the Terentian slave, and as was briefly mentioned in Chapter Two, the slave Parmeno in the *Eunuchus* is portrayed in a similar role to the one held by the Ovidian *praeceptor amoris*, cf. the young man Chaereas' outburst, *o Parmeno mi, o mearum uoluptatum omnium / inuentor inceptor perfector, scis me in quibu's sim gaudiis?* Ter. *Eun.* 1034–1035, 'Parmeno, my dear fellow, the deviser, the initiator, the perfector of all my delights, do you know how happy I am?'). James, arguing for a strong connection between the first book of the *Ars amatoria* and the *Eunuchus*, notes that 'Parmeno sets himself up as an advisor — a *praeceptor* — to the enamored *adulescens* Phaedria, and does so again shortly after, with Phaedria's younger brother Chaerea',[59] i.e. he sets himself up as Phaedria's advisor in the opening scene of the play, and does the same for the younger brother in the events that lead to the rape of the young *uirgo*. More recently, Hanses has suggested that both the slave Parmeno and the parasite Gnatho from the same play should be seen as among "Latin literature's original *praeceptores amoris*".[60]

I agree that Parmeno sets himself up as a *praeceptor*, and it is my opinion that this aspect of the comic slave is most thoroughly developed in this Terentian play. As shown in Chapter Three, Parmeno arguably holds a special position as the most developed advisor character in the Terentian corpus, as he takes on the role as the voice of reason with superior knowledge about love and women in the opening of the play,[61] and later as he brags about how he has taught the young man Chaerea to unlearn his love for *meretrices* in lines 923–940. James sees Parmeno as a cynical slave, hostile to both the subjects of love and *meretrices*.[62] Indeed, resentment towards prostitutes is a strong trait of the character, as becomes evident in both his attitude towards Thais in the opening,

---

58 Ter. *An.* 192 cf. Ov. *Ars am.* 2.744 and 3.812.

59 James 2016a, 87–88.

60 Hanses 2020, 335. For the full argument, see Hanses 2020, 333–353.

61 This is what Horace alludes to in *Satire* 2.3.

62 Resentment towards *meretrices* is, James argues, found in all the male characters in the play, and is mirrored in the Ovidian *praeceptor*'s attitude towards women of this class; in this way, Ovid sheds light on problematic male attitudes towards *meretrices*. See James 2016a. I treated Terentian allusions in the first book of the *Ars amatoria* in Chapter Two, where I point to the allusions as bringing out problematic and violent aspects of Rome's legendary history and the Roman marriage institution, and in the prolonging of this the Augustan moral laws, which stand in opposition to the elegiac notion of love.

where he (wrongly) sees her as the stock greedy *meretrix*,[63] and in his monologue across lines 923–940. Still, I believe that it is other aspects that Ovid invokes when he alludes to this character in the second book of the *Ars amatoria*,
namely the role Parmeno takes as an almost Stoic wise man in the opening scene. I will argue in the following, there is an allusion present that links Ovid's
praeceptor to this aspect of Parmeno when he advises young men to love wisely
(*sapienter amabit*, Ov. *Ars am.* 2.501 and 2.511). As will be demonstrated in the
following, this allusion forms part of what appears to be a contradiction in the
Ovidian text.[64]

One thing that is important to notice is that in Ovid's eroto-didactic works,
the comic 'splitting' of the lover into the *adulescens amator* and the slave work-
ing on his behalf, characters that are united in the elegiac lover, can be seen as
paralleled by the relationship between the young elegiac lovers and their advisor, the *praeceptor* or *magister*; the inexperienced lover and the advisor are in
the elegiac didactic works of Ovid not the same character, but are split into the
praeceptor and his target audience. The *praeceptor* or *magister amoris* is not just
(or even primarily in the contexts of an elegiac-didactic poem) a lover himself,
but is also a detached voice, teaching the lover to love in a wise manner. I believe that the opening scene of the *Eunuchus* demonstrates this connection between the slave and the *praeceptor* particularly well. Here, Phaedria turns to his
slave Parmeno for advice as he considers how to avoid being defeated by his
mistress by turning up at her door again after initially having refused to go back
there because of his earlier exclusion. Parmeno replies by stating that love lacks
logic, and hence cannot be controlled by logic, and goes on to list all of love's
flaws:

> ere: quae res in se neque consilium neque modum
> habet ullum, eam consilio regere non potes.

---

63 See Barsby 199, 100–101.

64 The allusions to the role of the Terentian slave might be seen as puzzling at first, as the
slave as the one who drives the action forward and solves the plot is a prominent figure strongly associated with the plays of Plautus, whereas this character is not as developed in Terence
(and Menander). See Barsby 1990, 4–5. On the Terentian slave as opposed to the Plautine, see
also Amerasinghe 1950. Ovid's preference for the Terentian slave might be compared to the
surprising choice of referring to Terence's *conuiuae* characters to invoke the comic hanger-on
in *Tristia* 2.359, *Accius esset atrox, conuiua Terentius esset* (Ov. *Tr.* 2.359, 'Else would Accius be
cruel, Terence a reveller'), treated in Chapter One, in spite of the fact that it is Plautus first and
foremost who is known for his use of this type; in fact, it has been argued that Terentian *conuiua* is also present in the *Ars amatoria*, in the same manner as the slave, as an aspect of the
praeceptor. See Janka 1997, 176–177, *ad* lines 197–202, and Labate 1984, 204–207.

in amore haec omnia insunt uitia: iniuriae,
suspicions, inimicitiae, indutiae,
bellum, pax rursum.

Ter. Eun. 57–61

Master, when a thing has no logic to it and no means of control, you can't rule it by logic. A love affair has all these symptoms: wrongs, suspicions, quarrels, truces, war, peace again.

Amerasinghe characterises the situation as a 'strange phenomenon' within the New Comic context, as the slave here is actually 'lukewarm to his master's cause',[65] i.e. he is seemingly not willing to help him to secure the relationship, as he is apparently against it, and as Barsby notes, Parmeno here and in the lines that follow 'adopts a superior pedagogic role in which he assumes a greater knowledge of the ways of the world and of the nature of love than his younger master'.[66] The scene was interpreted in this way already by Horace, who adapts the opening scene in *Sat.* 2.3 to illustrate a Stoic point, that those who are not wise are mad, presenting the slave as wiser than his master. The context of the adaptation of the scene is that Damasippus quotes to Horace from the Stoic philosopher Stertinius, who parallels the foolishness of the lover with childishness, basing the argument on the conversation between Phaedria and Parmeno at *Eun.* 46–63:[67]

porrigis irato puero cum poma, recusat:
'sume, catelle!' negat: si non des, optet: amator
exclusus qui distat, agit ubi secum, eat an non,
quo rediturus erat non arcessitus, et haeret
inuisis foribus? 'nec nunc, cum me uocet ultro,
accedam? an potius mediter finire dolores?
exclusit; reuocat: redeam? non si obsecret.' ecce
seruus non paulo sapientior: 'o ere, quae res
nec modum habet neque consilium, ratione modoque
tractari non uult. in amore haec sunt mala, bellum,
pax rursum: haec si quis tempestatis prope ritu
mobilia et caeca fluitantia sorte laboret
reddere certa sibi, nihilo plus explicet ac si
insanire paret certa ratione modoque.'

Hor. Sat. 2.3.258–271

---

65 Amerasinghe 1950, 66.
66 Barsby 1999, 91.
67 As Muecke points out, the opening scene of the *Eunuchus* can easily be recognised as source for the passage in Horace. Muecke 1993, 160–161. See also Barsby 1990, 5–6.

When you offer apples to a sulky child, he refuses them. 'Take them, pet.' He says, 'No.' Were you not to offer them, he would crave them. How differs the lover who, when shut out, debates with himself whether to go or not to where, though not invited, he meant to return, and hangs about the hated doors? 'Shall I not go even now, when she invites me of her own accord? Or rather, shall I think of putting an end to my affliction? She shut me out. She calls me back. Shall I return? No — not if she implores me.' Now listen to the slave, wiser by far of the two: 'My master, a thing that admits of neither method nor sense cannot be handled by rule and method. In love inhere these evils — first war, then peace: things almost as fickle as the weather, shifting about by blind chance, and if one were to try to reduce them to fixed rule for himself, he would no more set them right than if he aimed at going mad by fixed rule and method.'

To take on such a role in relation to the young man comes very close to the relationship between the *praeceptor amoris* and his target audience. A passage that demonstrates the affinity between the role of Parmeno as adviser in love and the Ovidian *praeceptor* particularly well is found in the second book of the *Ars amatoria*, where advice is offered on how to overcome love's many sorrows, as e.g. being shut out by the mistress, which he here uses as an example, and it is my opinion that also Ovid here invokes the Terentian passage:

> ad propiora uocor; quisquis sapienter amabit,
>   uincet et e nostra, quod petet, arte ferret.
> credita non semper sulci cum fenore reddunt,
>   nec semper dubias adiuuat aura rates.
> quod iuuat, exiguum, plus est, quod laedat amantes:
>   proponent animo multa ferenda suo.
> quot lepores in Atho, quot apes pascintur in Hybla,
>   caerula quot bacas Palladis arbor habet,
> litore quot conchae, tot sunt in amore dolores;
>   quae patimur, multo spicula felle madent.
>
> Ov. Ars am. 2.511–520

To nearer matters am I called. Whoever loves wisely will be victorious, and by my art will gain his end. Not always do the furrows repay their trust with interest, not always does the wind assist perplexed vessels; what aids lovers is but little, more there is to frustrate them; let them make up their minds to many a trial. As many as the hares that feed on Athos, or the bees on Hybla, as many as the berries that the blue-grey tree of Pallas bears, or the shells that are on the shore, so many are the pains of love; the darts that wound us are steeped in much poison.

In addition to the verbal resemblance, the *praeceptor* here describes and gives advice in a situation of striking similarity to the one in the opening of the *Eunuchus*, which involves what to do when faced with the flaws of love.

As Barsby notes on the Terentian text, the list of the flaws of love, introduced at line 59, 'sounds like a stock rhetorical theme',[68] and points to a similar
but lengthier list in Plautus' *Mercator* at lines 18–36, introduced by *nam amorem haec cuncta uitia sectari solent* (Plaut. *Merc.* 18, 'Well, normally all these
vices go hand in hand with love'), before he goes on to list the negative effects
of love such as worry, distress, excessive refinement, sleeplessness etc. Ovid
might also draw on such a stock rhetorical theme when he introduces this section on how to face different difficulties in love; he does not, however, provide a
list of *dolores* as such, but rather gives more lengthy advice on certain problems.
The context in Ovid is also effectively the same as that in Terence; in the *Mercator*, the list is part of the *adulescens* Charinus' opening monologue, whereas in
both Terence and Ovid the situation is that of giving advice, and both the *praeceptor* and the slave talk from a point of view of superior knowledge and reason
to a shut-out young lover. Thus, Ovid's choice of words in line 2.519 compared
to line 59 of the *Eunuchus* strongly suggests an allusion to the Terentian passage
and the slave Parmeno's parallel role as advisor.

It is also worth noting in this passage that the *praeceptor*'s advice to love
wisely, *sapienter* at 2.511, and with the help of *ars* to win or be on the victorious
side of love, *uincet* at 2.512, mirrors Phaedria's fear of being defeated by Thais,
uictum at line 55, if he goes to her later, uninvited, as he will not be able to endure this situation, *pati non poteris* at line 52. In the Ovidian version, the lesson
is that the lover must endure the problems of love to be victorious, cf. *quae
patimur* at 2.520. The problems to be endured are the same as those Phaedria is
faced with; the first flaw mentioned is being denied access to the beloved (lines
520–532, quoted above), which is also the case in the Terentian scene. Ovid then
goes on to treat the issue of the rival and jealousy, *riualem patienter habe: uictoria tecum / stabit* (Ov. *Ars am.* 2.539–540, 'endure a rival patiently: victory will
be on your side'), which is exactly the issue that Phaedria is facing. Ovid's *sapienter* also reflects Parmeno's claim that he is attempting to make Phaedria into a
wise lover towards the end of the scene: *si sapis, / neque praeter quam quas ipse
amor molestias / habet addas, et illas quas habet recte feras* (Ter. *Eun.* 76–80, 'If
you've any sense, you won't add more troubles to those love brings anyway,
and you'll bear the ones it does bring philosophically.'). *Si sapis* is a common
phrase, but as Barsby points out, it here also carries with it an allusion 'to the
philosophical truths that Parmeno is about to impart',[69] which is the aspect of

---

68 Barsby 1999, *ad loc.*
69 See Barsby 1999, *ad loc.*

the scene that I believe Ovid is also alluding to as part of the characterisation of the *praeceptor* as a wise man in the field of love.[70]

However, as it turns out, Parmeno is neither a Stoic wise man nor a particularly successful *praeceptor*, and his advice ends up being both ambiguous and of little aid to his young master;[71] in the end he is himself tricked by the maid Pythias, and ridiculed for not being the typical *seruus callidus* of the genre after all (*at etiam primo callidum et disertum credidi hominem*, Ter. *Eun.* 1011, 'Yet once I even believed you a clever capable sort of a fellow.').[72] That Ovid lets this character represent elements of the *praeceptor* in a section that urges the reader to love wisely, I believe, should not necessarily be taken at face value, but rather brings out important differences between the genres.

It has been noted how Ovid in his eroto-didactic works challenges elegiac convention when he teaches young lovers to love wisely; as Conte points out, the diligent student of the *Ars amatoria* would then in fact turn out very different from the elegiac lover, i.e. he would not end up unhappy and tormented, if he were to follow the the *praeceptor*'s advice on this point.[73] Indeed, the *praeceptor* admits shortly after that he has not been able to love wisely himself: *hac ego, confiteor, non sum perfectus in arte; / quid faciam? monitis sum minor ipse meis* (Ov. *Ars am.* 2.547–548, 'In this art, I confess, I am not perfect; what am I to do? I fall short of my own counsels.'). For a young man in an elegiac love relationship, loving wisely is not always achievable. This brings out an apparent contradiction in the text; to love wisely is apparently not the elegiac way of loving, or even possible. However, it is important to notice that Ovid as *praeceptor* gives advice based on his personal insight as a now experienced lover,[74] and that the experienced lover would be able to curve his temper in such situations,

---

70 However, Parmeno's advice is also here ambiguous; see Barsby 1999, 97, *ad* lines 77–78.

71 As Barsby notes to e.g. Parmeno's advice to Phaedria to 'buy back his freedom' in line 74, 'the image is not altogether apt, as a lover can scarcely buy himself out of a courtesan's clutches (...)'. See Barsby 1999, *ad loc.* Furthermore, even though being in possession of superior knowledge is the impression that Parmeno wishes to give in the opening, he eventually ends up as the typical 'bungling slave'. See Barsby 1990, 7–10. See also Hanses 2020, 343.

72 As Barsby notes, Pythias is adding to Parmeno's humiliation over being tricked, at the same time as Terence draws attention to the reversal of the cunning slave character by deploying the standard epithet *callidus*. See Barsby 1999, *ad loc.*

73 See Conte 1989, 458.

74 Cf. the *Amores*, where the *praeceptor amoris* speaks from the point of view of being an experienced elegiac lover himself, ref. e.g. *Vsus opus mouet hoc: uati parete perito; / uera canam. coeptis, mater Amoris, ades* (Ov. *Ars am.* 1.29–30, 'experience inspires this work: give ear to an experienced bard; true will be my song: favour my enterprise, O mother of Love.'). I am indebted to Thea Selliaas Thorsen for pointing this out to me.

e.g. accept that the door might be closed to him from time to time, and love more wisely, as becomes evident in Book Three: *ille uetus miles sensim et sapienter amabit / multaque tironi non patienda feret* (Ov. *Ars am.* 3.565–566, 'But the veteran will come gradually and prudently to love, and will bear much a recruit would not endure;').[75] This is a crucial difference between the comic slave advisor and the *praeceptor amoris*: the *praeceptor* ultimately speaks from a point of experience and hindsight; his own as a lover in the *Amores*, but also on a generic level as the successor of Gallus, Tibullus and Propertius. This is not the case for the comic *seruus* Parmeno, whose advice ends up being unsuccessful, just as he ends up an unsuccessful *seruus callidus*.[76] Furthermore, not to be able to love wisely might have more serious and dangerous outcomes within the Ovidian intratextual nexus; in *Her.* 2, Phyllis states that her only mistake had been not to love wisely (*dic mihi, quid feci, nisi non sapienter amaui?* Ov. *Her.* 2.27, 'Tell me, what have I done, except not love wisely?'), which ultimately leads to her death by suicide.[77] In the third book of the *Ars amatoria*, the *praeceptor* suggests the 'veteran' lover, who will love the *puella* wisely, *sapienter*, as a way to avoid amatory violence; as the young lover burning with passion is more likely to be jealous, break down her doors and tear her hair and clothes; the wise lover is a much safer choice (lines 3.565–576).[78]

A crucial difference between elegy and the comic genre is that the conventions of comedy demand that all love plots be solved within proper societal boundaries. The solution to the Phaedria-Thais plot in the *Eunuchus* comes as a surprise; in the end, Phaedria takes advice from another comic *praeceptor*-like character, the parasite Gnatho,[79] who presents him with the wisest way to handle the situation, that is to accept his rival as long as the latter pays the bill for them both (lines 1049–1094).[80] The solution comes across as rather cynical, in light of the fact that Thais is not the typical greedy *meretrix* of the genre and has

---

75 This section is closely linked to *militia amoris* and will be treated more closely in the next chapter.

76 And is thus no longer associated with the playwright, or, as formulated by Sharrock, '(a)s regards his relationship with the audience, his knowing, cynical commentary on the play, and his superior attitude to other stock characters, Parmeno appears to be written in the tradition of Pseudolus and to act as the eyes and mouth of the poet — until Terence kicks him beneath the belt.' Sharrock 2009, 152; see also pages 152–155.

77 I am grateful to Thea Sealliaas Thorsen for pointing out this intratextual implication to me.

78 The passage is also closely linked to *militia amoris,* and will be treated in Chapter Five.

79 See Hanses 2020, 333–342.

80 A link between the Ovidian *praeceptor* and the comic flatterer has been suggested in Janka 1997, 176–177, *ad* lines 197–202, and Labate 1984, 204–207.

no wish to continue her relationship with the soldier (which is the very reason why Phaedria can safely keep him around).[81] This has nothing to do with loving in a wise and patient way in the manner of Ovid's veteran lover; it is a mere question of financing the relationship.

Notably, the advice on how to love wisely, which Ovid admits to not have been able to follow in his younger days, is to endure one's rival (*riualem patienter habe*, *Ars am.* 2.539, 'endure a rival patiently'):[82]

> oscula uir dederat, memini, suus; oscula questus
>   sum data: barbaria noster abundat amor.
> non semel hoc uitium nocuit mihi; doctior ille,
>   quo ueniunt alii conciliante uiri.
>
> Ov. Ars am. 2.551–554

> Her own husband, I remember, had kissed her: I complained of the kisses; my love is full of savagery. Not once only has this fault done me harm: wiser he by whose complaisance other men come to his mistress.

This is exactly how Phaedria curbs his love troubles and regains control in the final scene of the *Eunuchus*: by taking the advice to keep the soldier as his rival (*militem riualem ego recipiundum censeo*, Ter. *Eun.* 1072, 'I propose that you accept the soldier as a rival'), as discussed above. Even though the solution is surprising, the notion of Thais having multiple lovers would not have been perceived as problematic as such, in the sense that she is a *meretrix*; with this, the plot thus reaches a satisfactory conclusion.[83] In the Ovidian text, the situation is more complex. The message is that one should allow one's *puella* to have multiple lovers, but the term *uir* here can indicate both the man currently in possession of her, but also her husband, which becomes especially relevant in light of the blurred status of the *puella*. To disclose one's jealousy in this situation would be unwise and harmful indeed, both to the *puella* and to the lover

---

81 On the surprising conclusion of the play, see also Barsby 1999, 280–283.
82 The quoted passage refers to Ov. *Am.* 1.4. There, it is strongly suggested that the *uir* is the *puella*'s husband: *oscula iam sumet, iam non tantum oscula sumet: / quod mihi das furtim, iure coacta dabis* (Ov. *Am.* 1.4.63–64, 'Then he will take kisses from you, yes, then he will take not only kisses; what you give me in secret, you will give him as a right, because you must.'). Then it would indeed be harmful and unwise for the lover to reveal their relationship by expressing jealousy. However, see McKeown 1989, *ad loc.*, for the reading that the girl is a freedwoman and the *uir* her patron.
83 See Barsby 1999, 281.

himself, as adultery was a serious crime, punishable by law.[84] This shows the many layers of the Ovidian work; the *praeceptor* and his advice can be read in light of the humorous characters, but given the crucial issue of status in the *Ars amatoria*, the text simultaneously and inextricably displays a deeper and more complex meaning. I would argue that the Terentian echoes highlight this aspect of the text by creating a contrast between the clearly defined characters of comedy and the not so easily defined Ovidian *personae*, here the *seruus* versus the *praeceptor*, the *meretrix* and her lovers versus the *puella*, her lover and her *uir*.

Conclusion

In this chapter I have demonstrated on the one hand that Ovid makes certain twists to the elegiac image of *seruitium amoris*, and thus develops it from its conventional form, and that he deploys Terence as he does so. On the other hand, I have shown that in Terence, in the *Eunuchus* in particular, one can find clear prefigurations of what will become central notions of the image of *seruitium amoris* in general, and as this is developed by Ovid in particular. One of these prefigurations is connected to a version of the *paraclausithyron*, that is the young man Phaedria in the *Eunuchus* as the *exclusus amator*, shut out due to a *diues amator*; both become important figures in Roman love elegy. Furthermore, I have argued that in the *Eunuchus* one finds the clearest example in the Roman Comic genre of a man of high status that is willing to take on the role as slave (though temporary) and perform slave duties to obtain access to a woman. This act is what gives name to the play, as the young citizen Chaerea poses as a slave eunuch and takes orders from a *meretrix* and her slaves, all to gain access to the girl Pamphila. As I argued, this reading is supported by an allusion to Chaerea's scheme in Horace's *Sat.* 2.7, and Ovid picks up on the concept, i.e. that the lover should not be ashamed to take on the role as slave and perform typical slave duties to get close to his beloved; slaves, after all, enjoy an enviable (to the lover) proximity to the object of desire, a concept well explored in the *Eunuchus*. However, within the comic universe, the proper social order with its clear lines between social classes is always at some point reestablished. This is also the case in the *Eunuchus* — as is fitting for the genre; such issues are never as simple within the bounds of Ovid's elegiac universe. On the other hand, marriage is

---

84 I believe that the blurred meaning of the term *uir* is invoked intentionally in this passage. On the Augustan law on marriage and adultery, see Chapter Two. Cf. also Thorsen 2018a on the danger of marriage as the deeper meaning of the *Ars amatoria*.

seemingly the goal in one of the most recognized examples of *seruitium amoris* in Ovid, found in the double *Heroides*, in letters of Acontius and Cydippe (*Her.* 20/21), as Acontius tricks Cydippe into promising to marry him. As I have argued, Ovid puts his own twist on the conventional elegiac notion of *seruitium amoris* as he plays with the stock comic *seruus callidus* in his portrayal of the trickster lover Acontius, in a storyline that fits well with the typical New Comic rape-marriage plot, with Cydippe in the role of the raped high-status *uirgo*, but not so much with the elegiac ideal of reciprocity. One of the most conspicuous examples of *seruitium amoris* in Ovid, represented by Acontius, is really a mock version of it. Another aspect of the comic slave, often described as a magister for his young master in matters of love, can be found in Ovid's elegiac didactic. As I have argued, this is most prominent in Parmeno in the *Eunuchus*, who takes on the role of a (mock) Stoic wiseman. This reading of Parmeno is also present in Horace's *Sat.* 2.3, and is picked up by Ovid in the second book of the *Ars amatoria*, and in his concept of loving wisely. However, Ovid's work is much more complex than the more strictly defined bounds of comedy, with its ever-present deeper meanings and strong connection to current societal issues, as can be seen in the double meaning of the notion of loving wisely.

5 Poetic imagery: militant love

Introduction

Militia amoris is a favourite metaphor of the elegiac writers, and though present in all of them in various forms, it is most developed in Ovid.[1] As Drinkwater observes, 'as Propertius is the master of *seruitium*, so Ovid's favourite weapon is *militia*'.[2] The usage of military imagery for describing matters of love, or *militia amoris*, is commonly seen as a particular Roman metaphor in its most developed form, mainly found in Roman comedy and love elegy.[3] It is, just as the notion of *seruitium amoris*, closely linked to the backdrop of real life social practice, and the metaphor can be said to mirror Rome's strong overall militarism, which is highly relevant in the context of both genres.[4] Still, as Barsby points out, military metaphors describing aspects of love are rarely found in Plautus and the fragments of Menander, whereas such images are present in Terence and the opening of the *Eunuchus*, and it is likely that Terence played a significant part in the development of this image.[5] In addition to the military language

---

1 See e.g. Murgatroyd 1975; Cahoon 1988. *Militia amoris* is first found in a basic form in Greek lyric and elegy (Sappho fr. 1, Anacreon 46 (B), Theognis 1285–94). On the further tradition and development of *militia amoris,* see e.g. Murgatroyd 1975, Lyne 1980, 71–78. Drinkwater 2013 treats the image in the Roman elegists. See also Gale 1997 for a summary of the image as deployed by Tibullus and Propertius. McKeown 1995 treats Ovid's *Amores* 1.9, arguably one of the most exhaustive treatments of the image.
2 Drinkwater 2013, 195.
3 Lyne 1980, 71.
4 On Roman militarism in the republican period in general, see e.g. Harris 1985. On the Roman societal backdrop of e.g. war in Roman comedy, see Leigh 2004.
5 Barsby 1999, 93. Fantham 1972, when treating military imagery, points out that 'love as warfare does not seem to feature in Plautus, largely because his plots favour unanimity of the lovers against a common foe; even *Truculentus*, in which the *meretrix* defeats her military foe, fails to exploit its metaphorical potential.' Fantham 1972, 32. Lyne, however, points to the popularity of the image in Plautus; see Lyne 1980, 71–72. No examples are provided in Lyne. Murgatroyd points to three passages in Plautus that he considers significant innovations in the image from the Republican period, and that although the point is not fully worked out, the idea that the lover is a soldier under the mistress's command, her role being similar to that of a general, is present, and that 'the concept that the lover is in some kind of military service is given concrete expression for the first time': *at confidentia / illa militia militatur multo magi' quam pondere* (Plaut. *Pers.* 231–232, 'But that fight is fought with self-confidence much more than weight'), *numquam amatoris meretricem oportet caussam noscere, / quin, ubi nil det, pro infrequente eum mittat militia domum* (Plaut. *Truc.* 229–230, 'A prostitute ought never to take notice of a lover's circumstances; rather, when he doesn't give anything, she should send him

https://doi.org/10.1515/9783111308036-005

of love deployed in the opening of the *Eunuchus*, the opening of the *Hecyra* has been recognised as using terms of military combat about matters of love, as it prominently displays the other side of 'the battle of the sexes', as the older *meretrix* Syra in military terms instructs the younger Philotis on how to deal with lovers, *amatores*, also labelled enemies (*aduersarios*, Ter. *Hec.* 72). This constitutes an interesting parallel to the Ovidian notion of being a *praeceptor* or *magister* to both men and women, a role paralleled by both slaves and prostitutes in the Terentian universe, as discussed in Chapters Three and Four.

Much research has been conducted on the elegists' use of *militia amoris* and their connection to the previous Greek and Roman tradition of using military terms for the description of love-affairs; as McKeown notes, 'military imagery had been used sporadically in earlier love poetry, but almost always it served as a merely decorative figure of speech. The elegists, however, developed the metaphor of love as warfare into a symbol of their non-conformist way of life.'[6] It is generally agreed that it is Ovid who devotes most attention to the idea and gives it the most exhaustive treatment,[7] as in e.g. *Amores* 1.2, 1.9, 2.12 and 3.8. As already mentioned, it is mainly in the Roman comic genre that the notion can be found in a more developed version prior to the elegists, and according to Murgatroyd, 'the concept that the lover is in some kind of military service' was first given concrete expression in Plautus.[8] However, as Fantham points out, Plautus does not exploit its 'metaphorical potential',[9] and it is again in Terence that a more extensive incorporation of military terminology and concepts into different aspects of love and the dynamics of interactions between men and women can be traced.

In this chapter, the most famous Terentian instances of *militia amoris* will be treated, including the opening scenes of the *Eunuchus* and *Hecyra*. My discussion will focus on their reception in Ovid in particular, and how, as I argue, his reception of the traits of *militia amoris* in Terence adds to this literary image.

---

back home as a deserter from military service'), *custos erilis, decu' popli, thesaurus copiarum, / salus interior corporis amorisque imperator* (Plaut. *Asin.* 655–656, 'guardian of your master, glory of the people, storehouse of riches, inner salvation of the body and commander of love'). From Terence is mentioned the use of military language in the opening of the *Hecyra* and the dialogue between the *meretrices* Syra and Philotis, and in the opening scene of the *Eunuchus*. Murgatroyd 1975, 66–67.

6 McKeown 1989, 258.

7 E.g. Murgatroyd 1974; Cahoon 1988.

8 Murgatroyd 1975, 67. The three passages from Plautus mentioned by Murgatroyd are quoted in Chapter Five, note 5 above.

9 Fantham 1972, 32.

The opening scene of the *Eunuchus* was treated also in the previous chapter, as it is also closely linked to the notion of *seruitium amoris*. A similar connection between *militia* and *seruitium* is moreover evident in the elegiac genre, where the tropes of *seruitium amoris* and *militia amoris* are sometimes seen as overlapping; this might reflect a kinship between slavery and warfare, offering a rich language for metaphors, as both concepts provide a vocabulary of dominance and submission, or of conquering and being conquered.[10] This link also occurred in real life, where slaves were often prisoners of war; this is duly reflected in the opening scene of the *Eunuchus*, where Phaedria is fittingly advised to find his way out his love troubles by buying his freedom back like a prisoner of war.[11] The connection is particularly evident in Ovid, where examples can be found in the second book of the *Ars amatoria* of the *praeceptor* suggesting slavish behaviour as a strategy to be victorious in love at 2.511–534, also treated in the previous chapter in relation to *seruitium amoris* and to the Terentian version of the image, and, as Murgatroyd points out, shortly before at 2.233–250, where it is fused with the myth of Apollo's enslavement.[12] Furthermore, some attention will be devoted to the real soldier characters of the two genres, as it will be argued that the portrayal of the *miles* Thraso of the *Eunuchus* is mirrored in Ovid's soldier lover in *Amores* 3.8, and thus constitutes the closest comic parallel to the soldier rival of the elegiac lover.

The opening of the *Hecyra* gives a female perspective on the battle of the sexes, and how women should be strategic in the same way as the enemy, that is men. The scene also establishes the theme for the play, that is women's sufferings due to male misperceptions and wrongdoing. This finds an interesting thematic parallel in Ovid's *Ars amatoria*, where he provides 'arms' for both men and their enemies, i.e. women, in the battle of love. Such provision is designed to allow for a 'fair fight', as it is in the end women that are most often deceived by men, and not the other way around.[13] Furthermore, I argue that the opening of the third book of the *Ars amatoria* also contains an allusion that latches on to the allusive nexus treated in Chapter One and Chapter Two, which connects the *Ars amatoria* to the *Eunuchus,* and the portrayal of problematic aspects of men's

---

10 See Cahoon 1988.

11 *te redimas captum* (Ter. *Eun.* 74, 'ransom yourself from your captivity'). As Barsby notes, the image seems to be connected to that of buying back prisoners of war for a ransom, which is confirmed also by Donatus, who says that this is a continuation of the military metaphors present in the scene. See Barsby 1999, *ad loc.*

12 Murgatroyd 1975, 79.

13 Ov. *Ars am.* 3.1–56.

violence towards women from a female perspective through the plays' female characters.

A prominent aspect of *militia amoris* in the elegiac genre is amatory violence, as in e.g. Tibullus 1.10, Propertius 2.5 and Ovid *Ars am.* 3.565–576. Furthermore, there is a connection between these three sections, or, in the words of Gibson, they partake in an 'elegiac dialogue',[14] discussing the use of 'rustic' amatory violence against the *puella*. This includes the practice of physical attacks on doors to get to the beloved, a practice that is part of the Roman *paraclausithyron* from its early form.[15] Violence against the beloved is, as discussed in Chapter Two, a feature of elegy that is often seen as a sign of influence from the New Comic genre; it is, as was argued there, a particularly prominent feature of the comedies of Terence, where actions such as rape and tearing the hair and clothes of the victim are presented in the worst possible light. In the present chapter, it will be argued that the elegiac discourse in Tibullus 1.10, Propertius 2.5 and Ovid *Ars am.* 3.565–576 on the use of violence, including breaking in doors and tearing of the beloved's clothes, can be traced back both thematically and textually to Terence's *Adelphoe*, where the *adulescens* Aeschinus' violent attack on a pimp's door (and on the pimp himself) to get to a girl is debated by his biological father and his adoptive father, the *senes* Demea and Micio; they both think the attack is a case of amatory violence, and they disagree as to whether it is acceptable for a young man to behave in such a manner.

Aspects of Terentian *militia* in Ovid's *Amores* 1.9 and 3.8

As one of two scenes that have been prominently associated with *militia amoris* in Terence, the general influence of the opening scene of the *Eunuchus* on the *topos* has already been recognised in research.[16] In the following, I would like to suggest a connection between the play's opening dialogue between the *adulescens* Phaedria and the slave Parmeno, and Ovid's *Amores* 1.9, which, to my knowledge, has not yet been commented upon. The connection is the notion that love is unstable, demonstrated by a play on the changeability that is common to love and war, a motif that occurs in both texts. The situation in the play's opening scene, also treated in the previous chapter, is that Phaedria has

---

14 Gibson 2003, 321.
15 As Copley notes, this element 'was present in the dramatic tradition of the Greek *paraclausithyron* but played little or no part in its non dramatic form'. Copley 1956, 40.
16 E.g. Murgatroyd 1975; Barsby 1999, 93.

been shut out of the *meretrix* Thais' house in favor of his rival, the soldier Thraso. The *Eunuchus* is the only Terentian comedy that features a soldier as a rival lover on stage, and notably, the plot comes very close to the situation lamented by Ovid as poet-lover in *Amores* 3.8; in the following, I will argue that Ovid's soldier rival is strongly influenced by the Terentian character.

It is evident that the memorable opening scene of the *Eunuchus* had a strong influence on later Roman literature and the development of a number of themes:[17] as Barsby points out, lines 59–63 are quoted by Cicero (*Tusc.* 4.76) to illustrate the fickleness of love,[18] and Horace's *Sat.* 2.3 also contains multiple verbal echoes of the opening scene.[19] As discussed in the previous chapter, the opening of the *Eunuchus* displays emotions and concepts that point forward to what becomes *seruitium amoris* in the elegiac writers, as Phaedria, a young man of citizen status, fears the consequences of losing control, of being beaten by and in the control of his *meretrix* mistress. Furthermore, as was treated in Chapter Four, this play seems to have played a part in the Roman development of the *paraclausithyron*. As also discussed there, the scene seems to be picked up by Ovid in the second book of the *Ars amatoria* at 2.511–534, a section that displays a fusion of the images of the lover as slave and the lover as soldier, and of love itself as war. In the Ovidian section, the objective is also to win at love (*uincet* at *Ars am.* 2.512; cf. *uictum* at Ter. *Eun.* 55), though by acting the slave.

In the same way, the Terentian opening scene can also be said to display simultaneously notions of *seruitium amoris* and *militia amoris*; just as vocabulary reminiscent of slavery can be detected, there is present a clear and extensive image of love qua military battle, where there is a fine line between victory and defeat and where one must meticulously plan one's tactics to ensure that one has the upper hand or to avoid being beaten. It is arguably one of the most exhaustive occurrences of the image of *militia amoris* within the New Comic genre:

> *exclusit; reuocat: redeam? non si me obsecret.*
> *siquidem hercle possis, nil prius neque fortius.*
> *uerum si incipies neque pertendes gnauiter*
> *atque, ubi pati non poteri', quom nemo expetet,*
> *infecta pace ultro ad eam uenies indicans*
> *te amare et ferre non posse: actumst, ilicet,*
> *peristi: eludet ubi te uictum senserit.*
>
> Ter. *Eun.* 49–55

---

17 E.g. Barsby 1999, commentary to line 53.
18 Barsby 1999, *ad loc.*
19 See Muecke 1993, 131 and 161.

She shut me out, she calls me back: shall I go? No, not if she implores me. If only you could, by god, this would be the best course, and the bravest. But if you start on it and haven't the strength to carry it through, and, when you can't endure it, when nobody wants you, you go to her of your own accord with no terms negotiated, making it quite clear that you love her and can't bear it — you've had it, it's all over, you're done for; she'll taunt you once she sees you beaten.

The bravest (*fortius*) course to take would be to keep one's distance, Phaedria initially concludes, but this is also a dangerous course to take, as it might not be endurable, and he might go to her later *infecta pace*, with no peace terms agreed, and thus be beaten (*uictum*).[20] Both being brave and being beaten are aspects of battle and warfare, and, as Barsby notes, *infecta pace* is a technical military term.[21]

The martial setting in the opening scene of the *Eunuchus* is sustained and further highlighted in the slave Parmeno's reply, and the military metaphors are prominent also in this section. Furthermore, there is made a clear link between war and the concept of love itself:

> *ere, quae res in se neque consilium neque modum*
> *habet ullum, eam consilio regere non potes.*
> *in amore haec omnia insunt uitia: iniuriae,*
> *suspiciones, inimicitiae, indutiae,*
> *bellum, pax rursum: incerta haec si tu postules*
> *ratione certa facere, nihilo plus agas*
> *quam si des operam ut cum ratione insanias.*
>
> <div align="right">Ter. <i>Eun.</i> 57–63</div>

> *quid agas? nisi ut te redimas captum quam queas*
> *minimo;*
>
> <div align="right">Ter. <i>Eun.</i> 74–75</div>

Master, when a thing has no logic to it and no means of control, you can't rule it by logic. A love affair has all these symptoms: wrongs, suspicions, quarrels, truces, war, peace again. If you try to impose certainty on uncertainty by reason, you'd achieve no more than if you set about going insane by reason.

What to do? What else but ransom yourself from your captivity at the lowest possible price?

---

20 As treated in the previous chapter, this might also be an allusion to losing a gladiator battle.
21 Barsby 1999, *ad loc*. As noted in the previous chapter, the phrase *eludet ubi te uictum senserit* seems to be an allusion to gladiatorial battles.

Here, it becomes clear that the slave Parmeno recognises changeability as a natural part of love, and he uses the unpredictability of war and the shifting between war and peace (*bellum, pax rursum*) as a fitting image for this changeability. His reply fits well with the military terminology deployed by Phaedria as he talks about himself as a soldier,[22] and Parmeno follows up again shortly after as he compares him to a prisoner of war, who should pay ransom to buy back his freedom, to put an end to love and his own misery. What can be seen here in the opening of the *Eunuchus* is a comprehensive imagery where the likeness of war and love affairs is exploited for literary effect in both Phaedria's speech and Parmeno's reply. Murgatroyd sees here an innovation in the *militia amoris*, namely the notion that if love is a war then there it must also have periods of peace,[23] and as Barsby points out, Terence and this section did most likely play a significant part in the development of this literary image.[24]

In addition to the lines pointed out by Barsby (*infecta pace* at line 53, *bellum, pax rursum* at line 61, *redimas captum* at line 74 in particular) as having had a general influence on the later image, the specific Terentian image of love as being unstable like the constant shift between war and peace seems to be picked up again in Ovid's central *militia* poem *Amores* 1.9. The comic scene had been established as a demonstration of love's changeability by Cicero, who quotes lines 59–63 and adds *haec inconstantia mutabilitasque mentis quem non ipsa prauitate deterreat?* (Cic. *Tusc.* 4.76,[25] 'Such inconsistency and capriciousness of mind — whom would it not scare away by its very vileness?'), and the notion of love's changeability is picked up by the elegists more generally, as e.g. in Propertius: *omnia uertuntur: certe uertuntur amores. / uinceris aut uincis: haec in amore rota est* (Prop. 2.8.7–8, 'all things change, and loves not least of all: you lose to those you vanquished — so turns the wheel of Luck in love').[26] Notably, the notion of love's changeability is again connected to *militia amoris* in *Amores* 1.9: *Mars dubius, **nec certa Venus*** (Ov. *Am.* 1.9.29, 'Mars is doubtful, and Venus, too, not sure.'). As McKeown notes, the uncertainty of war is proverbial,[27] and Ovid exploits this and makes the connection between the proverbial

---

22 As will be further highlighted later in this chapter, the soldier imagery is present from the very outset of the first scene.

23 Murgatroyd 1975, 66.

24 Barsby 1999, *ad* lines 74–75. The *militia* aspect of love and the comparison between love and war in the opening scene of the *Eunuchus* was alluded to also by Horace to demonstrate the foolishness of the lover in *Sat.* 2.3, see above.

25 My text for Cic. *Tusc.* is Pohlenz 1918.

26 Propertius 2.8 also mentions the *inimicitiae* of love at line 3; cf. Ter. *Eun.* 60.

27 McKeown 1989, *ad loc.*

instability of war and the nature of love. This comparison is the same as the one that is made by Terence, that is that love is *incerta* (line 61) and thus by nature cannot be made stable, *certa* (line 62), as he deploys the proverbial instability of war and the shift between war and peace to demonstrate the natural changeability of love.[28] Terence utilizes the proverbial changeability of war to illustrate the uncertainty of a love affair in a very similar manner to that which is picked by Ovid in *Amores* 1.9; the point is virtually the same, i.e. that love, just like war, will always contain an element of uncertainty.

Although Ovid dedicates *Amores* 1.9 to demonstrating how love is like war and that the lover thus leads a life much like the life of a soldier, the elegiac soldier of love is still very different from the notion of real soldiers as lovers within the genre. The concept of the crude soldier as a lover is present in both comedy and elegy, and when a soldier takes on the role as lover within the two genres, it is predominantly as a rival to both the comic *adulescens* and the elegiac lover, something that has been identified as a connecting trait between the genres.[29] Being a standard rival of the comic *adulescens*, the soldier is featured in several plays within the genre, mainly in Plautus (e.g. in *Bacchides*, *Poenulus*, *Truculentus*, *Miles Gloriosus*), whereas the rival soldier in only presented on stage in one Terentian play, that is the *Eunuchus*. The *miles* is pictured as a contrast to the *adulescens*, and he is typically boastful, arrogant, unrefined and stupid, but with money to spend (as in *Truculentus* and *Eunuchus*).[30] Within the elegiac genre, there are soldier rivals present in e.g. Prop. 1.8 and 2.16 (an Illyrian praetor), in Tib. 2.3 (a rich former slave, most likely a soldier)[31] and, famously, the newly rich soldier in Ovid's *Amores* 3.8 (see below). The comic soldiers and their elegiac counterparts share general common traits, such as having the financial upper hand in contrast to the poet-lover, who has only his love and poetry to offer, and they are generally presented as unworthy lovers for the *puella*.

Even though the comic soldier type is most conspicuously featured in Plautus, the closest connection between the elegiac soldier rival and the Roman comic universe is arguably found in Ovid's *Amores* 3.8 and the poem's affinity with Terence's *Eunuchus* and the play's soldier Thraso.[32] The situation lamented

---

28 As Barsby note, that lovers quickly reconcile again after quarrels was proverbial in antiquity; cf. e.g. Men. fr. 567 K-T, Plaut. *Amph*. 938–943, Ter. *An*. 555. However, the link to war and peace is made by Terence.
29 See e.g. James 2012, 256.
30 On the *miles* in Roman comedy, see Duckworth 1994 [1952], 264–265.
31 See Maltby 2002, 404–405, commentary on lines 33–34.
32 See also James 2012, 259.

by the poet lover is effectively the same as for Terence's Phaedria in the first
scene of the play, that is being shut out of the beloved's house for the benefit of
a richer soldier lover:

> *cum pulchre dominae nostri placuere libelli,*
> *quo licuit libris, non licet ire mihi;*
> *cum bene laudauit, laudato ianua clausa est:*
> *turpiter huc illuc ingeniosus eo.*
> *ecce recens diues parto per uulnera censu*
> *praefertur nobis sanguine pastus eques.*
>
> Ov. Am. 3.8.5–10

When my little books have won my lady, where my books could go, I may not go myself;
when she has praised me heartily, to him she has praised the door is closed. Disgracefully
hither and thither I go, for all my poet's gift. Look you, a newly-rich, a knight fed fat on
blood, who won his rating by dealing wounds, is preferred to me!

The lover is in the situation of the shut-out lover, ref. *ianua clausa* at line 7, and
he is not allowed to enter his mistress' house. As already demonstrated in Chapter Four, there are multiple references to the door being shut for Phaedria
throughout the *Eunuchus*,[33] and the reason for his exclusion is, as Phaedria sees
it, that Thais prefers the soldier (*ego excludor, ille — recipitur. qua gratia? | nisi si
illum plus amas quam me.* Ter. *Eun.* 159–160, 'I'm shut out, he's let in. Why?
Unless you love him more than me.'). There is also in Terence a strong focus on
gifts and the soldier's wealth; this is the very reason that he has been let in by
Thais, i.e. that he has been able to secure the girl Pamphila as a gift for her (CH:
quis is tam potens cum tanto munere hoc? PA: *miles Thraso, | Phaedriae riuali'.*
Ter. *Eun.* 353–354, 'CH: What man has the means to give a gift like that? PA: The
soldier Thraso, Phaedria's rival.').

The notion that the soldier is unworthy of the *puella*'s affections becomes
clear over the next lines:

> *qua periit aliquis, potes hanc contingere dextram?*
> *heu, ubi mollities pectoris illa tui?*
> *cerne cicatrices, ueteris uestigia pugnae:*
> *quaesitum est illi corpore, quidquid habet.*
> *forsitan et quotiens hominem iugulauerit ille*
> *indicet: hoc fassas tangis, auara, manus?*
>
> Ov. Am. 3.8.17–22

---

33 In Chapter Four, I argued for a connection between the shut-out lover at *Ars am.* 2.521–534
and Thais closing the door on Phaedria in the Terentian play.

The hand by which someone has died — can you touch that right hand? Alas! where is the tenderness of heart you had? Look at those scars, marks of the bygone fight — that man has earned with his body whatever he has. Perhaps he could even tell you how many times he has plunged the steel in a human throat. Do you touch, greedy girl, hands that tell such tales?

The concept of the crude soldier, bragging about his military exploits, as Ovid pictures him in *Amores* 3.8, can easily be traced back to the comic universe. Maybe most famous is Plautus' *Miles Gloriosus* and the soldier Pyrgopolinices, who constantly and proudly brags about his military exploits (and his own good looks) to his hanger-on Artotrogus.

As Duckworth points out, Terence's Thraso actually differs from the Plautine type, as he does not boast of his military achievements, but rather of his wit and his ability to outsmart people with words.[34] This is, however, not the impression that Parmeno tries to give Thais of the soldier, as he tries to highlight the benefits of choosing Phaedria instead: *neque pugnas narrat neque cicatrices suas / ostentat neque tibi obstat, quod quidam facit* (Ter. *Eun.* 482–483, 'He doesn't narrate his battles or parade his scars, or get in your way, as a certain person does.'). This comes very close to Ovid's description of the soldier as one who brags about violent battles, simultaneously drawing attention to scars. As Barsby notes on lines 482–483, to brag about military exploits is the typical behaviour of the comic *miles*, whereas there are fewer examples of showing off scars, though this might also have been typical behaviour for the character within the New Comic genre.[35] Notably, Parmeno's speech does not necessarily refer to the actual behaviour of the soldier within the play; it is a play on the typical characteristics of the stock comic *miles*, addressed to Thais to make Thraso seem repellent and thus put Phaedria in a better light. One of the features that is brought up is the soldier's many scars, drawing attention to something that maybe would have been perceived as off-putting, which would reflect the intention of Parmeno's speech. This is very similar to what Ovid does in *Amores* 3.8 in the lines quoted above; the lines are addressed directly to the *puella* to demonstrate the crudeness and repelling qualities of the soldier lover. To depict him as the stock braggart soldier of comedy should thus be effective.

---

34 Duckworth 1994 [1952], 265.
35 Barsby 1999, *ad loc.*

The battle of the sexes: a matter of perspective

The second Terentian passage associated with *militia amoris* is the opening scene of the *Hecyra* (58–75) and the dialogue there between two *meretrices*, Philotis and the older Syra. In this stock scene of new comedy, that of an older *meretrix* or *lena* instructing a younger one in matters of love,[36] love is portrayed as a battle, as Syra constantly speaks in military terms (underlined) to convince Philotis that men, without exception, are the enemy, and that one should take care to plot back against them:

> nam nemo illorum quisquam, scito, ad te uenit
> quin ita paret sese abs te ut blanditiis suis
> quam minimo pretio suam uoluptatem expleat.
> hiscin tu amabo non contra **insidiabere**?
>
> <div align="right">Ter. <i>Hec.</i> 67–70</div>

> Not one of them, I assure you, comes to you without the intention of talking you into satisfying his desires at the lowest possible price. Are you not going to do some counterplotting against such people, my darling?

And

> iniurium autem est ulcisci **aduorsarios**,
> aut qua uia te **captent** eadem ipsos **capi**?
>
> <div align="right">Ter. <i>Hec.</i> 72–73</div>

> Not fair to get revenge on your enemies or to catch them out in the same way as they try to catch you?

Even though the dialogue between the two *meretrices* is considered a stock scene for the genre, the battle between the sexes is also programmatic for the play, as Goldberg points out.[37] The humour of the play is largely based on the two *senes'* stereotypical conceptions about women and mothers-in-law (the *senex* Laches believes that wives are always opposed to their husbands, *uiris*

---

36 E.g. Plaut. *Cist.* 78–81, *Asin.* 504–544, *Mostell.* 184–247. However, the *meretrices* in the Terentian opening scene and what they represent will be significant for the play; see Gilula 1980, 153–154; McGarrity 1980, 150–151; Sharrock 2009, 242–243; Goldberg 2013, 96.
37 Goldberg 2013, commentary on line 72.

aduorsas at 202), whereas it is the two *matronae* and the other female characters of the play who drive the plot forward and gain the sympathy of the audience.[38]

Murgatroyd points to the use of the term 'spoil' in the opening scene of the *Hecyra*, *spolies mutiles laceres quemque nacta sis* (Ter. *Hec.* 65, 'strip, flay, and fleece every one you get'); the concept is first found in Asclepiades, who describes the lover as the spoil of Aphrodite, whereas in Plautus' *Trinummus* at line 239 Lysiteles describes Amor as a *despoliator* who ensnares men and makes them prone to give the beloved whatever she asks for, which is similar to the notion in Terence, where the idea is to secure as much money from one's lover as possible.[39] However, in Terence, the focus is on the woman herself and how she should play an active role in securing for herself the 'spoils of war', which is in line with the programmatic struggle for power that will take place throughout the play. The idea of spoils in love reappears in Propertius and Ovid,[40] at Prop. 2.14.23–24, where the poet compares his victory over Cynthia with a triumph (*haec mihi deuictis potior uictoria Parthis, / haec spolia, haec reges, haec mihi currus erunt*, Prop. 2.14.23–24, 'This is a greater victory for me than the defeat of the Parthians: this shall be booty, captive kings, and chariot for me'),[41] and at 3.13.11–12, where matrons are described as showing of the 'spoils of adultery' (*matrona incedit census induta nepotum / et spolia opprobrii nostra per ora trahit*, Prop. 3.13.11–12, 'Matrons step forth arrayed in the fortunes of spendthrifts and flaunt the spoils of dishonour before our eyes.'). The closest parallels to the Terentian context of the battle between the sexes are still, I propose, found in Ovid, who famously ends both his love advice to men, at the end of the second book of the *Ars amatoria*, and to women, at the end of the third, with a reference to the spoils to which his instructions might lead: *sed quicumque meo superarit Amazona ferro, / inscribat spoliis NASO MAGISTER ERAT* (Ov. *Ars am.* 2.743–744, 'But whosoever shall by my steel lay low the Amazon, let him inscribe upon his spoils "Naso was my teacher."') and *ut quondam iuuenes, ita nunc, mea turba, puellae / inscribant spoliis NASO MAGISTER ERAT* (Ov. *Ars am.* 3.811–812, 'As once the youths, so now let the girls, my votaries, write upon their spoils, Naso was our teacher.').

---

38 Norwood says of the play that '[i]t is a woman's play — not feminist, not expounding any special doctrine, but with women as the chief sufferers, the chief actors, the bearers here of the Terentian *humanitas*.' Norwood 1923, 91. See also Goldberg 2013, 18–25.
39 Murgatroyd 1975, 65–66. See also Goldberg 2013, *ad loc.*
40 *spolium/spoliare* does not occur in Tibullus.
41 See also e.g. Camps 1967, *ad loc.*, Richardson 1976, *ad loc.*, and Murgatroyd 1975, 70.

Notably, the opening scene of the *Hecyra* is effectively a reversal of the *adulescens* Chaerea's speech in the *Eunuchus*, as he, from the male point of view, tries to justify his plan to sneak his way into the house of the *meretrix* Thais, which again leads to his rape of the *uirgo* Pamphila:[42]

> *an id flagitiumst si in domum meretricam*
> *deducar et illis crucibu', quae nos nostramque adulescentiam*
> *habent despicatam et quae nos semper omnibus cruciant modis,*
> *nunc referam gratiam atque eas itidem fallam, ut ab is fallimur?*
>
> Ter. Eun. 382–385

Is it an outrage if I'm taken into a courtesan's house and pay back those crosses, who hold us young men in contempt and torture us in every possible way? If I cheat them in the same way that they cheat us?

The image of lovers being enemies is an implicit component of the image of *militia amoris*, and is present in e.g. Propertius 2.14, as the poet celebrates his victory over Cynthia like a military victory (see below). This framework is explicitly clear in Ovid's *Ars amatoria* and the opening of its book 3, where the poet proclaims his intentions and anticipates male objections to these, i.e. his arming of their opponents:

> ARMA *dedi Danais in Amazonas; arma supersunt,*
> *quae tibi dem et turmae, Penthesilea, tuae.*
> *ite in bella pares; uincant, quibus alma Dione*
> *fauerit et toto qui uolat orbe puer.*
> *non erat armatis aequum concurrere nudas;*
> *sic etiam uobis uincere turpe, uiri.*
> *dixerit e multis aliquis 'quid uirus in angues*
> *adicis et rabidae tradis ouile lupae?'*
>
> Ov. Ars am. 3.1–8

I have armed the Danai against the Amazons; there remain arms which I must give to you, Penthesilea, and to your troop. Go into battle on equal terms; let those conquer whom kind Dione favours, and the boy who flies all over the world. It were not just that defence-less girls should fight with armed men; such a victory, O men, would be shameful for you also. Some one or other may say to me, 'Why do you add gall to serpents, and betray the sheepfold to the mad she-wolf?'

The opening scene of the *Hecyra* and the reversal of it in Chaerea's speech in the *Eunuchus* makes an interesting thematic parallel to the third book of the *Ars*

---

42 As James 2016 points out, line 385 is picked up by Ovid in *Ars am.* 1.645 (see below).

amatoria and its relationship to book one and two. As Gibson points out, Ovid as advisor of a female audience takes on a role that is normally reserved for women, i.e. the *lena* of comedy and mime,[43] and his target audience is women that have been deceived and abandoned by men; cf. lines 29–42 and the catalogue of abandoned heroines from the *Heroides*. This mirrors the situation in the opening scene of the *Hecyra*, where the fact that the *adulescens* Pamphilus has abandoned his *meretrix* girlfriend Bacchis by marrying another woman, despite promising not to do so, has inspired Syra's lecture on the infidelity of lovers (*Per pol quam paucos reperias meretricibus / fidelis euenire amatores, Syra.* Ter. *Hec.* 58–59, 'Heaven knows, you can find precious few lovers who turn out faithful to their mistresses, Syra.').

There is a connection between the openings of the third and the first book of the *Ars amatoria*, and their shared Terentian allusive nexus; at *Ars am.* 3.31, Ovid states that it is men that most often deceive women, and that this is his reason for teaching them how to love: *saepe uiri fallunt, tenerae non saepe puellae / paucaque, si quaeras, crimina fraudis habent.* (Ov. *Ars am.* 3.31–32, 'Often do men deceive, tender girls not often; should you inquire, they are rarely charged with deceit.'). As Gibson points out, the sentiment here contradicts lessons from book one, where women are presented as the deceivers that should be deceived back:[44]

> *ludite, si sapitis, solas impune puellas:*
> *hac minus est una fraude tuenda fides.*
> *fallite fallentes; ex magna parte profanum*
> *sunt genus: in laqueos, quos posuere, cadant.*
> Ov. Ars am. 1.643–646

If you are wise, cheat girls only, and avoid trouble; keep faith save for this one deceitfulness. Deceive the deceivers; they are mostly an unrighteous sort; let them fall into the snare which they have laid.

As James argues, '*Eunuchus* provides the source of the most disturbing passage of Ovid's *Ars amatoria* book 1, namely the injunction to deceive (1.645) and rape women (1.669–706)',[45] and posits that *fallite fallentes* at line 1.645 is an allusion to Chaerea's speech and *Eun.* 385, quoted above. I would like to point out here that **ludite** ... *solas* **impune puellas** at line 1.643 closely mirrors line 942 in the same play: *ego pol te pro istis dictis et factis, scelus, / ulciscar, ut **ne inpune** in nos*

---

43 See Gibson 2003, 19–21.
44 Gibson 2003, *ad loc.*, notes that the *praeceptor* adapts to his new audience.
45 James 2016, 86.

inluseris (Ter. *Eun.* 941–942, 'I'll punish you, by heaven, you villain, for those words and deeds of yours; you won't get away with making fools of us.').

By this allusion, I submit, Ovid adds another element, or a question mark, to the *praeceptor*'s statement; the Terentian lines belong to Thais' maid Pythias, and the *scelus* referred to here is the slave Parmeno, whom she believes is the mind behind Chaerea's trick to sneak into their house dressed as a eunuch and his subsequent rape of the citizen *uirgo* kept there. As discussed in Chapter Two, Pythias represents the victim of the rape and thus the female perspective throughout the play, and from this viewpoint, such actions should not go unpunished at all. The *praeceptor*'s statement is then not as straightforward as it seems at first reading. I would like to argue that there is a dialogue between these lines in the first book of the *Ars amatoria*, lines 31–32 of the third book and the *Eunuchus*; even though the statement at lines 3.31–32 contradicts lines 1.643–646, it is important to notice that Ovid's perspective in book 3 has changed to a female one, and that this creates a tension, just as Chaerea's argument in the *Eunuchus* to 'cheat women just as they cheat men' to justify his actions are not justified in the eyes of the women of the play.[46] This is also mirrored in the opening of the Hecyra, where the female perspective of the battle between the sexes is represented.

In the name of love: amatory violence and attacks on doors

Another trait of elegiac *militia amoris* that is influenced by the practice of new comedy and, as I suggest, Terence's *Adelphoe* in particular, is the part of the Roman *paraclausithyron* that pictures the lover as violently breaking down the doors of the beloved's house, as e.g. described in Ovid's *Amores* 1.9. A parallel between the lover and the soldier pointed out in Ovid's famous poetic discourse on the similarities between the life of the soldier and that of the lover is the fact that they are both on guard duty; the soldier guards his general's, the lover his mistress's doors: *ille fores dominae seruat, at ille ducis* (Ov. *Am.* 1.9.8, 'the one guards his mistress's door, the other his captain's'.). This is a twist on the usual

---

46 It is interesting to note that Chaerea's justification is based on Thais being a greedy *mala meretrix*, a stock character of the genre. This is not the case, as Terence has already made explicit his departure from the stock type in Thais' exit monologue over lines 197–206: *me miseram, fors[it]an hic mihi paruam habeat fidem / atque ex aliarum ingeniis nunc me iudicet* (Ter. *Eun.* 197–198, 'Oh dear! It looks as if he has little trust in me and is judging me by the character of other women.'). See Barsby 1999, commentary on line 198. Play with expectations about stock characters is also a theme throughout *Hecyra*.

picture of the *exclusus amator,* who tries to gain access to his mistress' house as in e.g. *Amores* 1.6.[47] However, this soon shifts, as the more violent, military version of the *paraclausithyron* is introduced shortly after: *ille graues urbes, hic durae limen amicae / obsidet; hic portas frangit, at ille fores* (Ov. *Am.* 1.9.19–20, 'The one besieges mighty towns, the other the threshold of an unyielding mistress; the one breaks in doors, the other, gates.').

The image of the lover violently breaking down doors is a feature that is associated with the Roman version of the *paraclausithyron,* and it is first found in a Roman context in Plautus' *Persa:*[48]

> TO: *si hanc emeris,*
> *di immortales! nullus leno te alter erit opulentior.*
> *euortes tuo arbitratu homines fundis, familiis;*
> *cum optumis uiris rem habebis, gratiam cupient tuam:*
> *uenient ad te comissatum.* DO: *at ego intro mitti uotuero.*
> TO: *at enim illi noctu occentabunt ostium, exurent fores:*
> *proin tu tibi iubeas concludi aedis foribus ferreis,*
> *ferreas aedis commutes, limina indas ferrea,*
> *ferream seram atque anellum; ne sis ferro parseris*
>
> Plaut. *Pers.* 564–572

TO: If you buy her — immortal gods! — no pimp will be better off than you. You'll turn men out of their estates and households as you please; you'll have dealings with men of the highest rank, they'll be keen on your favour and come to you for their drinking parties. DO: Well, I won't let them in.
TO: Well, they'll serenade your door at night and burn down its panels. So you should have your house closed with an iron door, you should change your house to an iron one, put in an iron lintel and threshold and an iron bar and door ring. Please don't be economical with iron.

---

47 In *Am.* 1.9.8, Ovid actually pictures himself as in the role of the (slave) *ianitor* rather than the one of the lovers; cf. *non te formosae decuit seruare puellae / limina* (Ov. *Am.* 1.6.63–64, 'Not you were the one to be given ward of my beautiful lady-love's threshold.'). The connection between *militia* and *seruitium* again becomes very clear, and is also highlighted by using *domina* to describe the *puella* at *Am.* 1.9.8.
48 Copley states that the violent element of physical attacks on doors was present also in the dramatic tradition of the Greek *paraclausithyron,* but that it played little or no part in its non-dramatic form. He adds that it might be that Plautus is translating the lines from the Greek, but that either way 'they demonstrate the existence of a second concept of the *paraclausithyron* (...)', which foreshadows the later development of the Roman version of it. Copley 1956, 40–42. Certain features of the *paraclausithyron* are explained as being derived from corresponding features of the ancient κῶμος, see e.g. Copley 1942. On the *kōmos*-chorus in Menander, see Lape 2006.

Here, violent behaviour by the doors of the beloved (or her pimp's doors) is foreshadowed as something that might occur, and it is associated with drunkenness, and thus introduces a concept that later will become standard in the Roman tradition of love elegy. I would, however, like to suggest that the most elaborate instances of such behaviour by the lover are found in Terence, where it actually occurs, and furthermore that Terence's language lays the foundation for the later elegiac descriptions of the same *topos*.[49]

In the *Adelphoe*, there are three references to the young man Aeschinus breaking into a pimp's house to obtain a girl, all made within a discussion between his biological father Demea and Demea's brother and Aeschinus' adoptive father Micio:

> DE: *fores effregit atque in aedis inruit*
> *alienas; ipsum dominum atque omnem familiam*
> *mulcauit usque ad mortem; eripuit mulierem*
> *quam amabat. clamant omnes indignissume*
> *factum esse.*
> Ter. Ad. 88–92

He's broken down a door and forced his way into someone else's house. He's beaten the master and the whole household practically to death. And he's abducted a girl he'd taken a fancy to. Everybody is protesting that it's outrageous behaviour.

And again, shortly after, as Micio defends Aeschinus' behaviour:[50]

> *non est flagitium, mihi crede, adulescentulum*
> *scortari neque potare: non est; neque **fores***
> ***effringere**. haec si neque ego neque tu fecimus,*
> *non siit egestas facere nos. tu nunc tibi*
> *id laudi duci' quod tum fecisti inopia?*
> *iniuriumst; nam si esset unde id fieret,*
> *faceremus. et tu illum tuom, si esses homo,*
> *sineres nunc facere dum per aetatem decet*
> *potius quam, ubi te expectatum eiecisset foras,*
> *alienore aetate post faceret tamen.*
> Ter. Ad. 101–110

---

49 There might, however, as we shall see in the following, be one Plautine case that is of interest with regard to the development of the vocabulary.

50 Aeschinus actually breaks in to secure a girl for his brother Ctesipho, but this is unknown to the *senes* Demea and Micio.

It's not a scandal, believe me, for a young lad to chase after girls or go drinking. It really isn't, nor to break down a door. If you and I didn't do these things, it was because we couldn't afford them. Are you now claiming credit for behaviour forced on you by poverty? That's not reasonable. If we'd had the means to do these things, we would have done them. And, if you had any humanity, you would allow that son of yours to do them while he has the excuse of youth, rather than have him do them at a less appropriate age when he has at long last seen you to your grave.

And:

> amat; dabitur a me argentum dum erit commodum;
> ubi non erit fortasse excludetur foras.
> **fores effregit**: restituentur; discidit
> uestem: resarcietur
>
> <div align="right">Ter. <i>Ad.</i> 118–121</div>

He's in love: I'll keep him in funds as long as it suits me; when it doesn't, maybe he'll be thrown out. He's broken down a door: it can be repaired. He's torn some clothes: they can be mended.

Here, the notion of breaking down doors is used in an erotic context, and notably, with the same alliterative effect as in Ovid, with *fores effregit* at lines 88 and 120; cf. *frangit ... fores* at *Amores* 1.9.20. The expression *fores effringere/frangere* occurs on several occasions also in Plautus,[51] and in one instance it does have erotic implications, though as part of a scam: the prostitute Acroteleutium, dressed as a matron and set to trick the soldier Pyrgopolinices into thinking that she is very much in love with him, states in a dialogue with her maid Milphidippa, loudly so that the soldier will hear it, that she is willing to break down his doors to get to him (MI: *occlusae sunt fores*. AC: *effringam*. Plaut. *Mil.* 1250, 'MI: The door is locked. AC: I'll break it open.'). This constitutes an interesting female version of the image, even if the setting is different here than in Terence and the later elegiac writers, where it also carries military connotations as part of the *topos* of *militia amoris*. It should also be noticed that already in Terence, as is evident in the section from *Adelphoe* quoted above, the expression is connected to the use of other forms of amatory violence, here the tearing of clothes, and that this behaviour is set in the context of being *exclusus* in line 119 and, notably, associated with youth at 108.[52] As will be demonstrated in the following, all

---

51 E.g. Pl. *Amph.* 1022; 1026, *Asin.* 384; 388, *Bacch.* 586, *Stich.* 326, *Mostell.* 453; 456.
52 Violence such as tearing clothes and hair in itself occurs as part of the stock new comic rape/marriage plot at e.g. Ter. *Eun.* 646. See also Men. *Epit.* 486–490. On the use of *excludere* in Terence, see also on pages 106–107.

these traits reappear in what has been termed as an 'elegiac dialogue',[53] rooted in the *topos* of *militia amoris*, between Tib. 1.10., Prop. 2.5 and Ov. *Ars am.* 3.565–576.

In addition to several occurrences in Ovid, the image of the lover breaking down his mistress' door occurs in both Tibullus and Propertius, e.g. Tib. 1.1.73, 1.10.54, Prop. 2.5.22.[54] The image has, as in Ovid, clear military connotations, particularly in Tib. 1.10.54 in his poem against war, where it is included in his description of the ideal life in a rural landscape in peacetime in contrast to the life of a soldier, which he currently leads. Here, the poet treats love as a blessing of peacetime, but with a focus on love quarrels to bring out the similarities between love and war in the form of the elegiac *topos militia amoris*, though he states that fights between lovers should be restrained and that excessive physical violence such as beating one's beloved should be rejected, being described as more fitting for a soldier than a lover. As in Terence (ref. line 102), being drunk is part of the image:[55]

> *rusticus e lucoque uehit, male sobrius ipse,*
>   *uxorem plaustro progeniemque domum.*
> *sed ueneris tunc bella calent, scissosque capillos*
>   *femina,* **perfractas** *conqueriturque* **fores;**
> *flet teneras subtusa genas sed uictor et ipse*
>   *flet sibi dementes tam ualuisse manus.*
> *at lasciuus Amor rixae mala uerba ministrat,*
>   *inter et iratum lentus utrumque sedet.*
> *a lapis est ferrumque, suam quicumque puellam*
>   *uerberat: e caelo deripit ille deos.*
> *sit satis e membris tenuem* **rescindere uestem,**
>   *sit satis ornatus dissoluisse comae,*
> *sit lacrimas mouisse satis: quater ille beatus*
>   *quo tenera irato flere puella potest.*
> *sed manibus qui saeuus erit, scutumque sudemque*
>   *is gerat et miti sit procul a Venere.*
>
>   Tib. 1.10.51–66

And the yeoman drives back from the grove, himself half sober, with wife and offspring in his wain. Then love's war rages hotly; and women lament that hair is torn and doors are broken. The fair weeps for the buffets on her tender cheek; but the conqueror weeps too

---

53 I borrow this expression from Gibson 2003, 321. See Gibson 2003, 320–321, *ad* Ov. *Ars am.* 3.565.
54 For more examples of lovers breaking down doors in Love elegy, see e.g. Maltby 2002, *ad* Tib. 1.1.73 and 1.10.54, Fedeli 2005, *ad* Prop. 2.5.21–24, McKeown 1989, *ad* Ov. *Am.* 1.6.57–58 and 1.9.20. On the different forms of violence in elegy, see also James 2003, 185–98.
55 See Murgatroyd 1980 and Maltby 2002 *ad* Tib. 1.10.

that his mad hands were so strong; while freakish Love feeds the feud with bitter speeches, and sits in unconcern between the angry pair. Ah, he is stone and iron who would beat his girl: this is to drag the gods down from the sky. Be it enough to tear the light robe from her limbs, and to disorder the fair arrangement of her hair: enough to cause her tears to flow. Four times happy he whose anger can make a soft girl weep! But he whose hands are cruel should carry shield and stake and keep afar from gentle Venus.

It has been noticed that the military connotations of the image of the lover breaking down doors as an aspect of *militia amoris* was anticipated by Horace (*Carm.* 3.26.6–8), who describes himself as having been a soldier in his pursuit of women:[56]

> *Vixi puellis nuper idoneus*
> *et militaui non sine Gloria;*
> > *nunc arma defunctumque bello*
> > *barbiton hic paries habebit,*
> *laeuum marinae qui Veneris latus*
> *custodit. hic, hic ponite lucida*
> > *funalia et uectis et arcus*
> > *oppositis foribus minaces.*
>
> Hor. Carm. 3.26.1–8

Till recently I lived in a fit condition to take on the girls, and I campaigned not without distinction. Now this wall that guards the left flank of seaborn Venus will have my weapons, including the lyre whose fighting days are over. Here, here, put the yellowing tapers, and the crowbars and axes that posed such a threat to stubborn doors.

In elegy 2.5 Propertius looks to punish the unfaithful Cynthia, though not with violent actions such as breaking in her doors, but rather with words:

> *nec tibi periuro **scindam** de corpore **uestes**,*
> > *nec mea praeclusas **fregerit** ira **fores**,*
> *nec tibi conexos iratus carpere crines,*
> > *nec duris ausim laedere pollicibus.*
> *rusticus haec aliquis tam turpia proelia quaerat,*
> > *cuius non hederae circuiere caput.*
>
> Prop. 2.5.21–26

I shall not tear the clothes from your perjured body, nor let my anger shatter your locked door, nor bring myself in my rage to pull at your plaited hair, nor hurt you with brutal thumbs. Let some boorish clown pick these vulgar quarrels, one whose head no ivy has ever circled.

---

56 Barsby 1973, 111. See also Nisbet and Rudd 2004, *ad Carm.* 3.26.7–8.

It has been noted that Propertius 2.5 works as a critique of the amatory violence described at Tib. 1.10.61–6., in the light of the repetition of Tibullus' *rusticus* of 1.10.51 in Prop. 2.5.25–6; whereas Tibullus rejects violence such as hitting a woman, Propertius seems here to reject also the milder forms, such as breaking down doors and tearing clothes, as vulgar (*turpia*) and suitable only for a *rusticus*.[57] A similar notion might be detected in Ovid in the third book of the *Ars amatoria*, where he teaches the *puella* the benefits of choosing an older lover:

> ille uetus miles sensim et sapienter amabit
>   multaque tironi non patienda feret;
> nec **franget postes** nec saeuis ignibus uret
>   nec dominae teneras appetet ungue genas
> nec **scindet tunicasue** suas tunicasue puellae,
>   nec raptus flendi causa capillus erit.
> ista decent pueros aetate et amore calentes;
>   hic fera composita uulnera mente feret.
> ignibus heu lentis uretur, ut umida faena,
>   ut modo montanis silua recisa iugis.
> certior hic amor est, grauis et fecundior illo:
>   quae fugiunt, celeri carpite poma manu.
>
> Ov. Ars am. 3.565–576

But the veteran will come gradually and prudently to love, and will bear much a recruit would not endure; he will not break doors nor burn them with fierce flames, nor attack with his nails the soft cheeks of his mistress, nor rend his own nor his girl's clothes, nor will torn tresses be a cause of weeping. Such doings suit lads aflame with youth and love; but he will bear bitter smarts composedly, he will burn, ah, with slow fires like damp hay, like timber lately cut from the mountain ridge. Such love is surer; the other is richer but brief; pluck with quick hand the fruit that quickly passes.

The section is also strongly connected to the image of *militia amoris*, the more mature lover being described as a veteran soldier. As Gibson notes, there are connections between Ovid's *uetus miles* and Horace's description of himself as now a veteran soldier in *Carm.* 3.26 (quoted above) whose fighting days are over,[58] but that the section most closely recalls Prop. 2.5.21, as he transforms the violence deemed fitting for a *rusticus* by Propertius into the violence of young and inexperienced lovers.[59] It also recalls Ovid's regret over his own behaviour

---

57 On Propertius' criticism of Tibullus in this passage, see Solmsen 1961, 273–276.
58 Cf. also *Am* 1.9.3, on how young age is fitted for both fighting in wars and for love: *quae bello est habilis, Veneri quoque conuenit aetas* (Ov. *Am.* 1.9.3, 'The age that is meet for the wars is also suited to Venus').
59 Gibson 2003, *ad* 565–576.

as a younger lover in *Amores* 1.7, where he describes how he has assaulted his *puella* as some kind of madman or boor (*quis mihi non 'demens', quis non mihi 'barbare' dixit?* Ov. *Am.* 1.7.19, 'Who did not say to me: "Madman!" who did not say: "Barbarian!"').[60]

It seems to me that the elegiac discussion of the use of amatory violence, such as the *exclusus* breaking in doors to get to the beloved, which ends with Ovid recommending a more mature lover, is rooted in the New Comic universe and the formulation of this image as it is described in the *Adelphoe*. In the *Adelphoe*, amatory violence, including the breaking in of doors, is not directly associated with *militia* in the way that it is in the elegiac discourse, but Aeschinus' behaviour is seen as a result of the burning passion of youth, in a manner very similar to Ovid's depiction:

> MI: (...)
>   *etsi Aeschinus*
> *non nullam in hac re nobis facit iniuriam.*
> *quam hic non amauti meretricem? Aut quoi non dedit*
> *aliquid? postremo nuper (credo iam omnium*
> *taedebat) dixit uelle uxorem ducere.*
> *sperabam iam deferuisse adulescentiam:*
> *gaudebam. ecce autem de integro!*
>   Ter. *Ad.* 147–153

> MI: (...) But it's true that Aeschinus is treating me pretty badly in this. Is there a girl in town he hasn't taken a fancy to and spent money on? In the end, just recently — I suppose he was getting bored with the lot of them — he told me he wanted to take a wife. I hoped that the flames of youthful passion had died down, and I was delighted. But here he goes all over again!

Conventionally for both the comic and the elegiac genre, mature age would not be seen as fit for elegiac love; this notion is clear in Ter. *Ad.* 107–110 (quoted above)[61] and is reflected in Tib. 1.1.71–74:[62]

> *iam subrepet iners aetas, nec amare decebit,*
>   *dicere nec cano blanditias capite.*

---

60 I treat *Amores* 1.7 in Brecke 2021.

61 The idea that old age is unfit for love is also prominent in e.g. Plautus' *Mercator*, where the *senex amator* occurs: *tun capite cano amas, senex nequissime?* (Plaut. *Merc.* 305, 'You with your grey head are in love, you wicked old man?').

62 Hanses suggests that Tib. 1.1.73–74 echoes Ter. *Ad.* 120 (quoted above), see Hanses 2020, 318.

> *nunc leuis est tractanda uenus, dum frangere postes*
> *non pudet et rixas inseruisse iuuat.*

Tib. 1.1.71–74

Soon will steal on us the inactive age, nor will it be seemly to play the lover or utter soft speeches when the head is hoar. Now let gay love be my pursuit while it is no shame to break a door down and a joy to have plunged into a brawl.

It is also reflected in *Am*. 1.9, where youth is seen as preferable for being both a lover and a soldier (*quae bello est habilis, Veneri quoque conuenit aetas: / turpe senex miles, turpe senilis amor. Ov. Am.* 1.9.3–4, 'The age that is meet for the wars is also suited to Venus. It is unseemly for the old man to soldier, unseemly for the old man to love.').[63] Now, however, Ovid seems to take on a more positive view of the mature lover. This change of heart might be motivated by the fact that Ovid himself now speaks from the point of view of being a more experienced and wise lover, as discussed in the previous chapter, but it also provides him with the opportunity to teach women a way to love more safely and avoid suffering violence, that is by choosing a more mature and patient lover, who does not burn with the same uncontrollable passion that causes the inexperienced lover to be violent.

In Terence's *Adelphoe*, the whole idea of the young man, burning with passion, breaking in doors and conducting amatory violence is coherently formed in the conversation between Demea and Micio, and it is my belief that this has influenced the later elegiac discourse. This might not be so surprising, given that violence against the beloved is common within the comic genre, as an important plot element, and that violence against the *puella* within elegy is often seen as a trait adopted from new comedy.[64] There are, however, important differences in the way the theme is treated within the two genres. As discussed in Chapter Two, the violence is generally not problematised within the comic genre, as all such problematic aspects are solved toward the end of the plays, conventionally with marriage. The 'elegiac dialogue' between Tibullus, Propertius, and Ovid, however, addresses the topic and to different degrees displays an ideal of love without (excessive) violence.[65]

---

63 See Murgatroyd 1980, *ad loc.* and McKeown 1989, *ad loc.*
64 See e.g. McKeown 1989, commentary on Ov. *Am*. 1.7.
65 As was also demonstrated in Chapter Two, excessive violence towards the beloved is a particularly prominent feature in Terence, and the focus is on the disturbing effect it has on the victim. This is picked up by Ovid in his treatment of the Sabine rape, to demonstrate how the theatre might be an unsafe place for women, also at a generic level, in what I believe is criticism of the rustic violence inherent to the Roman marriage institution. This makes an interest-

Even though Aeschinus' attack on the door in *Adelphoe* has not, to my knowledge, been linked to *militia amoris* as such, such a link might still be detected; I would like to argue that the military aspect is also strongly present here, and thus that all of the three Terentian *paraclausithyra* can be interpreted as *militia*. There is a version of the more violent *paraclausithyron* in Terence that is closely link to military combat, that is the soldier Thraso's attack on Thais' house and plan to attack Thais herself in the *Eunuchus*. As Copley points out, Terence refers to the *paraclausithyron* twice in the *Eunuchus*, i.e. Phaedria in the first act (Ter. *Eun.* 46–49, 81–83, and 155–161), and to a parody of it, i.e. the soldier Thraso's attack on Thais' house (Ter. *Eun.* 771–816).[66] Copley finds no new independent additions to the motif by Terence, as the versions are the usual Greek ones, but it is, however, my belief that the violent 'mock' *paraclausithyron* in the *Eunuchus* is interesting to see in the context of the other Terentian *paraclausithyra* and the notion of the later development of *militia amoris*.

In the scene that Copley defines as a parody of the *paraclausithyron* in the *Eunuchus*, the soldier Thraso plans a violent attack on Thais' house; the reason is jealousy, as he believes that she has brought another lover, Chremes, who is actually the girl Pamphila's brother, to a party at his house earlier in the day. He has now come to force his way into her house, beat her up, and reclaim his gift to her, the girl Pamphila. He has brought his 'army', consisting of household slaves, armed with a crowbar and a brush or sponge, and is ready to attack:

> THR: *hancin ego ut contumeliam tam insignem in me accipiam, Gnatho?*
> *mori me satiust. Simalio, Donax, Syrisce, sequimini.*
> *primum aedis expugnabo.* GN: *recte.* THR: *uirginem eripiam.* GN: *probe.*
> THR: *male mulcabo ipsam.* GN: *pulchre.* THR: *in medium huc agmen cum uecti, Donax;*
> *tu, Simalio, in sinistrum cornum; tu, Syrisce, in dexterum.*
> *cedo alios: ubi centuriost Sanga et manipulus furum?* SA: *eccum adest.*
> THR: *quid, ignaue? peniculon pugnare, qui istum huc portes, cogitas?*
> SA: *egon? imperatoris uirtutem noueram et uim militum:*
> *sine sanguine hoc non posse fier: qui abstergerem uolnera?*
> THR: *ubi alii?* GN: *qui malum 'alii'? solu' Sannio seruat domi.*
> THR: *tu hosce instrue; ego hic ero post principia: inde omnibus signum dabo.*

---

ing comparison to the 'elegiac dialogue' between Tib. 1.10.51–65, Prop. 2.5, and Ov. *Ars am.* 3.565–576, which departs from the rejection of amatory violence and Tibullus' *rusticus*, who conducts violence towards his wife as he is drunk after a rustic festival, which can be seen as closely mirroring the stock New Comic rape marriage plot (and a festival would also be an occasion to see a comic play on stage). This is the same type of rustic violence that Ovid is criticising in his treatment of the Sabine rape (which also took place at a rustic festival) and that he here teaches women how to avoid.

66 Copley 1956, 43.

GN: *illuc est sapere: ut hosce instruxit, ipsu' sibi cauit loco.*
THR: *idem hoc iam Pyrru' factitauit. GH: uiden tu, Thais, quam hic rem agit?*
nimirum consilium illud rectumst de occludendis aedibus.
TH: *sane quod tibi nunc uir uideatur esse hic, nebulo magnus est:*
ne metuas. THR: *quid uidetur?* GN: *fundam tibi nunc nimi' uellem dari,*
ut tu illos procul hinc ex occulto caederes: facerent fugam.
THR: *sed eccam Thaidem ipsam uideo.* GN: *quam mox inruimus?* THR: *mane.*

Ter. *Eun.* 771–788

THR: The very idea that I should put up with such a palpable insult, Gnatho! I'd rather die. (to the slaves) Simalio, Donax, Syriscus, follow me. First I'll storm the house.
GN: Right!
THR: I'll carry off the girl.
GN: Excellent!
THR: I'll give the mistress a good thrashing.
GN: Brilliant!
THR: Donax, in the centre of the line with your crowbar. You, Simalio, on the left wing. You, Syriscus, on the right. Bring on the others. Where is centurion Sanga and his company of thieves?
SA: (coming forward) Present.
THR: What, you useless creature? Are you proposing to fight with a sponge? I see you're carrying one with you.
SA: Me? I knew the valour of the general and the violence of the soldiers. This operation cannot take place without blood. How else was I to wipe the wounds?
THR: (to Gnatho) Where are the others?
GN: What others, damn it? There's only Sannio and he's on duty at home.
TH: You draw up these. I'll be here behind the front line. I'll give the signal to everybody from there.
GN: (aside) There's a wise man for you. He's drawn up the troops to protect himself.
THR: Pyrrhus did the same before me.
CH: (to Thais) Thais, do you see what he's doing? It was surely a good idea to bolt the door.
TH: (to Chremes) The truth is, though he may seem now to you a real man, he's a great fairy. Don't be afraid.
THR: (to Gnatho) What do you think?
GN: I only wish you had a sling, so that you could cut them down in hiding from a distance. That would put them to flight.
THR: But look, there's Thais.
GN: (mischievously) How soon do we attack?
THR: Wait!

As Barsby points out, Donatus claims the opening line, i.e. the talk of not enduring insults, is military (*proprie et ut miles*). If so, it is the first of many indications in this section that Thraso is treating the mission as a military operation, as the scene is packed with military language (*expugnabo, agmen, cornum, cen-*

turio, manipulus, imperatoris uirtutem, uim militum, uolnera, instrue, principia, signum dabo, instruxit, fundam, ex occulto, caederes, fugam, inruimus).[67]

Both the *paraclausithyron* in the opening scene of the same play and Aeschinus' attack on a pimp's house in the *Adelphoe* are partially mirrored in this scene. The opening line recalls Phaedria's similar complaint at the opening of the play, *an potius ita me comparem / non perpeti meretricum contumelias?* (Ter. *Eun.* 47–48, 'Should I rather take myself in hand and refuse to endure the insults of courtesans?'), and, I submit, connects the two scenes together. This again adds to the military setting and image of love as war in the opening scene, as discussed in this chapter, and to the overall connection between the Terentian *paraclausithyra* and the concept of *militia amoris*. Similar connections can also be made between the 'mock' *paraclausithyron* and the attack on the pimp's house in *Adelphoe*, where much the same type of military language may also be detected. Aeschnius has made an attack on the house, *fores effregit atque in aedis inruit / alienas* (Ter. *Ad.* 88, 'He's broken down a door and forced his way into someone else's house'), cf. *inruimus* at Ter. *Eun.* 787, and he has given the people of the household a beating, *ipsum dominum atque omnem familiam mulcauit usque ad mortem* (Ter. *Ad.* 89–90, 'He's beaten the master and the whole household practically to death'), cf. *mulcabo* at Ter. *Eun.* 774. As Barsby noted, there might also here be a hint at the military sense of rout,[68] which might be transferred to *Adelphoe* as well, given the similarities in the situations; notably, both Aeschinus and Thraso attack in order to take back a girl: *eripuit mulierem* at Ter. *Ad.* 90 cf. *uirginem eripiam* at Ter. *Eun.* 773. Thus, the scenes in which the *adulescentes* Phaedria and Aeschinus are depicted as shut-out lovers both have elements of *militia* in them. This military element of Aeschinus' attack in order to get to a woman, and the use of what is depicted as excessive military force, makes the scene a fitting fundament for the later elegiac dialogue on *militia* and violence.

Conclusion

As I have aimed to show in this chapter, Terence stands in a special position in developing the Roman image of *militia amoris*, which becomes a stock trait of Roman love elegy, arguably most developed in Ovid. I believe that one can trace a connection between Ovid's version of *militia amoris* and notions that can be

---

67 Barsby 1999, *ad loc.*
68 Barsby 1999, *ad loc.*, cf. OLD 1b = worst (in battle).

traced back to Terence and passages rich in military language in the *Eunuchus*, as seen in e.g. *Amores* 1.9 and 3.8. The idea that constitutes the background for the image of *militia amoris* is the notion that love is war between the sexes; and interestingly, both Terence and Ovid are famous for conveying both the male and the female perspective. Shifting between male and female perspective can be said to be a common tread in Ovid's elegiac authorship, as is clearly demonstrated in his *Heroides* and the *Ars amatoria* in particular, whereas Terence includes strong female voices conveying the impact of male actions towards women in both his *Eunuchus* and *Hecyra*. The battle between the sexes is programmatic for the latter comedy, and I believe that there is a strong affinity between it and Ovid's third book of the *Ars amatoria*, where love in a similar manner is portrayed as a battle and the aim of the work is to provide women with the right weapons to secure a fair fight. The issue of the male versus female perspective is further highlighted by the striking allusive play between Ov. *Ars am.* 3.31, 1.642 and Ter. *Eun.* 941–942. Furthermore, Terence seems to have played an important role in the development of the imagery connected to what becomes Roman elegiac *militia* in general, as has perhaps been most widely recognized in the *Eunuchus*; in addition, as I aimed to demonstrate in the last section of this chapter, the *Adelphoe* in particular seems to have functioned as a backdrop for what has been termed an 'elegiac dialogue' between Tibullus, Propertius, and Ovid on amatory violence, a dialogue that includes breaking in doors (e.g.) and debating whether, or under which circumstances, such behaviour can be justified.

6 Ovid's Terence: *omnia mutantur, nihil interit*

The relationship between Ovid and Terence is a close yet complicated one, and the elegist's reception of the playwright is both extensive and multifaceted. As I hope to have demonstrated, to fully understand the works of Ovid, Terence is crucial reading material. There are, on the one hand, some obvious similarities between their genres on a more general note, but on the other hand there are also some crucial differences, and the connection between them is anything but straightforward. The most obvious of such differences are perhaps the role of marriage, the elegiac artistic 'I' and the strong voice of the beloved, and perhaps also the clearly defined stock comedy characters versus the more blurred elegiac personas such as the the *puella*, and the rival, the *puella*'s *uir*. In comedy, every issue and confusion, such as the rape of a woman who turns out to be of citizen status, is resolved in the end, often with marriage and perhaps the birth of a legitimate child. Such solutions are in line with the convention of the genre, but also with conservative and traditional values: whatever has occurred during the action of the play, the proper societal order is generally re-established in the end, at least on the surface.

Within the generic boundaries of elegy, such solutions do not exist, and there is a highly notable gap between reciprocal elegiac love, the comic rape-marriage plot, and traditional Roman family values, especially in light of their legal reinforcement under the rule of Augustus. When Ovid then alludes to a Terentian rape-marriage plot in the opening of the *Ars amatoria*, and later again in exile in the opening address to Augustus in his defence of the very same work in *Tristia* 2, this cannot straightforwardly be explained as a result of influence from comedy upon the elegiac way of living and loving. Here, I believe, one must look for other factors to explain why Ovid opts for Terence and the *Eunuchus* as his allusive source. A hint might be found in the main model for *Tristia* 2, Horace's epistle 2.1,[1] also addressed to Augustus; here, in a catalogue of playwrights and their foremost literary qualities, it is claimed that Terence is known for his *ars*.[2] As I hope to have demonstrated throughout the preceding chapters, there can be detected in Ovid an appreciation for that which might be considered to be particularly Terentian, such as his elegance and style, and his *humanitas* and the way in which he provides the reader (or viewer) with insight into the nature of his characters and their actions, from the deep-felt terror of a

---

1 See Barchiesi 2001 [1993], 79–104.
2 Hor. *Epist.* 2.1.59.

https://doi.org/10.1515/9783111308036-006

victim of rape and the brutality of such actions to the emotions and frustrations that follow from being in love or from being a parent or someone's partner. That is, everything that constitutes the particular *ars* of Terence.

It is hard not to read the Latin love elegists in light of their socio-political context, not only e.g. when it comes to images of war and love categorised as *militia amoris*, but also when it comes to their anti-marital ideal of reciprocal love for its own sake, explained by Thorsen as love with 'no explanation; it appears as its own cause and effect and seems self-sufficient.'[3] This stands in contrast to current political affairs and Augustus' attempt to control matters such as sexuality, marriage and childbirth by law, which of course becomes particularly clear in Ovid in light of his exilic works and the way in which he partially explains his exile as a result of his *Ars amatoria* and Augustus' alleged (mis-)reading of it as prompting immoral behaviour and thus breaking the *Lex Iulia de adulteriis coercendis*. Ovid's apparent *apologia Tristia* 2, addressed to Augustus, is no straightforward defence of himself and for the *Ars amatoria*; it also hints at the emperor's double standards when he exiled Ovid for his *crimen*, as the very same content can be found in other artistic productions of the period, openly enjoyed and promoted by Augustus himself, and even in the Roman legend of the Sabine Women deployed in the legitimation of Augustan rule.

As I argued in Chapter One, it is to this aspect of the poem that an allusion to Terence and his most shocking rape-marriage plot adds, as Ovid urges Augustus to follow the ways of Jupiter. To act like Jupiter will always carry a double meaning in the Ovidian corpus, the god being the supreme deity on the one hand and a 'serial adulterer' or rapist on the other. The latter is a feature of the god that is ever-present in Ovid's oeuvre. The rape scene in the Eunuchus is also alluded to in the opening of the first book of the *Ars amatoria*, in an intricate play with the status of the desired object; here Ovid urges young men to hunt for women in the same manner as Romulus and the first Romans hunted down and captured the Sabine Women for the sake of marriage and childbirth, in what might be described as an Ovidian rape-marriage plot. The allusions, I believe, are meant to hint at the *crimen* that is imminent in the Roman tradition and legend, and the violent origin of Roman marriage — newly reinforced by Augustus by law. This is supported by the fact that formulations that belong to the same allusive nexus occur in other places as well, such as in e.g. the *Remedia amoris* and *Heroides* 20–21, in passages that comment on matters such as marriage and harmful 'love'. Terence, who on the one hand is known for his problematic and shockingly violent rape-marriage plots, in the *Eunuchus* and the

---

3 Thorsen 2013, 2.

Hecyra in particular, but who on the other hand writes within a genre that always chases a conventional ending that is perfectly in line with traditional Roman values, is an apt source for Ovid's allusive play which creates tension in the text.

That Ovid mentions Terence by name in his defence for the poetry and the poet in *Tristia* 2 is hardly a coincidence. Notably, one of the things that Terence is known for is his defence of himself and his works in the prologues to his plays. They are unique in the comic genre as they differ in content and style from any predecessor, and he deploys them to defend himself and his artistic choices from accusations from anonymous critics; in the prologue to the *Hecyra*, he even attacks the audience at an earlier performance of the play with accusations of being 'stupid' for preferring other (and lower) forms of entertainment. This was also picked up by Horace in his defence of himself as poet and contemporary poetry in epistle 2.1, and it is hard not to see Ovid's mentioning of Terence in *Tristia* 2 in connection with Horace's statement that Terence is known for his *ars* in contemporary Rome and his allusion to the 'stupidity' of the audience known from the prologue of *Hecyra*. As I aimed to demonstrate in Chapter Three, this is also not the first time that Ovid invokes Terence in such a defence, as a similar defence, inspired by the Terentian prologue, against accusations from an anonymous critic is also featured in the *Remedia amoris*.

On a concluding note, I believe that the repeated use of the Terentian prologue in these settings indicates that it has gained a special literary position and influence at Ovid's time, and I find it interesting to see the deployment of it by the poets in light of Goldberg's study of the Terentian prologue and a possible non-dramatic model: contemporary Roman oratory. As Goldberg argues, 'Terence's need to win his audience has led to an oratorical prologue',[4] and furthermore, his prologues' 'singular fusion of rhetoric and drama showed the first signs of a style with influence beyond the occasion.'[5] As Goldberg also points out, Terence makes the accusations against him memorable, but without really intending to refute them, which may seem strange, as this will apparently just make the audience aware of the existence of such accusations. However; the reason for this is rhetorical; by phrasing the accusations as extravagantly as possible, their absurdity will rebound on the accusers.[6] Thus, the prologue functions to announce the play and secure an audience for it in an effective manner, which is the primary purpose of the prologue in the first place. I find it interest-

---

4 Goldberg 1983, 209.
5 Goldberg 1983, 210.
6 After the model of Cato the elder; see Goldberg 1983, 206–211 for the full argument.

ing to compare this tactic with Ovid's defence of his *Ars amatoria* in the *Remedia amoris*, and e.g. the statement *nuper enim nostros quidam carpsere libellos, / dummodo censura Musa proterua mea est* (Ov. *Rem. am.* 361–362, 'For certain folk of late have found fault with my writings, and brand my Muse as a wanton.'). *Proterua* is a strong expression; as Henderson points out, Ovid's muse is accused not only of being immoral, but of flaunting her immorality.[7] Ovid then goes on to dismiss his accusers as just a mere handful (*unus et alter* at line 364).[8] Just as with Terence, one might ask why Ovid chooses to include such accusations against himself in such a prominent manner, and the answer is, most likely, that the passage has a rhetorical function, that is, to secure an audience. It is a very similar tactic to the one established by Terence.

Traces of what became stock elegiac *topoi* can in fact be found in new comedy, and this has been an important factor in the establishment of the view that Latin love elegy is inextricably connected to this genre; the three last chapters have been dedicated to the exploration of such themes, namely the literary image of love as an illness and the related concepts of *seruitium amoris* and *militia amoris*. The image of love as a disease is rooted in the Greek literary tradition and occurs in a number of genres. It is evident in the Roman tradition from Plautus and onward, and it is prominently present in Terence, where it is arguably more elaborate than in Plautus. Among the elegists, it is undoubtedly in Ovid that the image of love as a sickness is most developed, and his *Remedia amoris* is dedicated solely to it and to its potential cures. As I have argued, I believe that there are in Terence some specific notions that point forward to the Ovidian development of the more thorough version of the image. As I suggested, one can see in the *Eunuchus* in particular an almost programmatic connection with the *Remedia amoris*, exploiting the Stoic philosophical tradition with the slave in the role of (mock) Stoic wiseman and 'the voice of reason', cast in a role that parallels the role of the Ovidian *praeceptor*; these characters are, as I also argued in Chapter Four, generally closely connected. On the other hand, the image of love as an illness also demonstrates the differences between the genres of new comedy and Latin love elegy when it comes to the fundamental subject that is love: in the comic universe, the conventional 'cures' for love are marriage and the re-establishment of the proper societal order, all in line with the bounds

---

7 Henderson 1979, *ad loc.* compares the expression with Cic. *Pro Cael.* 49, *ut non solum meretrix, sed etiam proterua meretrix procaxque uideatur*, 'proclaim her to be not only a courtesan, but also a shameless and wanton courtesan.'.
8 See Henderson 1979, *ad loc.*

of the genre. In love elegy, there is no real cure for love, as proper love elegy would then find it hard to exist.

Seruitium amoris is not generally considered a trait of the comic genre as such, but examples of various forms of the image do occur in both Plautus and Terence, and both playwrights feature versions of the *paraclausithyron* in their comedies. In Terence, one can find the *exclusus amator*, shut out due to a *diues amator*, a setting that is closely linked to the *seruitium amoris* in the elegists, including Ovid. Among the Roman elegists, it is not primarily Ovid who is known for deploying this image, but as I have argued, he makes certain twists to it, and I believe that his doing so is inspired by Terence and developments that might be considered particularly Terentian. However, the result is not necessarily what is considered conventional *seruitium amoris*. In the *Eunuchus*, we find a prominent example of a young man who takes on the role of a eunuch slave to gain access to his beloved, due to the enviable proximity to her that this type of slave would enjoy; I have argued that an allusion in Horace supports this reading, and that Ovid picks it up in the second book of the *Ars amatoria* in particular; it mirrors an idea that is evident throughout Ovid's elegiac output, namely that it is slaves after all that have direct access to the *puella*. I believe that this particular Ovidian development of *seruitium amoris* is much indebted to influence from Terence. It is, however, not conventional *seruitium amoris*, defined as the lover giving up control and surrender to love and the *puella*, as he, both in Terence and Ovid, intentionally takes on a role and temporarily *acts* the slave in order to gain something for himself. The same goes for one of the most famous *seruitium* passages in Ovid, found in *Heroides* 20, the letter of Acontius to Cydippe, as Acontius describes himself as willing to undergo servile punishment due to his love for her. As I hope to have shown, he is described in terms associated with the stock comic *seruus callidus*, which is fitting, as he has tricked Cydippe into promising to marry him. The notion of *seruitium* here is really a mock *seruitium*, and in the end, Acontius re-establishes his position as Cydippe's *dominus*.

Whereas *seruitium amoris* in its conventional form is not primarily associated with Ovid among the elegists, he is recognised as the foremost exponent of *militia amoris*, an image that in previous research has been associated with Terence, who most likely played an important role in the development of this particularly Roman image. This can be seen in linguistic and thematic links between Terence and the larger elegiac context, e.g. in the elegiac dialogue about the use of amatory violence and the *topos* of knocking down doors to get to one's beloved. In addition, I have found in Ovid military metaphors for love that I believe are inspired directly by Terentian concepts; one crucial factor that particularly unites Ovid and Terence, I believe, is the shifting between male and female perspectives and the programmatic conveying of 'the battle between the sexes, and the way in which both authors convey the impact of male actions towards women and the emotional and physical dangers faced by women in particular in matters of love and sexuality.

Terence and Ovid are two of Roman literature's greatest authors, and they have had an immense influence on the Western dramatic and literary tradition from antiquity to the present day.[9] A number of factors separate them, such as social rank and position, genre, time, and the socio-political context of their writings. Yet, as I have demonstrated, they are intricately connected, perhaps mainly by their keen observations on society and human life and nature. It has been my hope to show that the only mention of Terence by name in the entire Ovidian corpus in *Tristia* 2 is a gateway to a new world of understanding when it comes to Ovid's text, a world consisting of a nexus of allusions that touch upon that which relates to everyday life and concerns, but also imperative matters such as the position of art and the freedom of the artist, love, life and death.

---

9 See e.g. Miller and Newland 2014; Knox 2009, 395–484, (on reception of Ovid); Augoustakis, Traill and Thorburn 2013, 341–481 (on reception of Terence); Dinter 2019, 259–366 (on reception of Roman comedy).

Bibliography

Acosta-Hughes, B. 2009. 'Ovid and Callimachus: rewriting the master', in: P.E. Knox (ed.),
  A Companion to Ovid, Chichester, U.K./Malden, MA: Wiley-Blackwell, 236–251.

Adams, J.N. 1982. *The Latin Sexual Vocabulary*, London: Duckworth.

Amerasinghe, C.W. 1950. 'The part of the slave in Terence's drama', *Greece and Rome* 19(56):
  62–72.

Anderson, W.S. 1984. 'Love plots in Menander and his Roman adapters', *Ramus* 13(2): 124–134.

Augoustakis, A./Traill, A./Thorburn, J. (eds.) 2013. *A Companion to Terence*, Chichester, U.K./
  Malden, Mass.: Wiley-Blackwell.

Bailey, C. (ed.) 1922. *Lucreti* De Rerum Natura: *Libri Sex*, 2nd ed., Oxford: Oxford University
  Press.

Bailey, D.R.S. 2003. *Statius Volume III: Thebaid, Volume II, Books 8–12; Achilleid*, Cambridge,
  Mass: Harvard University Press.

Barchiesi, A. 2001. *Speaking Volumes: Narrative and Intertext in Ovid and Other Latin Poets*,
  London: Duckworth.

Barsby, J. 1979 [1973]. *Ovid's* Amores. *Book one*, Bristol: Bristol Classical Press.

Barsby, J. 1990. 'The characterisation of Parmeno in the opening scene in Terence's *Eunuch*',
  Prudentia 22(1): 4–12.

Barsby, J. 1996. 'Ovid's *Amores* and Roman Comedy', in: F. Cairns/M. Heath (eds.), *Papers of
  the Leeds International Latin Seminar 9*, 135–157.

Barsby, J. (ed.), 1999a. *Terence* – Eunuchus, Cambridge: Cambridge University Press.

Barsby, J. 1999b. 'Love in Terence', in: S.M. Braund/R. Mayer (eds.), *Amor Roma. Love and
  Latin Literature: Essays Presented to E. J. Kenney on his Seventy-Fifth Birthday*, Cambridge
  Philological Society, Supplementary Volume no. 22: 5–29.

Barsby, J. 2001 (ed. and trans.). *Terence. Phormio, The Mother-in-law, The Brothers*. Loeb
  Classical Library. Cambridge, Mass.: Harvard University Press.

Barsby, J. 2001 (ed. and trans.). *Terence. The Woman of Andros, The Self-tormentor, The Eunuch*. Loeb Classical Library. Cambridge, Mass.: Harvard University Press.

Beacham, R.C. 1991. *The Roman Theatre and its Audience*, London: Routledge.

Beacham, R.C. 2005. 'The Emperor as Impresario: producing the pageantry of power', in:
  K. Galinsky (ed.), *The Cambridge Companion to the Age of Augustus*, Cambridge: Cambridge University Press, 151–174.

Bessone, F. 2013. 'Latin percursors', in: T.S. Thorsen (ed.), *The Cambridge Companion to Latin
  Love Elegy*, Cambridge: Cambridge University Press, 39–56.

Bing, P./Höschele, P. 2014. *Aristaenetus: Erotic Letters*, Atlanta: SBL Press.

Bollinger, T. 1969. *Theatralis licentia: die Publikumsdemonstrationen an den öffentlichen
  Spielen im Rom der früheren Kaiserzeit und ihre Bedeutung im politischen Leben*, Win-
  terthur: Hans Schellenberg.

Boyd, B.W. (ed.) 2002. *Brill's Companion to Ovid*, Leiden: Brill.

Boyd, B.W. 2009. '*Remedia amoris*', in: P.E. Knox (ed.), *A Companion to Ovid*, Chichester, U.K./
  Malden, MA: Wiley-Blackwell, 104–119.

Boyd, B.W. 2017. *Ovid's Homer. Authority, Repetition, and Reception*, Oxford: Oxford University
  Press.

Brecke, I. 2017. *Terents – Evnukken*. Kanon. Antikkens litteratur på norsk, Oslo: Gyldendal
  norsk forlag.

Brecke, I. 2018. *Terents – Svigermora*. Kanon. Antikkens litteratur på norsk, Oslo: Gyldendal norsk forlag.

Brecke, I. 2021. 'Rape and violence in Terence's *Eunuchus* and Ovid's love elegies', in: T.S. Thorsen/S. Harrison/I. Brecke (eds.), *Greek and Latin Love: The Poetic Connection*, Berlin: De Gruyter, 83–103.

Brothers, A.J. 1988. *Terence – The self-tormentor*, Warminster: Aris & Phillips.

Brown, P.G.McC. 2001. 'Love and marriage in Greek New Comedy', in: E. Segal (ed.), *Oxford Readings in Menander, Plautus and Terence*, Oxford: Oxford University Press, 53–64.

Bömer, F. 1957. *P. Ovidius Naso. Die Fasten. Band I. Einleitung. Text und Übersetzung*, Heidelberg: Carl Winter Universitätsverlag.

Bömer, F. 1958. *P. Ovidius Naso. Die Fasten. Band II. Kommentar*, Heidelberg: Carl Winter Universitätsverlag.

Cahoon, L. 1988. 'The bed as battlefield: erotic conquest and military metaphor in Ovid's *Amores*', *Transactions of the American Philological Association* 118: 293–307.

Cain, A. 2013. 'Terence in late antiquity', in: A. Augoustakis/A. Traill/J. Thorburn (eds.), *A Companion to Terence*, Chichester, U.K./Malden, Mass.: Wiley-Blackwell, 380–396.

Camps, W.A. 1967. *Propertius – Elegies, Book II*, Cambridge: Cambridge University Press.

Caston, R.R. 2006. 'Love as illness: poets and philosophers on romantic love', *The Classical Journal* 101(3): 271–298.

Christenson, D.M. 2013. '*Eunuchus*', in: A. Augoustakis/A. Traill/J. Thorburn (eds.), *A Companion to Terence*, Chichester, U.K./Malden, Mass.: Wiley-Blackwell, 262–280.

Claassen, J.-M. 2012 [2008]. *Ovid Revisited: The Poet in Exile*, London: Bristol Classical Press.

Cole, S.G. 1984. 'Greek sanctions against sexual assault', *Classical Philology* 79: 97–113.

Conte, G.B. 1986. *The Rhetoric of imitation: Genre and poetic Memory in Virgil and Other Latin Poets*, Ithaca: Cornell University Press.

Conte, G.B. 1989. 'Love without elegy: the *Remedia amoris* and the logic of a genre', *Poetics Today* 10(3): 441–469.

Conte, G.B. 1994. *Genres and readers: Lucretius, Love Elegy, Pliny's Encyclopedia*, Baltimore, Md: The Johns Hopkins University Press.

Cooper, T. 1852. *The Institutes of Justinian: With Notes*. Third Edition, with additional notes and references by a member of the New York Bar, New York: John S. Voorhies, Law Bookseller and Publisher.

Copley, F.O. 1942. 'On the origin of certain features of the *paraclausithyron*', *Transactions and Proceedings of the American Philological Association* 73: 96–107.

Copley, F.O. 1947. '*Servitium amoris* in the Roman elegists', *Transactions and Proceedings of the American Philological Association* 78: 285–300.

Copley, F.O. 1956. Exclusus Amator: *A study in Latin Love Poetry*, New York: The American Philological Association.

Cornish, F.W./Postgate, J.P./Mackail, J.W. (trans.) 2017. *Catullus. Tibullus. Pervigilium Veneris*, Second Edition, revised by G.P. Goold, reprinted with corrections. Loeb Classical Library. Cambridge, Mass.: Harvard University Press.

Csillag, P. 1976. *The Augustan Laws on Family Relations*, Budapest: Akadémiai Kiadó.

Dalzell, A. 1996. *The Criticism of Didactic Poetry: Essays on Lucretius, Virgil, and Ovid*, Toronto: University of Toronto Press.

Davis, J.T. 1989. *Fictus Adulter. Poet as Actor in the* Amores, Amsterdam: Gieben.

Day, A.A. 1938. *The Origins of Latin Love-Elegy*, Oxford: Blackwell.

De Melo, W. (ed. and trans.) 2011. *Plautus. Amphitryon, The Comedy of Asses, The Pot of Gold, The Two Bacchises, The Captives*. Loeb Classical Library. Cambridge, Mass.: Harvard University Press.

De Melo, W. (ed. and trans.), 2011. *Plautus. Casina, The Casket Comedy, Curculio, Epidicus, The Two Menaechmuses*. Loeb Classical Library. Cambridge, Mass.: Harvard University Press.

De Melo, W. (ed. and trans.), 2011. *Plautus. The Merchant, The Braggart Soldier, The Ghost, The Persian*. Loeb Classical Library. Cambridge, Mass.: Harvard University Press.

De Melo, W. (ed. and trans.) 2013. *Plautus. Stichus, Three-dollar-day, Truculentus, The Tale of a Traveling-bag, Fragments*. Loeb Classical Library. Cambridge, Mass.: Harvard University Press.

Dinter, M.T. 2019. *The Cambridge Companion to Roman Comedy*, Cambridge: Cambridge University Press.

Drinkwater, M.O. 2013. *'Militia amoris*: fighting in love's army', in: T.S. Thorsen (ed.), *The Cambridge Companion to Latin Love Elegy*, Cambridge: Cambridge University Press, 194–206.

Drinkwater, M.O. 2015. 'Irreconcilable differences: pastoral, elegy, and epic in Ovid's *Heroides* 5', *Classical World* 108(3): 385–402.

Duckworth, G.E. 1994 [1952]. *The Nature of Roman Comedy: A Study in Popular Entertainment*, Second Edition, with a foreword and bibliographical appendix by Richard Hunter, Norman: University of Oklahoma Press.

Eder, W. 2005. 'Augustus and the power of tradition', in: K. Galinsky (ed.), *The Cambridge Companion to the Age of Augustus*, Cambridge: Cambridge University Press, 13–32.

Fairclough, H.R. (trans.), 1929. *Horace. Satires. Epistles. The Art of Poetry*, revised and reprinted. Loeb Classical Library. Cambridge, Mass.: Harvard University Press.

Fantham, E. 1972. *Comparative Studies in Republican Latin Imagery*, Toronto: University of Toronto Press.

Fantham, E. 1984. 'Roman experience of Menander in the late republic and early empire', *Transactions of the American Philological Association (1974–)* 114: 299–309.

Fantham, E. 2011. *Roman Readings: Roman Response to Greek Literature from Plautus to Statius and Quintilian, Beiträge zur Altertumskunde Bd. 277*, Berlin: De Gruyter.

Faraone, C.A. 2006. 'Magic, medicine and eros in the prologue to Theocritus *Id*.11', in: M. Fantuzzi/T.D. Papanghelis (eds.), *Brill's Companion to Greek and Latin Pastoral*, Leiden: Brill, 75–90.

Fedeli, P. 2005. *Properzio. Elegie. Libro II: introduzione, testo e commento*, Cambridge: Francis Cairns.

Fitzgerald, W. 2000. *Slavery and the Roman Literary Imagination*, Cambridge: Cambridge University Press.

Fitzgerald, W. 2019. 'Slaves and Roman Comedy', in: M.T. Dinter (ed.), *The Cambridge Companion to Roman Comedy*, Cambridge: Cambridge University Press, 188–199.

Foster, B.O. 1919. *Livy, History of Rome, Books I–II*, Loeb Classical Library. Cambridge, Mass.: Harvard University Press.

Frazer, J.G. (trans.), 1996. *Ovid*. Fasti, 2nd ed., revised by G.P. Goold, reprinted with corrections. Loeb Classical Library. Cambridge, Mass.: Harvard University Press.

Friedländer, L. 1908–1913. *Roman Life and Manners Under the Early Empire, Authorized Translation of the Seventh Enlarged and Revised Edition of the Sittengeschichte Roms by Leonard A. Magnus*, London: G. Routledge/New York: E.P. Dutton.

Fulkerson, L. 2004. '*Omnia vincit amor*: why the *Remedia* fail', *The Classical Quarterly* 54(1): 211–223.

Fulkerson, L. 2013. '*Seruitium amoris*: the interplay of dominance, gender and poetry', in: T.S. Thorsen (ed.), *The Cambridge Companion to Latin love elegy*, Cambridge: Cambridge University Press, 180–193.

Funke, H. 1990. 'Liebe als Krankheit in der griechischen und römischen Antike', in: T. Stemmler (ed.), *Liebe als Krankheit: 3. Kolloquium der Forschungsstelle für europäische Lyrik des Mittelalters*, Mannheim, Tübingen: G. Narr, 11–30.

Gale, M.R. 1997. 'Propertius 2.7: *militia amoris* and the ironies of elegy', *The Journal of Roman Studies* 87: 77–91.

Gardner, R. (trans.), 1958. *Cicero. Pro Caelio. De Provinciis Consularibus. Pro Balbo*, Loeb Classical Library. Cambridge, Mass.: Harvard University Press.

Garrod H.W./Wickham, E.C. (eds.), 1963. *Q. Horati Flacci Opera*, Oxford: Oxford University Press.

Germany, R. 2016. *Mimetic Contagion: Art and Artifice in Terence's Eunuch*, Oxford: Oxford University Press.

Gibson, R.K. (ed.), 1998. '*Meretrix* or *matrona*? Stereotypes in Ovid, Ars Amatoria 3', *Papers of the Leeds International Latin Seminar* 10: 295–312.

Gibson, R.K. 2003. *Ovid – Ars Amatoria book 3*, Cambridge: Cambridge University Press.

Gibson, R.K. 2006. 'Ovid, Augustus, and the politics of moderation in *Ars Amatoria* 3', in: R.K. Gibson/S.J. Green/A. Sharrock (eds.), *The Art of Love: Bimillennial Essays on Ovid's Ars Amatoria and Remedia Amoris*, Oxford: Oxford University Press, 121–142.

Gibson, R.K./Green, S.J./Sharrock, A. 2006. *The Art of Love: Bimillennial Essays on Ovid's Ars Amatoria and Remedia Amoris,* Oxford: Oxford University Press.

Gilula, D. 1980. 'The concept of the *bona meretrix*. A study of Terence's courtesans', *Rivista di Filologia e di Istruzione Classica* 108: 142–165.

Gold, B.K. (ed.), 2012. *A Companion to Roman Love Elegy*, Oxford: Blackwell.

Goldberg, S.M. 1983. 'Terence, Cato, and the rhetorical prologue', *Classical Philology* 78(3): 198–211.

Goldberg, S.M. (ed.), 2013. *Terence – Hecyra*, Cambridge: Cambridge University Press.

Goold, G.P. (ed. and trans.), 1999. *Propertius. Elegies*. Revised Edition. Loeb Classical Library. Cambridge, Mass.: Harvard University Press.

Griffin, J. 1985. *Latin Poets and Roman Life*, London: Duckworth.

Griffiths, J.G. 1990. 'Love as a disease', in: S. Israelit-Groll (ed.), *Studies in Egyptology: Presented to Miriam Lichtheim*, Jerusalem: Magnes Press, 349–364.

Grimal, P. 1967. *Love in Ancient Rome*, New York: Crown Publishers.

Hanaghan, M. 2017. 'Micro allusions to Pliny and Virgil in Sidonius's Programmatic Epistles', *International Journal of the Classical Tradition* 24(3): 249–261.

Hanses, M. 2014. 'Plautinisches im Ovid: the *Amphitruo* and the *Metamorphoses*', in: I.N. Perysinakis/E. Karakasis (eds.), *Plautine Trends: Studies in Plautine Comedy and Its Reception*, Berlin: De Gruyter, 223–256.

Hanses, M. 2020. *The Life of Comedy after the Death of Plautus*, Ann Arbor: University of Michigan Press.

Hardie, P. 1988. 'Lucretius and the delusions of Narcissus', *Materiali e discussioni per l'analisi dei testi classici* 20/21: 71–89.

Hardie, P. 1995. 'The speech of Pythagoras in Ovid *Metamorphoses* 15: Empedoclean Epos', *The Classical Quarterly* 45(1): 204–214.

Hardie, P. 2002. *The Cambridge Companion to Ovid*, Cambridge: Cambridge University Press.

Hardie, P. 2007. 'Lucretius and later Latin literature in antiquity', in: S. Gillespie/P.R. Hardie (eds.), *The Cambridge Campanion to Lucretius*, Cambridge: Cambridge University Press, 111–127.

Harries, B. 1990. 'The spinner and the poet: Arachne in Ovid's *Metamorphoses*', *Proceedings of the Cambridge Philological Society* 216(NS 36): 64–77.

Harris, W.V. 1985. *War and imperialism in Republican Rome, 327–70 B.C.*, Oxford: Clarendon Press/New York: Oxford University Press.

Harrison, S.J. 2002. 'Ovid and genre: evolutions of an elegist', in: P. Hardie (ed.), *The Cambridge Companion to Ovid*, Cambridge: Cambridge University Press, 79–94.

Harrison, S.J. 2007a. *Generic Enrichment in Vergil and Horace*, Oxford: Oxford University Press.

Harrison, S.J. 2007b. 'Introduction by Stephen Harrison', in: G.B. Conte/S.J. Harrison (eds.), *The Poetry of Pathos: Studies in Virgilian Epic*, Oxford: Oxford University Press, 1–22.

Harrison, S.J./Frangoulidis, S./Papanghelis, T.D. (eds.), 2018. *Intratextuality and Latin Literature*, Berlin: De Gruyter.

Hejduk, J.D.D. 2011. 'Death by elegy: Ovid's Cephalus and Procris', *Transactions of the American Philological Association* 141(2): 285–314.

Hemker, J. 1985. 'Rape and the founding of Rome', *Helios* 12: 41–47.

Henderson, A.A.R. 1979. *P. Ovidi Nasonis* Remedia amoris, Edinburgh: Scottisch Academic Press.

Hersch, K.K. 2010. *The Roman Wedding: Ritual and Meaning in Antiquity*, Cambridge: Cambridge University Press.

Hersch, K.K. 2014. 'Introduction to the Roman wedding: two case studies', *The Classical Journal* 109(2): 223–232.

Heslin, P.J. 2005. *The Transvestite Achilles: Gender and Genre in Statius'* Achilleid, Cambridge: Cambridge University Press.

Heyworth, S.J. 2007. *Sexti Properti* Elegos, Oxford: Oxford University Press.

Heyworth, S.J. 2019. *Ovid. Fasti III*, Cambridge: Cambridge University Press.

Hill, D.E. 1992. *Ovid* – Metamorphoses. *V–VIII*, Warminster: Aris & Phillips.

Hill, G.T./Turner, A. (eds.), 2015. *Terence Between Late Antiquity and the Age of Printing: Illustration, Commentary and Performance*, Leiden: Brill.

Hinds, S.E. 1987. *The metamorphosis of Persephone: Ovid and the Self-Conscious Muse*, Cambridge/New York: Cambridge University Press.

Hinds, S.E. 1998. *Allusion and Intertext: Dynamics of Appropriation in Roman Poetry*, Cambridge: Cambridge University Press.

Hollis, A.S. 2009 [1977]. *Ovid* – Ars Amatoria. *Book 1*, Oxford: Clarendon Press.

Ingleheart, J. 2010. *A Commentary on Ovid*, Tristia, *Book 2*, Oxford: Oxford University Press.

Ingleheart, J. 2019. '*Vates Lesbia*: images of Sappho in the poetry of Ovid', in: T.S. Thorsen/ S. Harrison (eds.), *Roman Receptions of Sappho*, Oxford: Oxford University Press, 205–226.

Jacobson, H. 1974. *Ovid's Heroides*, Princeton: Princeton University Press.

Jacoby, F. 1905. 'Zur Entstehung der römischen Elegie', *Rheinisches Museum* 60: 38–105.

James, S.L. 1998a. 'Introduction: constructions of gender and genre in Roman Comedy and elegy', *Helios* 25: 3–16.

James, S.L. 1998b. 'From boys to men: rape and developing masculinity in Terence's *Hecyra* and *Eunuchus*', *Helios* 25(1): 31–47.

James, S.L. 2003. *Learned Girls and Male Persuasion: Gender and Reading in Roman Love Elegy*, Berkeley/London: University of California Press.

James, S.L. 2006. 'A Courtesan's choreography: female liberty and male anxiety at the Roman dinner party', in: C. Faraone/L. McClure (eds.), *Prostitutes and Courtesans in the Ancient World*, Madison, Wis.: The University of Wisconsin Press, 224–262.

James, S.L. 2012. 'Elegy and New Comedy', in: B.K. Gold (ed.), *A Companion to Roman Love Elegy*, Oxford: Blackwell, 253–268.

James, S.L. 2016a. '*Fallite fallentes*: rape and intertextuality in Terence's *Eunuchus* and Ovid's *Ars amatoria*', *Eugesta* 6: 86–111.

James, S.L. 2016b. 'Rape and repetition in Ovid's *Metamorphoses*: myth, history, structure, Rome', in: L. Fulkerson/T. Stover (eds.), *Repeat Performances: Ovidian Repetition and the Metamorphoses*, Madison, Wis.: The University of Wisconsin Press, 154–175.

Janka, M. 1997. *Ovid, Ars amatoria, Buch 2: Kommentar*, Heidelberg: Winter.

Johnson, P.J. 2008. *Ovid Before Exile: Art and Punishment in the Metamorphoses*, Madison, Wis./London: The University of Wisconsin Press

Kauer, R./Lindsay, W.M. (eds.), 1963. *P. Terenti Afri Comoediae*, Oxford: Oxford University Press.

Kenney, E.J. 1994. *P. Ovidi Nasonis* Amores; Medicamina faciei femineae; Ars amatoria; Remedia amoris, Oxford: Oxford University Press.

Kenney, E.J. 1996. *Ovid, Heroides, XVI–XXI*, Cambridge: Cambridge University Press.

King, J.E. (trans.) 1945. *Cicero.* Tusculan Disputations, Revised Edition. Loeb Classical Library. Cambridge, Mass.: Harvard University Press.

Knox, P.E. 1995. *Ovid.* Heroides. *Select Epistles*, Cambridge: Cambridge University Press.

Knox, P.E. 2009. *A Companion to Ovid*, Chichester, U.K./Malden, MA: Wiley-Blackwell.

Konstan, D./Raval, S. 2018. 'Comic violence and the citizen body', in: M.R. Gale/ J.H.D. Scourfield (eds.), *Texts and Violence in the Roman World*, Cambridge: Cambridge University Press, 44–62.

Konstan, D. 1983. *Roman Comedy*, Ithaca/London: Cornell University Press.

Konstan, D. 1986. 'Love in Terence's Eunuch: the origins of erotic subjectivity', *The American Journal of Philology* 107(3): 369–393.

Labate, M. 1984. *L'arte di farsi amare: modelli culturali e progetto didascalico nell'elegia ovidiana*, Pisa: Giardini.

Labate, M. 2006. 'Erotic aetiology: Romulus, Augustus, and the Rape of the Sabine women', in: R. Gibson/S. Green/A. Sharrock (eds.), *The Art of Love. Bimillennial Essays on Ovid's* Ars Amatoria *and* Remedia Amoris, Oxford: Oxford University Press, 193–215.

Lape, S. 2006. 'The poetics of the kōmos-chorus in Menander's comedy', *American Journal of Philology* 127(1): 89–109.

Leach, E.W. 1971. 'Horace's *Pater Optimus* and Terence's *Demea*: Autobiographical fiction and comedy in Sermo, 1.4', *American Journal of Philology* 92: 616–632.

Leigh, M. 2004. *Comedy and the Rise of Rome*, Oxford: Oxford University Press.

Leisner-Jensen, M. 2002. '*Vis comica*: consummated rape in Greek and Roman New Comedy', *ClMed* 53: 173–196.

Leo, F. 1895. *Plautinische Forschungen zur Kritik und Geschichte der Komödie*, Berlin: Weidmanns.

Lindheim, S. 2000. '*Omnia vincit amor*: or, why Oenone should have known it would never work out (*Eclogue* 10 and *Heroides* 5)', *Materiali e Discussioni per l'Analisi dei Testi Classici* 44: 83–101.

Lindsay, W.M. (ed.), 1905. *T. Macci Plauti Comoedia II*, Oxford: Oxford University Press.

Lindsay, W.M. (ed.), 1913. *Sexti Pompei Festi* De verborum significatu quae supersunt cum Pauli epitome, Leipzig: Teubner.

Lindsay, W.M. (ed.), 1903. *T. Macci Plauti Comoedia I*, Oxford: Oxford University Press.

Luck, G. 1959. *The Latin Love Elegy*, London: Methuen.

Lyne, R.O.A.M. 1979. '*Servitium Amoris*', *The Classical Quarterly* 29(1): 117–130.

Lyne, R.O.A.M. 1980. *The Latin Love Poets: From Catullus to Horace*, Oxford: Clarendon Press.

Maltby, R. 2002. *Tibullus*, Elegies: *Text, Introduction and Commentary*, Cambridge: Francis Cairns.

Maltby, R. 2006. 'Major themes and motifs in Propertius' love poetry', in: H. Günther (ed.), *Brill's Companion to Propertius*, Leiden: Brill, 147–181.

Maltby, R. 2012. *Terence* – Phormio, *Edited with Introduction, Translation and Commentary*, Oxford: Oxbow Books.

Manuwald, G. 2019. 'The reception of republican comedy in antiquity', in: M.T. Dinter (ed.), *The Cambridge Companion to Roman Comedy*, Cambridge: Cambridge University Press, 261–275.

Marti, H. 1974. 'Zeugnisse zur Nachwirkung des Dichters Terenz in Altertum', in: V. Reinhardt/ K. Sallmann (eds.), *Musa Iocosa: Arbeiten über Humor und Witz, Komik und Komödie der Antike*, Hildesheim; New York: Olms, 158–178.

Martindale, C. 1993. *Redeeming the Text: Latin Poetry and the Hermeneutics of Reception*, Cambridge: Cambridge University Press.

McCarthy, K. 2004. 'The joker in the pack: slaves in Terence', *Ramus–Critical Studies in Greek And Roman Literature* 33(1–2): 100–119.

Mcgarrity, T. 1980. 'Reputation vs. reality in Terence's *Hecyra*', *The Classical Journal* 76(2): 149–156.

McGinn, T.A.J. 1998. *Prostitution, Sexuality, and the Law in Ancient Rome*, New York: Oxford University Press.

McKeown, J.C. 1979. 'Augustan elegy and mime', *Proceedings of the Cambridge Philological Society* 205: 71–84.

McKeown, J.C. 1987. *Ovid*: Amores. *Volume I. Text and prolegomena*, Leeds: Francis Cairns.

McKeown, J.C. 1989. *Ovid*: Amores. *Volume II. A commentary on book one*, Leeds: Francis Cairns.

McKeown, J.C. 1995. 'Militat omnis amans', *The Classical Journal* 90(3): 295–304.

McKeown, J.C. 1998. *Ovid*: Amores. *Volume III: A commentary on book two,* Leeds: Francis Cairns.

Miller, F.J. 1977. *Ovid*. Metamorphoses, *Book 1–8, With an English Translation*, 3rd ed., revised by G.P. Goold, Loeb Classical Library. Cambridge, Mass.: Harvard University Press.

Miller, J.F./Newlands, C.E. (eds.), 2014. *A Handbook to the Reception of Ovid*, Chichester, UK: John Wiley & Sons, Inc.

Monda, S. 2015. 'Terence quotations in Latin grammarians: shared and distinguished features', in: G.T. Hill/A. Turner (eds.), *Terence Between Late Antiquity and the Age of Printing: Illustration, Commentary and Performance*, Leiden: Brill, 105–137.

Most, G.W. 1996. 'Reflecting Sappho', in: E. Greene (ed.), *Re-Reading Sappho: Reception and Transmission*, Berkeley: University of California Press, 11–35.

Mozley, J.H. (trans.), 1979. *Ovid. The Art of Love and Other Poems*, Second Edition, revised by Goold, G.P. Loeb Classical Library. Cambridge, Mass.: Harvard University Press.

Muecke, F. 1993. *Horace* Satires *II*, Warminster: Aris & Phillips.

Murgatroyd, P. 1975. '*Militia amoris* and the Roman elegists', *Latomus* 34: 59–79.

Murgatroyd, P. 1980. *Tibullus I: A Commentary on the First Book of the Elegies of Albius Tibullus*, Pietermaritzburg: University of Natal Press.

Murgatroyd, P. 1981. '*Seruitium amoris* and the Roman elegists', *Latomus* 40: 589–606.

Myerowitz, M. 1992. 'The domestication of desire: Ovid's *Parva tabella* and the theater of love', in: A. Richlin (ed.), *Pornography and Representation in Greece & Rome*, New York, Oxford: Oxford University Press, 131–157.

Müller, R. 2013. 'Terence in Latin literature from the second century BCE to the second century CE', in: A. Augoustakis/A. Traill/J. Thorburn (eds.), *A Companion to Terence*, Chichester, U.K./Malden, Mass.: Wiley-Blackwell, 364–379.

Mynors, R.A.B. (ed.), 1958. *C. Valerii Catulli* Carmina, Oxford: Oxford University Press.

Nisbet, R.G.M./Rudd, N. 2004. *A Commentary on Horace: Odes, Book III*, Oxford: Oxford University Press.

Norwood, G. 1923. *The Art of Terence*, Oxford: Blackwell.

Ogilvie, R.M. 1965. *A Commentary on Livy: Books 1–5*, Oxford: Clarendon Press.

Owen, S.G. (ed.), 1924. *P. Ovidi Nasonis* Tristium Liber Secundus, Reprint, Amsterdam: Adolf M. Hakkert, 1967.

Owen, S.G. (ed.) 1946 [1915]. *P. Ovidi Nasonis* Tristium Libri Quinque; Ibis; Ex Ponto Libri Quattor; Halieutica; Fragmenta, Oxford: Clarendon Press.

Palmer, A. (ed.)/Kennedy, D.F. (new introduction and bibliography), 2005 [1898]. *Ovid, Heroides. Volume I, Introduction and Latin Text, with Greek Translation by Maximus Planudes*, Exeter: Bristol Phoenix Press.

Paraskeviotis, G.C. 2013. 'Place and time of the rape scenes in Terence's comedies', *Acta Antiqua Academiae Scientiarum Hungaricae* 53(1): 47–59.

Parker, H. 1989. 'Crucially funny or Tranio on the couch: the *servus callidus* and jokes about torture', *Transactions of the American Philological Association (1974–)* 119: 233–246.

Pfeiffer, R. (ed.), 1985. *Callimachus Fragmenta*. 2 vols. Reissued after the 1949 edition. Oxford: Clarendon Press.

Philippides, K. 1995. 'Terence *Eunuchus*: elements of the marriage ritual in rape scene', *Mnemosyne* 48: 272–284.

Piazzi, L. 2013. 'Latin love elegy and other genres', in: T.S. Thorsen (ed.), *The Cambridge Companion to Latin Love Elegy*, Cambridge: Cambridge University Press, 224–238.

Pohlenz, M. 1918. *M. Tulli Ciceronis scripta quae manserunt omnia, Fasc. 44, Tusculanae disputationes*, Leipzig: Teubner.

Postgate, J.P. (ed.), 1924. *Tibulli aliorumque carminum libri tres. (Revised Edition)*, Oxford: Oxford University Press.

Rawson, E. 1987. 'Discrimina ordinum: the *Lex Julia theatralis*', *Papers of the British School at Rome* 55: 83–114.

Richardson, L. 1977. *Propertius. Elegies, I–IV*, Norman: University of Oklahoma Press.

Richlin, A. (ed.), 1992a. *Pornography and Representation in Greece & Rome*, New York/Oxford: Oxford University Press.

Richlin, A. 1981. 'Approaches to the sources on adultery at Rome', *Women's Studies* 8(1–2): 225–250.

Richlin, A. 1992b. 'Reading Ovid's rapes', in: A. Richlin (ed.), *Pornography and Representation in Greece & Rome*, New York/Oxford: Oxford University Press, 158–179.

Richlin, A. 2017. *Slave Theater in the Roman Republic: Plautus and Popular Comedy*, Cambridge: Cambridge University Press

Rosivach, V.J.J. 1998. *When a Young Man Falls in Love: The Sexual Exploitation of Women in New Comedy*, London: Routledge.

Rouse, W.H.D. (trans.), 1992. *Lucretius*. De rerum natura, revised by M.F. Smith, reprinted with revisions. Loeb Classical Library. Cambridge, Mass.: Harvard University Press.

Rudd, N. 1989. *Horace – Epistles, Book II; And, Epistle to the Pisones (Ars Poetica)*, Cambridge: Cambridge University Press.

Rudd, N. (ed. and trans.), 2012. *Horace*. Odes, Epodes, reprinted with corrections. Loeb Classical Library. Cambridge, Mass.: Harvard University Press.

Rynearson, N. 2009. 'A Callimachean case of lovesickness: magic, disease, and desire in 'Aetia' Frr. 67–75 PF', *The American Journal of Philology* 130: 341–365.

Shackleton Bailey, D.R. 2001. *Q. Horatius Flaccus Opera*, Editio 4., Monachii et Lipsiae: In aedibus K.G. Saur.

Sharrock, A. 1994. *Seduction and Repetition in Ovid's* Ars Amatoria *2*, Oxford: Clarendon Press.

Sharrock, A. 2002. 'Ovid and the discourses of love: the amatory works', in: P. Hardie (ed.), *The Cambridge Companion to Ovid*, Cambridge: Cambridge University Press, 150–162.

Sharrock, A. 2009. *Reading Roman Comedy: Poetics and Playfulness in Plautus and Terence*, Cambridge: Cambridge University Press.

Sharrock, A. 2013. 'Terence and non-comic intertexts', in: A. Augoustakis/A. Traill, A/J. Thorburn (eds.), *A Companion to Terence*, Chichester, U.K./Malden, Mass.: Wiley-Blackwell, 364–379.

Sharrock, A. 2021. '*Amans* et *Egens* and *Exclusus Amator*: The Connection (or not) between Comedy and Elegy', in: T.S. Thorsen/I. Brecke/S. Harrison (eds.), *Greek and Latin Love. The Poetic Connection*, Berlin: De Gruyter, 59–81.

Sharrock, A./Morales, H. 2000. *Intratextuality: Greek and Roman Textual Relations*, Oxford: Oxford University Press.

Shipp, G.P. 1960 [1939]. *P. Terenti Afri Andria*, Melbourne: Oxford University Press

Showerman, G. (trans.), 1977. *Ovid*. Heroides, Amores, Second Edition, revised by G.P. Goold, Loeb Classical Library. Cambridge, Mass.: Harvard University Press.

Strong, A.K. 2016. *Prostitutes and Matrons in the Roman World*, New York: Cambridge University Press.

Tarrant, R. 2002. 'Ovid and ancient literary history', in: P. Hardie (ed.), *The Cambridge Companion to Ovid*, Cambridge: Cambridge University Press, 13–33.

Tarrant, R. (ed.), 2004. *P. Ovidi Nasonis* Metamorphoses, Oxford: Oxford University Press.

Thorsen, T.S./Harrison, S. (eds.), 2019. *Roman Receptions of Sappho*, Oxford: Oxford University Press.

Thorsen, T.S. 2013a. *The Cambridge Companion to Latin Love Elegy*, Cambridge: Cambridge University Press.

Thorsen, T.S. 2013b. 'Ovid the love elegist', in: T.S. Thorsen (ed.), *The Cambridge Companion to Latin Love Elegy*, Cambridge: Cambridge University Press, 114–129.

Thorsen, T.S. 2014. *Ovid's early poetry: From his single* Heroides *to his* Remedia Amoris, Cambridge: Cambridge University Press.

Thorsen, T.S. 2016. 'Ovid's *Amores* 1.5 and the complex of Pompey', *Aevum Antiquum* NS 16, 159–181.

Thorsen, T.S. 2018a. 'The second Erato and the deeper design of Ovid's *Ars amatoria*: Unravelling the anti-marital union of Venus, Procris and Romulus', *Exemplaria Classica* 10: 141–168.

Thorsen, T.S. 2018b. 'Intrepid intratextuality: the epistolary pair of Leander and Hero (*Heroides* 18–19) and the end of Ovid's poetic career', in: S. Harrison/S. Frangoulidis/T.D. Papanghelis (eds.), *Intratextuality and Latin Literature*, Berlin: De Gruyter, 257–271.

Thorsen, T.S. 2019a. 'The newest Sappho (2016) and *Heroides* 15', in: T.S. Thorsen/S. Harrison (eds.), *Roman Receptions of Sappho,* Oxford: Oxford University Press, 249–264.

Thorsen, T.S. 2019b. 'Cydippe the poet', *The Classical Journal* 115(2): 129–145.

Thorsen, T.S. 2021. 'In sickness or in health? Love, Pathology and Marriage in the Letters of Acontius and Cydippe (Ovid's *Heroides* 20–1)', in: D. Kanellakis (ed.), *Pathologies of Love in Classical Literature*, Berlin: De Gruyter, 135–158.

Traill, A. 2001. 'Menander's 'Thais' and the Roman poets', *Phoenix–The Journal of The Classical Association of Canada* 55(3–4): 284–303.

Traill, A. 2005. 'Acroteleutium's Sapphic infatuation (*Miles* 1216–1283)', *Classical Quarterly* 55(2): 518–533.

Treggiari, S. 1991. *Roman Marriage: Iusti Coniuges from the Time of Cicero to the Time of Ulpian*, Oxford: Clarendon Press.

Watson, P. 1983. 'Puella and virgo', *Glotta* 61: 119–143.

Wessner, P. 1902–1908. *Aeli Donati quod fertur Commentum Terenti: Accedunt Eugraphi commentum et Scholia Bembina*, Lipsiae: Teubneri (3 vols.).

Wheeler, A.L. 1910. 'Erotic teaching in Roman elegy and the Greek sources. Part I', *Classical Philology* 5(4): 440–450.

Wheeler, A.L. 1911. 'Erotic teaching in Roman elegy and the Greek sources. Part II', *Classical Philology* 6(1): 56–77.

Wheeler, A.L. (trans.), 1996. *Ovid.* Tristia, Ex Ponto, Second Edition, revised by G.P. Goold, reprinted with corrections. Loeb Classical Library. Cambridge, Mass.: Harvard University Press.

White, P. 2002. 'Ovid and the Augustan milieu', in: B.W. Boyd (ed.), *Brill's Companion to Ovid*, Leiden: Brill, 1–25.

Whitton, C. 2018. 'Quintilian, Pliny, Tacitus', in: A. König/C. Whitton (eds.), *Roman Literature Under Nerva, Trajan and Hadrian*, Cambridge: Cambridge university Press, 37–62.

Whitton, C. 2019. *The Arts of Imitation in Latin Prose: Pliny's Epistles/Quintilian in Brief*, Cambridge: Cambridge University Press.

Williams, G.D. 1994. *Banished Voices: Readings in Ovid's Exile Poetry*, Cambridge: Cambridge University Press.

Yardley, J.C. 1972. 'Comic influences in Propertius', *Phoenix* 26(2): 134–139.

Yardley, J.C. 1978. 'The elegiac *paraclausithyron*', *Eranos: Acta Philologica Suecana* 76: 19–34.

Yardley, J.C. 1987. 'Propertius 4.5, Ovid *Amores* 1.6 and Roman Comedy', *Proceedings of the Cambridge Philological Society* 33: 179–189.

Zanker, P. 2003 [1988]. *The Power of Images in the Age of Augustus*, A. Shapiro (trans.), Ann Arbor: University of Michigan Press.

Ziogas, I. 2013. *Ovid and Hesiod: The Metamorphosis of the Catalogue of Women*, Cambridge: Cambridge University Press.

Ziogas, I. 2016. 'Love elegy and legal language in Ovid', in: P. Mitsis/I. Ziogas (eds.), *Wordplay and Powerplay in Latin Poetry*, Berlin: De Gruyter, 213–239.

Index Locorum

https://doi.org/10.1515/9783111308036-008

951	54		90	137
Mil.			101–110	128
1250	129		118–119	84
Mostell.			118–121	129
286	48		728	42
Pers.			*Eun.*	
231–232	113		47–48	137
564–572	127		49	84
Truc.			49–50	73
229–230	112		49–55	116
			55	82
Propertius			57–61	103–104
1.1.1	72		57–63	66, 117
1.1.3–8	65		64–70	74
1.1.25–26	53		65	84
2.1.65–66	53		70–72	72
2.5.21–26	131		74–75	83, 117
2.8.7–8	118		76–80	106
2.14.23–24	123		86–87	83
3.13.11–12	123		87–88	84
3.24.17–18	75		98	84
3.25.5	75		159–160	120
			187	76
Statius			197–198	126
Achil.			216	76
917	46		217–220	76
			225–227	63
Suetonius			293	38
Aug.			308–309	31, 36, 60
44	35		313	42
			319–320	34
Terence			322	38
An.			342	38
5–7	7		353–354	120
15–21	15–21		365–368	91
192	68		372–373	31, 36
192–193	61		375	96
306–309	62		382–385	124
386	84		385	99
558–560	61		436–439	64
560–562	62		480–485	86–87
828–831	63		482–483	121
943–944	63		484	87
Ad.			526	70
88	137		567–574	92
88–92	128		584–591	12
89–90	137		586–587	16

www.ingramcontent.com/pod-product-compliance
Lightning Source LLC
Chambersburg PA
CBHW030831090426
42737CB00009B/965